New Economic Windows

Even what seems simple in economics generally arises from behavior reflecting the enormous diversity of humanity in terms of knowledge, attitudes, and behaviors, which interact within an enormous range of institutional frameworks. Put briefly, the economy is a complex system. This complexity arises naturally. Economic agents, be they banks, firms, households, consumers, or investors, act with strategic behavior and foresight by considering outcomes that might result from behavior they might undertake. Furthermore, they continually adjust their market operations, buying decisions, prices, and forecasts to the situations that these operations, decisions, prices, and forecasts together create. This adds a layer of complexity to economics not experienced in the natural sciences. The recognition of such complexity has resulted in diverse new approaches to the analysis of economic phenomena. After two centuries of preferential study of static equilibrium models, economists are discovering models that contain discontinuity, nonlinearity, and a variety of phenomena that are not so easily predicted or understood. The New Economics Windows (NEW) series, derived from Massimo Salzano's ideas and work, comprises books that explore innovative perspectives and components of complexity theory in economics. They have in common an acceptance that economic phenomena should be investigated not as an outcome of deterministic, predictable, and mechanistic dynamics, but as history-dependent, organic, and continually evolving processes. Research fields covered by the series include in particular (but are not limited to): • Agent-Based Models • Nonlinear Economic Systems • Evolutionary Economics • Econophysics • Chaos Theory • Fractal Analysis • Neuroeconomics • Fuzzy Systems • Network Theory

Otto Loistl · Georg Behm · Sascha Bakry

Screen Based Trading and Open Order Book

From One-Sided Order Execution to Two-Sided Order Matching

Springer

Otto Loistl
Vienna University of Economics
and Business
Wien, Austria

Georg Behm
NEROM & Partner GmbH
Vienna, Austria

Sascha Bakry
Deloitte Financial Advisory GmbH
Vienna, Austria

ISSN 2039-411X ISSN 2039-4128 (electronic)
New Economic Windows
ISBN 978-3-031-99051-9 ISBN 978-3-031-99052-6 (eBook)
https://doi.org/10.1007/978-3-031-99052-6

This Springer imprint is published by the registered company Springer Nature Switzerland AG
The registered company address is: Gewerbestrasse 11, 6330 Cham, Switzerland

Prices are falling because there are more people on the market who want to sell than buy.

Old traders' wisdom

Competing Interests The authors have no competing interests to declare that are relevant to the content of this manuscript.

Contents

1 Preface: Beyond Markowitz: Trading Turns Volatilities into Profits 1

2 Introduction 7
- 2.1 Economic Evaluation of Trading 7
  - 2.1.1 Innovative Perception of Market Performance 7
  - 2.1.2 Capital Market Current Issues 8
  - 2.1.3 Asset Management Activities 12
- 2.2 Organised Trading Venues to Enhance Trading 18
  - 2.2.1 Organised Trading Venues and New Order Types 18
  - 2.2.2 Order Events and Codes 20
- 2.3 Risk Management by Trading: Portfolio Insurance Concept 20
  - 2.3.1 The Three Parameter Principle 20
  - 2.3.2 Two Different Scenarios to Derive Black and Scholes Formula 21

3 Decision-Making with Known Probabilities of Outcome 29
- 3.1 Decision-Making and Probabilities 30
  - 3.1.1 The Issue of Modelling Trader Behaviour 30
  - 3.1.2 A Brief History of Decision-Making According to Mean Variance 32
- 3.2 Calculation of the Expected Value of the Utility 34
  - 3.2.1 Bernoulli Principle: the Axioms 34
  - 3.2.2 Bernoulli Principle: the Constructive Formulas 38
- 3.3 Calculation via Taylor Series-Expansion 39
  - 3.3.1 Taylor Approximations Applied to Quadratic Utility Functions 39
  - 3.3.2 Expected Utility Value as a Function of the Central Moments of Probability Distributions 41
  - 3.3.3 Expected Utility Value and Continuous Distribution Moments 42
- 3.4 Numerical Examples 44
  - 3.4.1 Parameters of the Probability Function 44

3.4.2 Risk Aversion: Several Formulas ... 47
3.4.3 Certainty Equivalent: The Basis of the Mean–Variance Formula ... 49

4 Performance of Real Trading Venues ... 57
4.1 Overview ... 57
4.1.1 Meeting Place for Buyers and Sellers ... 57
4.1.2 Activities of the Traders: Information Processing and Order Selection ... 59
4.1.3 Algorithmic Trading Patterns in Xetra Orders ... 59
4.1.4 Real Time Messages and Traders Reaction ... 90
4.2 Information and Traders' Behaviour ... 92
4.2.1 Event Data ... 92
4.2.2 Empirical Results ... 93
4.2.3 Company-Specific Messages and Individual Stocks ... 93
4.2.4 Conclusion ... 95
4.3 Modelling Agents' Performance on Markets and Complexities ... 96
4.3.1 Modelling Agents' Actions and Interactions on Markets ... 96
4.3.2 Basic Requirements of the Individual Choice Behaviour Model ... 97
4.3.3 Independence from Irrelevant Alternatives Relevance for Trading ... 99
4.4 Organised Complexity to Model Interactions of Traders ... 100
4.4.1 Varying Complexities Require Different Probability Capabilities ... 100
4.4.2 Organised Complexity Appropriate to Model Interacting Agents ... 102
4.4.3 Market Modelling, Complexity and Paradigm Shifts ... 104
4.5 Market Transforms Subjective Values into Objective Prices ... 106
4.6 Big Data and Big Computer Enhance Order Investigation ... 108
4.7 Investor Decision-Making Today: Mean Variance vs Prospect Theory ... 111
4.8 Is There a Change of Paradigm: From Equilibrium to Emergence? ... 112

5 Discrete Choice Capabilities to Select Orders ... 115
5.1 Contractarian Approach to Model Individual Actions ... 116
5.1.1 Markets' Vital Function: The Matching of Opposite Orders ... 116
5.1.2 Matching of Orders Generates Transaction Prices ... 117
5.2 Frame of Microstructure Performance ... 118
5.2.1 Frame's Discrete Items Express Individual Traders' Endowments and Actions Explicitly ... 118

5.2.2 Integrating the Interaction Part into the Individual Decision Model ... 119
5.2.3 Social Interactions Deserve Mediation Features ... 121
5.2.4 Summarising the Proposed Solutions ... 122
5.3 Modelling Actions Any Agent Can Take ... 122
5.3.1 The Logit Formula ... 122
5.3.2 Coordination of Information Processing and Action Taking ... 124
5.3.3 The Milestones ... 124
5.4 Model's Capabilities to Explain Real Market Performance ... 125
5.4.1 Regulators' View on Best Execution Refers to Orders ... 125
5.4.2 Dynamic Cumulated Orders Book ... 126
5.4.3 Emergence of Cumulated Orders During Trading Time ... 127
5.4.4 Simulated Emergence of Dynamic Order Cumulation ... 127
5.5 Identification of Order Types ... 129
5.5.1 Descriptive Statistics of Orders ... 129
5.5.2 Order Types to be Investigated ... 132
5.5.3 The Statistical Formulas ... 132
5.5.4 The Set of Explanatory Variables ... 133
5.5.5 Descriptive Statistics: Outlier Check 0.001 ... 133
5.6 The Model's Power to Separating Orders ... 133
5.6.1 Significance of Variables' Coefficients: L/- vs L/I vs M/- ... 133
5.6.2 The Model's Separating Power ... 135
5.7 Summary ... 135
5.7.1 The Model's Explanatory Capabilities ... 135
5.7.2 Order Identification Capabilities ... 139

6 Decision Frame Modelling ... 141
6.1 Interactions of Agents on Markets ... 142
6.1.1 Integrating the Interaction Component into the Individual Decision Model ... 142
6.1.2 The Issue of Coordinating Actions and Processing Information ... 143
6.2 Explicit Decision Frame ... 143
6.3 Markov State Transition Probabilities Derived From an Action's Discrete Choice Utility: The DSMP Feature ... 145
6.4 DSMP Circumvents Markov's Principle of Constant Transition Probabilities ... 149
6.5 Isomorphic Modelling of Real Trading Venues ... 150

7 Entropy and Economic Efficiency ... 153
7.1 Meanings of Entropy ... 154
7.1.1 Entropy in Physics ... 154
7.1.2 Entropy in Information Theory ... 155

7.1.3 Entropy and Statistics 156
7.1.4 Entropy of Selected Probability Distributions 156
7.2 Entropy and Random Utility 157
7.2.1 Maximum Entropy and Actions Probability Formula 157
7.2.2 Entropy and Market Efficiency 157
7.2.3 Entropy Equals the Actions' Probability 158
7.3 Definition of Information Efficiency of Markets and Examples 159
7.3.1 Definition 159
7.3.2 Pure Insider Knowledge, Minimum Entropy and Minimum Information Efficiency of Markets 159
7.3.3 Pure Ignorance, Maximum Entropy and Maximum Information Efficiency of Markets 160
7.4 Market Equilibrium as Bose–Einstein Condensation 162
7.5 Entropy and Economic Efficiency—Two Suggestions 162
7.5.1 Entropy and Logit Model's Probability 162
7.5.2 Entropy and Aggregation of Individual Decisions to Collective Decisions 164
7.6 High-Dimensional Probability to Model Stochastic Processes 165

8 Outlook 167
8.1 Econophysics II 1: From the Overriding Equilibrium to Agents' Objectives 168
8.2 Econophysics II 2: Entropy Numbers to Evaluate Interactions' Resilience 173

References 177

Index 187

Preface: Beyond Markowitz: Trading Turns Volatilities into Profits

1

Abstract

This chapter explains the new perspective of the book with regard to the current developments in the trading venues. Trading has become a key instrument of risk management. Increased trading facilities provide opportunities to make profits at volatile markets. Variance of price quotation is not per se risky, but misestimation of prices is risky. Static diversification is replaced by dynamic revision. Order book management plays a key role.

Keywords

Orders • Finance paradigm

Finance paradigms—absence of arbitrage, equilibrium and mean/variance—are called into question.[1] Mainstream begins to challenge its fundamental axioms. Big data and powerful computers demand and enable alike a deeper view of economic events: Exploiting arbitrage opportunities are a substantial motivation of human actions, the equilibrium assumption is questioned since more than hundred years.[2] In spite of being "*unquestionable more preferable*" von Neuman and Morgenstern based their approach not on dynamic disequilibria, but chose the second best, the equilibrium approach. The authors' justification might have been appropriate at the time of the book's publication in the 1940s when the investigation of human decision-making was still in its infancy. Analogously, Markowitz's postulate "*that*

[1] Gallegati and Kirman (2019) and Colander et al. (2008).

[2] Fisher (1892, p. 103), von Neumann and Morgenstern (1944): "*A dynamic theory would unquestionably be more complete and therefore preferable*", p. 44. Landini et al. (2020) discuss comprehensively the tensions between individual decision and general equilibrium, referring to Goedel. But the relevance of Goedel's assumption for modeling markets does not seem to be answered.

O. Loistl et al., *Screen Based Trading and Open Order Book*, New Economic Windows,
https://doi.org/10.1007/978-3-031-99052-6_1

the investor ... should consider expected return a desirable thing and variance of return an undesirable thing"[3] might have been appropriate at the time of the article's publication in the 1950s. But today, a treasure trove of knowledge about human decision-making is available and successfully applied in many disciplines, but not yet in economics and finance. Variance itself is not risky, but wrong forecasts of future returns' fluctuations and that of trading possibilities alike bear the risks. Option pricing formulas prove that the value of derivatives increases when the underlying's variance increases.[4]

To be more precise, turning variance into profit means exploiting price fluctuations according to the famous rule: "buy low sell dear". It requires knowledge of price's peaks and troughs during the course of time. Contrary to the prevailing statistical techniques, the recently emerged issue of "high dimensional probability" is capable of identifying upper and lower bounds of stochastic processes. Thus, justifying the heading of preface. Greater details will be discussed in chapter 8, e.g. the appropriate meaning of "entropy". Professionals are well aware that risk evaluation must take account of trading possibilities on the markets and real trading behaviour. That justifies our investigation of traders' behaviour in detail: Traders signal their willingness to trade by placing orders and order monitoring instead of price monitoring provides a competitive advantage. The matching of two opposing orders produces a transaction and thus a market price. Prices are not generated by statistically extrapolating a time series or by throwing dice.

This book is a true description of the realistic performance of a markets' last mile of trading activities at the microlevel. The guidance for our model is the reality of market activities on the one hand and the successful modelling of human decision-making by behavioural finance on the other. We model human actions, interactions and emergence, i.e. consideration of the decision framework's change caused by these actions. We do not rely on mathematical statements and axioms that are outdated even in physics now. Renowned physicists emphasise: "*The transitions to the ageof emergence brings to an end the myth of the absolute power of mathematics*".[5] Warren Weaver (1948) and other scientists[6] noted that statistical tools like mean and variance are not appropriate to analyse same problems with "***emergence***" and "***organised complexity***". Actions modify the decision frame, that is relevant for other agents. Modelling the issue of interactions must implement that decision frame's change. That is at the core of emergence and of organised complexity as well, as Warren Weaver proved nearly 80 years ago. This demand requires knowledge of the real consequences of an action.

[3] Markowitz (1952, p. 77).

[4] The application of the Black and Scholes formula for the valuation of options went hand in hand with a change in the content of the term "variance". This can be clearly seen in the change in terminology from variance to volatility, converted to implied volatility and finally summarised in VIX, the volatility index. Further details can be found in chapter 2.3.2.4.

[5] Laughlin (2006, p. 209).

[6] So explicitly Hayek (1975), Hayek (1983), and Klir (2006).

Nobel Prize winner Alvin E. Roth[7] reaffirmed the importance of matching buyers' and sellers' orders on markets. The term "execution" disguises the concrete circumstances of matching the two. Roth, and later together with Sotomayor, restricted the investigations to bipartite situations where both partners are known due to the markets' rules. They declined to investigate the trading rules at financial markets because the second partner of the transaction was not known precisely in many cases. Indeed, the SEC rules give the broker a lot of discretionary power in organising the transaction, i.e. providing the opposite trader. Brokers are in charge to maintain an orderly market and they are obliged to document that the price charged to the customer corresponds to the specific market situation.

In electronic trading, the system matches suitable orders, basically according to the "price time priority rule". Our model pictures Xetra's computerised trading system; order limits and matching partners are well documented. In liquid markets, the matching occurs when the conditions of two orders match.

In nonliquid situations, the matching might be tedious. Xetra has installed the so-called "designated sponsor" to manage such non-liquid markets. His privileges and obligations are regulated quite comprehensively compared to the obligations of a US broker. But the US exchanges installed equivalent "designated market makers" now as well. We will investigate the impact of Xetra's "designated sponsors" in different market situations by simulation of the market's performance.

We reaffirm that reliable data is a basic prerequisite for meaningful studies. Due to a generous gift of Frankfurt Stock Exchange, we could rely on the completely recorded "DAX" tick by tick data of two batches of seven trading days each from Monday to next Monday included. Although the number of companies included in the DAX was increased from 30 to 40 stocks in the meantime, the quality of these time stamped tick by tick data is not outdated even today and the basic findings of the model remain valid. The SEC rule adjustments refer to such time stamped tick by tick data as well. But we must perceive that academic research is not yet advanced in some areas so far. Partly the adequate data is missing; partly the adequate methods are not common. Warren Weaver emphasised as early as 1948 that the conventional statistical methods were inadequate. We propose the application of adequate methods. The results might surprise scholars who are used in handling big data by averages.

The portfolio selection guideline "mean is good, variance should be avoided" might have been appropriate at the time of Markowitz's publication. But today, portfolio selection is extended to portfolio revision to convert fluctuations into returns. Trading has been a nearly neglected issue in finance textbooks until now. But in the current reality, many trading opportunities exist. Trading departments become profit centres, and the supervisory authorities are called upon to issue efficient regulations for orderly trading. Our approach can provide a basis for the development of a reliable set of rules. Examples are the simulative efficiency tests of Nasdaq rules in Chapter 6.

[7] Roth (2018), Roth (2015), and Roth and Sotomayor (1992).

Over the course of time, we have cooperated with competent experts on various topics. Together we were able to transfer the persistently presented economic and financial requirements into an adequate quantitative model. We thank Thomas Landes who proposed - after intensive discussions - the idea to combine discrete choice and Markov processes. The research project was funded by DFG (German Research Foundation) following an expert opinion by Heinz König and Artur Woll. The first results were achieved at a time when "discrete choice" was not yet successfully applied by professionals.[8] Nevertheless, we continued, encouraged by these experts and others, to explore the possibilities of modelling financial markets microstructure with discrete choice. The situation has now changed: These methods are now successfully applied in many disciplines,[9] but not yet in finance and economics.[10] Several generations of doctoral students - and of course the authors as well - refined that idea. We called that combination "Doubly Stochastic Markov Process", DSMP for short. The content of the model pictures the real processes on the microstructure of a stock exchange. The model's empirical impact has been reviewed by numerical checks. We could perform that tests with the help of Frankfurt Stock Exchange's data. Major results have been published, other results have been presented in working papers and on conferences. This book presents a consistent view of our research.

Up to our knowledge, the results are still valid, and no errors were detected. The file records order data, for each order the time point of submission, and the time point of its extinction. The complete recording of all trading events provides a comprehensive picture of the trading landscape that goes far beyond the picture provided by "averaging" orders and prices.

The innovative and comprehensive data set required adequate statistical tools. We thank Thomas Landes, Chris Adcock, Michael Huetl, Georgui Konstantinov, Johannes Prix and Emanuel Kopp, Bernd Schossmann, Alexander Veverka and Olav Vetter for fruitful cooperation and permanent willingness to engage in discussions, and for being able to quote from both published and non-published papers that we produced together. Thanks go to the journal's editors for generously granting to quote from the published articles. Many thanks go to Alexander Veverka for the cooperation in finding an operational definition of efficient markets. We got successfully inspired by the Bose–Einstein interpretation of entropy. Our discussion was animated by, at that time, current discussion of awarding the Physics Nobel Prize to Ketterle. But unfortunately, we had no opportunity to talk about the further discussions around Nobel Price awarded to Giorgio Parisi and the Abel Prize awarded to Michel Talagrand. The valuation and errors occurring in the description of these issues are solely our responsibility.

Finally, we would like to inform the potential reader about the content and what she may gain when reading the book: Basically, our book offers a culture dish for

[8] See Loistl and Landes editors (1989).

[9] Behavioural research history covers at least Thurstone (1927), Luce (2005), McFadden (2001) and Haghani et al. (2021) provide a comprehensive overview of the various fields of applications.

[10] Thaler (2017) regrets this omission.

modelling trading on markets. We start with the most transparent one, an electronic trading market. But the concept can also be used for modelling other markets.

New aspects:

- Our book examines the complete chain of individual steps to be taken till a transaction is completed: How orders are placed and how the order matching generates prices.
- Matching of orders to generate transactions is a bipartite issue. To perform a transaction, one needs both, a buyer and a seller. The frequently used expression of "executing an order" blurs the necessity of the counterpart: The market price as the compromise of both, buyer's and seller's subjective interests constitutes the objectification of their individual ratings.
- The required data was extracted from the Xetra trading file. It recorded within the investigation period all the buy and sell orders, time stamped by the timepoint of submission and the time point of execution. The data was anonymised.
- We display the complete order data dynamically as the real two pages of the order book.
- The decision of selecting and placing an order has been modelled according to the discrete choice or random utility approach. Our research results confirm that order specification could be explained up to 80 per cent by ex post micro data using that random utility approach.
- The random utility formula provides the utility for taking that action. This formula provides the probability to take that action too. The calculation of transition probability via Master equation is not necessary. Additionally, the formula equals Shannon's entropy definition.
- Entropy's threefold interpretation permits an operational interpretation of the efficient market hypothesis: Markets are efficient, when no participant has a reason to a further action. This is the case, when the utility/probability/entropy to take an action is equal for every action.

In summary, we present an innovative approach to modelling real market activities, focusing on placing and matching orders. The mathematics refers to basic analysis. The formulas are developed step by step. But the economic discussion of market activities is more thorough. We follow Alfred Marshall's advice: *Use mathematics as a shorthand language* - after the problem had been researched using ordinary language - *rather than as an engine for independent inquiry of the unknown.*

Otto Loistl Georg Behm Sascha Bakry

Introduction 2

Abstract

This chapter explains, why improved technical facilities und economic necessities enhanced trading. The world became much more volatile. The experts developed new instruments to counter these increasing risks. The commonly applied hedging procedure by diversification was no longer sufficient. Professionals voted for risk management by trading. The financial professionals sharpened their tools to manage volatility. They introduced options and futures to hedge volatility of spot instruments and established trading opportunities. That is the core message of Black Scholes option pricing formula.

Keywords

Capital market issues • Trading venues • Principle of asset management • Three parameter principle of risk management

2.1 Economic Evaluation of Trading

2.1.1 Innovative Perception of Market Performance

The perception of economic issues is changing: "...*ideas that previously have been considered the holy trinity in economics - rationality, greed,and equilibrium - are being modified, and the process is changing the very nature of economics*".[1] Thaler postulates to switch from "*homo economicus to homo sapiens.*"[2] According to

[1] Colander et al (2004, p. 3).

[2] Thaler (2000) article's title.

O. Loistl et al., *Screen Based Trading and Open Order Book*, New Economic Windows,
https://doi.org/10.1007/978-3-031-99052-6_2

Schumpeter,[3] every science passes two stages regarding the understanding of its research object: Firstly, starting with static relations and then in the second step formulating dynamic (inter)relations. Our understanding is that modelling a market's performance may now move from the static equilibrium approach to the realistic dynamic interactive approach. Several scientific disciplines have prepared appropriate tools. Their combination provides the instruments to take the second step according to Schumpeter.

The focus of our investigation is the innovative modelling of markets' recent performance. According to Gallegati (2018) the alteration of markets has implications on the other two holy trinity parts as well: "*Freed from the straitjacket of equilibrium... opened both, the opportunity and the necessity to deal with realmarket events*".[4] Several aspects of the great and complex issue have been worked out independently at an operational level. But until now an approach putting these fragments together has been missing. In the following, we will first describe the fragments and then use a very clear example—an electronic trading system—to show how a market really works.

2.1.2 Capital Market Current Issues[5]

At the beginning, we should explain the subject of our investigation. In principle, it is the physical or electronic place where shares are bought and sold. Behind this simple description lies an extensive industry. The following brief description positions our investigation within this industry.

1. Investors are buying and selling shares in different varieties. Investors range from big players like banks, insurances companies and funds to individuals. These different players have different interests, different means and different trading attitudes.

---

[3] Schumpeter (1965, p. 1172). The complete argument goes as follows: An observer just descended from the mars might comprehensively assume, that the human mind starts by the analysis of the real tangible phenomena and later, when more complicated relations must be investigated, to go over to abstract thinking, i.e. that he starts by dynamic relationships and then goes over to work out static relationships.

> "**Such a procedure however did not happen at any field of scientific research.**" (p 1172. Own translation. Emphasis added)

[4] Mauro Gallegati (2018, p. 53).

[5] A comprehensive description of the current trading issues at exchanges from a professional point of view brings: Francioni and Schwartz (2017). Our approach is devoted to establishing a quantitative model reflecting these professional perspectives.

2. Intermediaries. In most cases, buyers and sellers require support to come together. The intermediaries' help is needed especially in non-liquid markets and when trading large volumes. The intermediaries have different terms, e.g. brokers or market makers. They make money by charging a fee for every transaction they organise on the one hand and by buying and selling shares on their own account. This activity leads to conflicts of interests with their clients when they take positions in the share they are brokering. The rules these intermediaries must observe range from the general obligation "to maintain an orderly market" to specified rules for "designated market makers" at NYSE or "designated sponsors" at Xetra.
3. Trading venues. In order to make trading among those willing to trade efficient, these people met for organised trading meetings at fixed locations and at fixed times. They were termed in Anglo-Saxon "exchanges" after London's building and Bourse/Boerse in Continental Europe. The trading features changed during the time according to the trading needs and the technical facility. The need to adjust the rules and regulations was obvious whenever a crash disturbed the trading. Such crashes occur regularly when three circumstances unite with the ever-existing human factor greed. These circumstances are: The emergence of a new trading feature, the abundant availability of money and finally, the dominance of an optimistic view. The positive aspects of the trade function make it easy to promote, but the dangers are not known or are ignored. Talented speculators persuade profit maximising investors to buy investments with unknown risks. The crash follows.
4. The regulators. The description of the crash makes it clear that these trading facilities require rules and regulations. Regulation is multi-layered in many countries: the first layer is a law enacted by the government. This law regulates general circumstances regarding a company organising trading. The second layer is constituted by levels 2, 3, etc., regulation.
5. In the United States, the Security Exchange Act provides the general guidelines and has investor protection as its primary goal. It distinguishes between Self Regulating Organisations "SROs" like the New York Stock Exchange "NYSE" and Alternative Trading Systems "ATS"[6] like Nasdaq. Explaining the differences between the two goes beyond the scope of our investigation. The Security and Exchange Commission SEC is in charge of supervising the law's execution. The challenge is the adjustment of the law to adapt to new technological and financial instruments. If the SEC imposes too rigid controls on nascent developments too early in its emergence, a potentially desirable innovation may be prevented from coming into existence. On the other hand, if innovation is regulated too late or is not subjected to regulation at all, this may give way to a crash and hence impair financial stability.

[6] An ATS is a trading system that meets the definition of "exchange" under federal securities law but is not required to register as a national securities exchange if the ATS operates under the exemption provided under Exchange Act Rule 3a1-1(a), SEC (2024a).

6. The European capital market exhibits similarities and yet big differences. The EU is a supranational political and economic union of member states, each with their own jurisdiction. The EU has since its foundation taken steps to greater integration and the introduction of a common currency has been one of these great leaps. Yet, the unification of corporate laws is still "under construction" and hence each country oversees its own corporate laws (certain elements being transpositions of European law however). Each company in a set country must obey its own national corporate law. Therein lies the difference to the United States. While a company must comply with the corporate law of the state in which it is incorporated, and companies therefore favour states with less rigid regulations (e.g. Delaware), any company applying for interstate share trading must comply with national securities laws. This is different from Europe: Firstly, every company must comply with the corporate laws of the country in which it does business, regardless of where the company was founded. The European Commission has taken steps to unify both, capital market law and corporate law. We will concentrate on modelling the trading specifics of Xetra, that operates under the German Stock Exchange law. The reason for focussing on Xetra is that its regulation provides a transparent bipartite matching of orders. The fate of any order is transparently documented from submission until matching or withdrawal and that enables a clearcut modelling.

In the current situation, the SEC is confronted with big computer power and big data, and globalisation is changing trading venues in a similar way. The number of trading places has grown comparably. Additionally, modes and motives for trading shares have increased and diversified. Trading of options and exchange traded funds have influenced the mode of trading shares. Our focus is on the plain activity of trading shares. We intend to model the complete procedure from the traders' decision to buy/sell shares, the selection of an order and submitting that order at the trading venue, thus signalising his/her willingness to trade and -last but not least—the completion of the transaction by matching his/her order with an opposite order. The straight matching procedure follows the price time priority rule: Among those orders with equal price limit, that order will be matched first, that has been submitted at the earliest time point. If a trader wants to buy/sell his order immediately or at once, he/she should choose "best possible". He/she may receive the worst possible price. But in case, she has to hedge a future contract, that loss is equalised by a profit on the other side. Regarding the final step at any market, we follow Alvin E. Roth and investigate "*The (new) Economics of Matchmaking*".[7]

We investigate the matching of buy and sell orders. That's a difference to the wording of US exchanges and SEC wording; they use the word "execution".[8] But

[7] Roth (2015) Sub-Title of his book.
[8] Investor.gov U.S. Securities and Exchange Commission "Executing an Order", undated.

that word gives no information about the final fate of an order. Obviously, execution means that the order will be fulfilled. In fact, "execution" implies obviously just that the order's extinction. The way and manner of extinction is left open. Matching implies that the order will be brought together with an opposite order and that the other order complies with the first order's conditions. "Execution" leaves open who is the counter party and how it matches the other order's conditions. "Execution" that implies finding the appropriate counterparty or extinct the order otherwise is obviously market makers' or brokers' duty. But the human brokers compete now with electronic trading systems. Accordingly, the catalogue of trading facilities was enlarged comparably.

Regarding the trading places we observe a consolidation: The biggest might be ICE, Intercontinental Exchange. ICE has been generated to be a parent company of New York Stock Exchange (NYSE) and London Stock Exchange (LSE). The NYSE operates five equities exchanges, each purpose-built to meet the needs of corporate and ETF issuers and to offer greater choice to investors in how they trade. NYSE American market for small companies, NYSE Arca Equities, the first all-electronic exchange in the US, NYSE National, a fully electronic market National Chicago is a fully electronic equities exchange with unique features to support the Institutional Brokers serving the exchange-traded derivatives community, along with full NYSE Pillar order entry and execution functionality..., NYSE American Equities, NYSE Chicago. And NYSE National all operate using NYSE Pillar, our [i.e. NYSE's] integrated trading technology platform that is designed to improve efficiency and reduce complexity, while enhancing consistency, performance and resiliency".[9]

The US trading venues are dominated by human brokers that act on both sides. They can be buyers or sellers. The situation is even more complex because the other US trading places submit information about their trading performance into a common information platform termed "National Market Systems".

That interaction is not compatible with the basic game theoretic condition that the matching partner could be identified. This blurring condition has been a major reason that Alvin E. Roth avoided to investigate commodity markets. We investigate matching at capital market according the "Xetra" rules. Xetra is a pure electronic trading system with an electronic matching system of opposite orders. However, the management agreed that human intervention is appropriate in certain non-liquid situations. Therefore, the management introduced the "designated sponsor", analogously to the "designated market maker". But the rights and obligations of the designated sponsor are much more precise and he could be integrated in the Xetra matching system. His efficiency has been investigated by simulations in different market situation.

[9] NYSE, leaflet nyse.com/equities.

2.1.3 Asset Management Activities

In times of Algo-Trading, the question is how to integrate trinity of research, portfolio construction and trading into an efficient investment strategy. The relation among these three parts has been changing: The improvements in IT, the communication tools, the deregulation of the capital markets and finally, the introduction of a huge number of so-called derivative products led to a fundamental change in asset management. New investment instruments have been developed, and investors are not restricted to concentrate on long-only equity and fixed income investments or to trade on the local market only. The recent regulation initiatives—to further investor protection both in US and EU—will increase the importance of trading issues, e.g. best execution. The philosophy of buying a market portfolio and holding it till maturity is no longer the guideline, neither from the regulatory nor from the portfolio management point of view. The development of the active portfolio management strategy (Grinold and Kahn 2000) breaks fresh ground to portfolio management techniques and terms: Long/short equity, market neutral, managed futures and much more sophisticated strategies have been made available to a great variety of investors. The impressive developments of information communication technology enable investors to trade globally nearly all these instruments. They obtain information about all these investments nearly without any time delay.

The paradigm of the efficient market has been abandoned, at least in modern portfolio management. Active portfolio management has shown the superiority of portfolio selection and revision. The rise of hedge funds regarding number of funds and money invested is compelling evidence that there are inefficiencies in the market that can be exploited by sophisticated strategies. Even if the recent crises in hedge fund business underline that there is of course risk in the hedge fund business, the overall superiority of active sophisticated portfolio management is beyond any doubt.

However, exploiting these opportunities requires very sophisticated tools in all three segments of portfolio management, either research, portfolio construction or trading. The major challenge in the moment seems to be that these three chapters must be treated together to exploit the opportunities. We will term this combined approach Integrated Active Asset Management (IAAM). It is the real challenge we must cope with to take advantage of the opportunities offered by the recently available techniques. We will explain the individual steps firstly and discuss then the issue of integration.

Research

The advantage of a systematic investment strategy is the possibility of using complex quantitative approaches at every stage of the Integrated Active Asset Management Process.

The quantitative research strategy assumes that the future returns of an investment instrument can be modelled by a certain generation process, e.g. if the future asset returns are significantly influenced by the lagged relationship between various factors, the patterns of these indicators could be used to accurately predict the future returns. Hence, a combination of a systematic investment strategy and an accurate prediction of short-term future returns of financial assets embedded in an integrated active asset management is a convincing approach to market opportunities.

Such a quantitative approach makes high demands on active asset management. At a first stage, a financial forecasting system that predicts the future returns and the expected volatility of financial instruments has to be developed. Therefore, an analysis of the target process has to be defined and indicators influencing the target process have to be found. Dependencies between indicators and the target process have to be modelled mathematically and short-term forecasts predicting the future returns have to be generated.

Portfolio Construction

In the second step, a portfolio based on the predicted and historical returns has to be constructed. Following a purely quantitative approach the optimal asset allocation is determined by optimisation algorithms subject to linear constraints such as lower and upper limits for single assets or asset classes according to the requirements stated in the management mandate. The objective function is to maximise the expected portfolio return while minimising the expected portfolio risk and expected transaction costs. The resulting portfolio consists of a basket of long positions in those instruments with the highest expected returns and a basket of short positions in instruments with expected negative returns.

Trading

At a third stage, the systematic trading strategy must be implemented. The number of shares/securities determined in the portfolio construction step must be transformed in reality by buying/selling the appropriate number of shares.

Trading implies firstly determining the marketplace, secondly the timing and thirdly slicing of the entire amount into several tranches. Where, when and how to trade.

If the trades have been executed, this gives rise to monitoring of the trading procedure and the transaction costs. These lead to an integrated performance analysis as well as an efficiency analysis at each stage of the entire process.

We will discuss the tasks at the individual stages of the integrated process. We firstly will discuss the complexities of forecast generation and the portfolio construction process. As a result of new trends in trading, a more detailed analysis will be done for the implementation process.

Due to the short-term forecasts, a portfolio based on a systematic investment strategy must be rebalanced very often. Hence, transaction costs are a critical component for tactical asset management. There are various factors that influence transaction costs, e.g. trading costs, brokerage fees, price impact costs, slippage, implementation shortfall, etc. While some of the costs can be measured quite exactly (explicit costs), others cannot be quantified as easily (implicit costs). In our analysis we want to focus on the second. We want to have a detailed look at the prices at which we decide to execute an order (decision price) and the actual trading price. We will show that these price differences can be of relevant magnitude for some instruments and therefore we want to analyse the impact on the performance.

When analysing implementation shortfall, we focus on two major factors that significantly influence the price difference between decision price and trading price. First, we examine the impact of the amount invested in a portfolio. As the order size of high-volume portfolios can be very high, brokers are not capable to fulfil all the orders immediately. They split up big orders to packages that are traded separately.

Interactive decision-making comprises the following issues: For ease of argumentation, we introduce therefore the following symbols (Further details see chapter 5.2.2):

Agents: $A_1, A_i \ldots A_N$ taking.
Actions: a_{11}, a_{1j}, a_{ij} a_{nm}. Processing information about.
Decision frame changes from F_1 via F_k to F_K

1. We must model the decision any agent takes.
2. Then we need to model the selection of the agent whose action is taken over by the system and which has influence on the decision framework. In our market model, we must decide whose traders order will be placed in the order book. It will be done according to price time priority. In our model that activity will be selected that brings the highest utility.
3. What is the impact the activity selected has on the decision frame. In our model, the impact is either, it adds to the order book, or it generates a transaction, if the conditions of any buy or sell order match with the order under consideration placed. In any case, the order book will be adjusted accordingly.
4. The next step is, how the other agents get the information about the changed order book and how the other agents process the new information on the new order book and decide. Details will be explained later.
5. This design requires that the consequences of any action are known. That assumption is fulfilled in the segment we are investigating: the stock exchange. The cause-effect relations are transparent by the exact bookkeeping of all events.
6. Such transparency about the precise cause-effect information and the consequences is also required by the instruments we are applying: The random utility model.
7. In other cases, the cause-effect situation is not exactly known. In such cases, the formal modelling of cause-effect is displayed by mathematical function, sometimes by probability distributions. The reliability of the factual statement derived from such models however deserves a very careful check. This demand is even more important in case of probabilistic relations.
8. Another assumption must be mentioned: In any case the real cause-effect must be known and regarded by quantitative modelling. A straight translation of a

function developed for and successfully applied in case of physical relations should be checked even more carefully.

We must model the impact that action a_{11} has on the decision frame. It changes from F_0 to F_1 for ease of clarity we omit for the moment the fact, that the change is due to action of agents 1. Therefore there should be an additional index for the agents responsible for the Frame's change.

At an electronic trading system, the rules and regulations are transparent, any agent's actions are well known and their consequences are precisely recordable. The basic structure might provide a blueprint to model other markets as well. The following fragment might be identified:

1. Firstly, matching of opposite human interests is the key function of markets. Alvin E. Roth and Roth/Sotomayor promoted the analysis of markets[10] and affirmed the importance of matchmaking between opposite partners. Roth was awarded the Nobel prize for this innovative approach.
2. Secondly, agents indicate the willingness to trade by submitting buy or sell orders to the marketplace under consideration. Among the possible orders, a trader selects that order, that promises the highest utility in the sense of discrete choice. The utility formula equals physics' and statistic's entropy formula.
3. Matching of appropriate buy and sell orders generates the transaction of goods from seller to buyer and a market prize: Objective pricing occurs by matching opposite interests. The matching follows the rules and regulations of real markets, e.g. the Xetra electronic market. It follows by no means any artificial market. The results are relevant for a real-world market. The relevance for any artificial market will not be discussed.
4. The tools we rely on are successfully applied to manage many commercial issues. They are not used in finance and economics. Finance scholars until now display loyalty to the hypothesis that markets are efficient and in equilibrium and there do not exist arbitrage opportunities.

Until Roth's research, the analysis of markets performance and of matching opposite interests has been left to markets themselves. The basic assumption—it might be called an air castle—has been that markets are efficient and achieve and/ or are in equilibrium: According to this assumption the exploitation of market opportunities—of arbitrage opportunities—could be left to markets themselves and economists can omit the investigation of this decisive economic issue. Economists until now do not care about this vital economic activity: Exploitation of arbitrage opportunities is an essential economic motivation and motor of economic transformations. Economic modelling of markets begins until now only, when the essential economic activity has already happened: The exploitation of arbitrage opportunities. Model builders ignore the matching of supply and demand orders

[10] Alvin E. Roth (2015), Roth and Sotomayor (1992).

to generate transactions and prices as well. Regarding the application of mathematics, professionals felt authorised to proceed in this way by Jevons's statement: "*It is clear that Economics, if it is to be a science at all, must be a mathematical science.*"[11] It had the big advantage that professionals were authorised to apply their mathematical methods—they were used in physics already—to analyse economic/financial problems without checking, if these methods were appropriate to model economic/financial problems. They felt authorised by Jevons' dictum and disregarded Marshalls famous "six step recommendation": "*use mathematics as a shorthand language, rather than an engine of enquiry*".[12]

To avoid misunderstandings: Mathematical modelling per se has the big advantage in any science that mathematical models of any problem are clearcut and could be followed quite in detail. However, these mathematical models should provide an isomorphic picture of the real world under consideration.[13] That must be proven by extra investigations, and this prove should not be restricted to statistical tests. Alfred Marshall gave a further instruction: "*Induction and deduction are both needed for scientific thought as the right and left foot are both needed for walking.*"[14] Quantitative models of markets have until now been protected against a reality check of real markets performance by the already mentioned assumption that markets are efficient and/or in equilibrium. But the real implications of that assumption have not been checked either. "*Mainstream economists do use advanced mathematical techniques; only they use the wrong ones, because they don't consider economics to be a complex system, as it is composed of heterogeneous and interacting agents*".[15] The assumptions mentioned at the beginning are still regarded as the holy grail in economics and in finance, even if prominent scholars pointed towards the preliminary character of that assumption since more than a century. Just two quotes: "*The actual world both physical and economic has no equilibrium*" (Fisher (1892), 103). Von Neumann and Morgenstern (1944) conceded that economic modelling under the assumption of equilibrium is only second best: "*A dynamic theory would unquestionably be more complete and therefore preferable.*" They justified taking this second-best equilibrium approach by pointing towards the rudimentary exploration of real economics. "*For the real dynamics which investigates the precise motions, usually far from equilibria, a much deeper knowledge of these dynamic phenomena is required*" (von Neumann and Morgenstern 1944,

[11] Jevons (2020, p. 2).

[12] The complete recommendation is reported in footnote 15 in Chapter 8.

[13] Gallegati (2018, Preface).

[14] Alfred Marshall (1920, p. 24). An impressive example of suitable vs. unsuitable mathematics is the modelling of the planetary orbits. Modelling epicycles did not fit the astronomical data. Kepler applied an ellipsoid orbit and that fit the data. Regarding economics and finance, the discussion is in the state of transition from circular to ellipsoid orbit, i.e. from the assumption of equilibrium to the assumption of emergence and self-organisation. Formulating the deficits of the one approach and the necessities of the other is the first step. We propose the next step: an operational approach modelling a market's performance without equilibrium but with tested - not ad hoc assumed - models of human actions.

[15] Gallegati (2018, Preface, VII).

45). Indeed, the knowledge about economics' performance was not harmonised, but several confusing opinions were still around at this time. An English buzzword was common since the 1940s in London: "*If five economists were together, you hear six opinions – and two of them were from Keynes.*"

There is no doubt, von Neumann and Morgenstern's "game theory" milestone offered economists various suggestions for research directions and improved economics recognition comparably in different branches alike.

But it seems an open question, if this research success reduced the number of different opinions. Anyway, mathematical economic modelling got a push. Several Game Theory researchers were honoured with Nobel Prizes in Economics. Among the decorated researchers, Alvin E. Roth must be mentioned in the context of our topic. He investigated the explicit conditions under which opposite interests can be matched on the markets. He analysed and solved the task, how study places should be allocated among students. Another issue was to allocate kidneys among patients. He made only a cursory remark concerning capital markets. He found "markets are everywhere". He especially reaffirmed that the core feature of markets is the matching of agents' opposite interests and that this core feature has to be modelled: Traders disclose their willingness to pay or to sell by submitting buy or sell orders to the trading venue. Deals are completed and transactions generated by matching opposite orders.

He published, together with Marilda A. Oliveira Sotomayor (1992) the comprehensive synopsis of matching on markets. But they explicitly left commodity markets (and implicitly capital markets alike) unconsidered, but left it for further research. The reason was, that at these markets the sets of buyers and of sellers could not always be strictly separated. Alvin E. Roth broke fresh ground and sharpened the awareness that the real matching among two opposite groups of market participants is a vital part of any market's performance. In economic and finance markets buyers act on one side and sellers on the other. The situation is clear cut at capital markets in case of an electronic market. Traders submit their orders, either buy or sell orders. If a trader wants to switch, he withdraws his order and resubmits an opposite one.[16]

Even if Roth did not investigate capital markets by means of game theory, he reaffirmed the vital significance of matching of interests on markets. We strongly believe that game theoretic skills will help to establish rules even in complex markets like US New Market System.[17] Verbal description of (capital) markets familiarise with the (capital) markets performance. There exist also publications describing capital markets by means of time series of prices. But prices are the vital product of a market's performance, not the true performance of human beings acting on markets. Human beings are the core driving element on markets. Even electronic trading systems support, but not yet substitute, human agents as traders.

[16] The situation is different, when brokers are in charge to provide an orderly market. They can submit buy and sell orders all the time. But they must reckon their activities' efficiency, at different markets at different strictness..

[17] Recent research shows that the symmetry assumption can be mitigated. See Kirman et al. (2023).

Human traders tell programmers how to program the electronic trading systems. We will describe and model human beings matching their orders, thus generating prices and transactions. That is a big leap forward from leaving markets by themselves.

We believe that science has acquired sufficient knowledge about market's dynamic and about human behaviour alike that the modelling of market's performance without equilibrium should be possible. Trying to make a step forward beyond equilibrium.

Giving up the "equilibrium straight jacket" (Gallegati 2018), we are facing the big problem: How to fill the free space resulting from removing the "equilibrium straight jacket", how to model an agent's actions reliably. Under the dominating equilibrium condition, it does not matter too much, how an agent is assumed to act: He is always forced to pursue the equilibrium condition. Without the equilibrium condition, he follows his own will, whatever that might be. He will select that activity that brings the highest utility to him. Regardless, if that individual activity attains the overall equilibrium. In real world, there does not exist any rule that forces the acting agents to attain an overall equilibrium. We are not aware of a given procedure that measures in a method consistent with theory if equilibrium has been attained. We will propose a rule that is derived from watching the real-world behaviour.

2.2 Organised Trading Venues to Enhance Trading

2.2.1 Organised Trading Venues and New Order Types

Risk Management by Trading requires well organised trading venues. A trading venue is a physically or electronically organised place where people come together having the intention to trade, either they want to buy some goods or to sell some goods. These meetings are commonly called markets. We intend to describe and model markets where securities are traded. The basic principles are relevant for any market where transactions are settled quickly and without any disputes that would delay the transaction settlement. Such trading venues are commonly called exchanges or bourses and access to the trading place is permitted only to persons that possess personal reputation and solid financial standing.

Traders must be informed about the quality, quantity and price of the good to be traded. To make such information easier to achieve, the items traded at a trading venue are standardised. Regarding securities, every security is carefully examined, if it fulfils the appropriate legal and quality requirements.

Therefore, every buyer can be sure, that the good or security he buys, fulfils the qualities any item of the category to which it belongs. Vice versa, any seller can expect to get the money agreed in the transaction.

To increase the trading speed further, the trading venues under consideration prescribe certain types of offers, buyers and/or sellers can choose. The simplest form is a market order: The traders want to have executed her order as quickly as possible at any price the market pays at the moment of the trade. The traders just specify the number of items. If the traders want 100 shares or a multiple of 100 shares, then he submits a round lot, in other cases he wants to buy/sell an odd lot of shares.

Electronic trading capabilities made further order differentiations possible[18]:

Boerse Frankfurt offers "intelligent order types".[19] Without going into details Frankfurt Exchange offers additionally:

- *Trailing-Stop-Orders*: The Limits of a stop loss order will be adjusted according to the changing price quotation.
- *One-cancels-Other*: Two orders will be submitted. If one order is executed, then the other will be cancelled.
- *Order-on-Event*: the order enters into force, when a third item, e.g. index or future quotation reaches a priori given level.

These order types increase the flexibility of trading. The orders can be adjusted to the course of the exchange.

The last-mentioned order type might be especially suited for attaining a hedged portfolio by the combination of options and shares. This assumption is vital for the fact that Black and Scholes' option price formula applies a risk-free discount rate. This replication possibility has been questioned.[20] We first examine what the trading feasibility should look like in order to enable such perfect replication. The order type "order on event" is certainly a step in the right direction. Besides the technicality of orders reacting instantaneously and incremental to the change of the share price, the existence of n is not sure. That is a basic principle throughout all exchanges: an exchange provides the conditions that the potential traders can submit their trading wishes as precise and detailed as possible. But not any exchanges guarantee that there is counterpart ready to finalise the trade to matching conditions. Exchanges do not take the risk to act as counterpart in case no external counterpart exists. Of course, exchanges are aware of that counterparty-risk, especially at non liquid markets. But instead of taking that risk themselves, they install the institution of a "broker"—that is a general label of that function—or a "designated sponsor"—that is the specified function of that intermediate at Frankfurt's Xetra. At New York Stock Exchange (NYSE), a broker is in charge "to maintain an orderly market". We will not go into modelling NYSE but concentrate on modelling Frankfurt's Xetra and investigate the designated sponsor's efficiency by simulating different market scenarios. The existence of an appropriate counterpart is not for sure.

[18] Frankfurt's commonly used orders are described in chapter 2.2.1.

[19] See Börse Frankfurt (2019).

[20] Derman and Taleb (2005, pp. 323) and Haug and Taleb (2011, pp. 97).

Table 2.1 Frequency of different events in the database

Event type	Event code	Absolute frequency
Order entry	1	2,284,628
Order modification	2	36,165
Order cancellation	3	1,626,896
Order filled completely	4	675,232
Order partially filled	5	373,760
Order deleted automatically	6	16,597
Technical entry	101	461
Technical cancellation	103	461

Note Data is adapted from Prix et al. (2007)

2.2.2 Order Events and Codes

See Table 2.1.

2.3 Risk Management by Trading: Portfolio Insurance Concept

2.3.1 The Three Parameter Principle

Risk management by flexible adjustments to decision frame changes is well known and practiced among professionals. But it is difficult to model by mathematics. Therefore, this problem is disregarded quite frequently among academics and/or quants. But its importance has been reaffirmed among academics and professionals alike when Black and Scholes promoted the risk-free application of the already well-known option pricing formula. The formula as such has been successfully applied by, e.g. Thorp and Kassouf before Black and Scholes' publication. Thorp mentions that he sent the formula to Fisher Black, who, together with Myron Scholes, promoted the use of this formula to create a risk-free portfolio. A risk-free portfolio was achieved by combining the corresponding number of shares with a short option. The portfolio could be made risk-free, even if the share price fluctuated according to a stochastic process. Black and Scholes assumed that the share price follows a stochastic process that fluctuates in an infinite number of incrementally small steps. Furthermore, they showed that a portfolio consisting of shares (long) and an option (short) can be made risk-free if the momentary and incremental fluctuations in the share price (long) can be offset by opposite momentary and incremental fluctuations in the option (short). They derived the formula by integrating the stochastic process according to the formula of Îto. Interestingly, the same formula could also be derived by discounting the option value.[21] Thorp and others used this formula some time before the publication of Black and Scholes.[22]

2.3.2 Two Different Scenarios to Derive Black and Scholes Formula

2.3.2.1 Derivation by Means of a Risk-Free Portfolio

Black and Scholes claimed to have proven that a risk-free discount rate can be used. Later, Kreps generalised that approach and extended the Arrow-Debreu formula to the effect that a risk-free portfolio can be formed if the state of nature is equal to the number of securities. Using the Black and Scholes formula, he showed that the two-parameter risk-free scenario can be extended to a three-parameter risk-free scenario: In addition to the number of states of nature and the number of shares, trading opportunities must also be considered.

In case of the Black and Scholes formula with two securities, a risk-free portfolio can also be achieved if the state of nature—according to the stochastic process—changes instantaneously in incremental steps, provided that such instantaneous and incremental trading opportunities exist. Even if trading opportunities exist under normal conditions, they may no longer exist in critical situations (as the failure of Long-Term Capital Management shows)[23] (Figs. 2.1 and 2.2).

A number of publications[24] address the shortcomings of the prevailing efficient market assumption, especially stating that it lacks the "physicists" way of approaching scientific problems, in particular a systematic comparison between "theory" and "experiments" (i.e. empirical results). "*[T]he whole pricing methodology is based on the construction of risk-free strategies. The idea of zero risk is counter-intuitive and the reason for the existence of these risk-free strategies in the Black–Scholes theory is buried in the premises of Itô's stochastic differential rules.*"[25] Bouchaud/Potters (2000) contrast Hull's (1997) basic statement "*The pricing of derivatives involves the construction of risk-free hedges from traded securities.*"[26] with the disclaimer found on most Chicago Board Options Exchange documents: Option trading involves risk![27]

The pricing concepts rely on the assumption of an arbitrage-free world.[28] This assumption provides the justification for neglecting the modelling of the real market forces: "*Prices are falling because there are more sellers than buyers in the*

[21] Derman and Taleb (2005) provide a sketchy derivation. A detailed derivation is provided below in our booklet.

[22] Haug and Taleb (2011) and the references therein.

[23] Dunbar (2000).

[24] See, for example, Ilinski (2001), Bouchaud and Potters (2000), and Kurz and Beltratti (1997).

[25] Bouchaud and Potters (2000, p. xi).

[26] Hull (1997, p. 539). For the fourth edition see Hull (2000).

[27] See Bouchaud and Potters (2000, p. 179).

[28] See, for example, Jarrow (2001, p. 75).

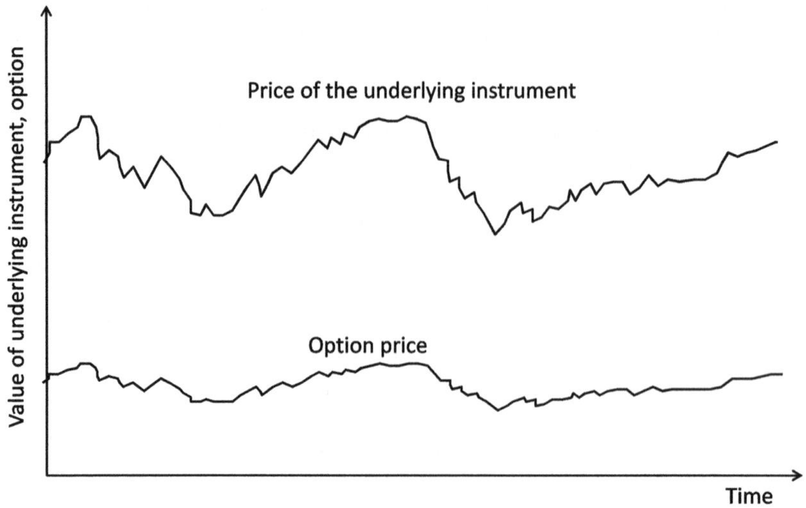

Fig. 2.1 Value correlation between share price and price of a call option[29]

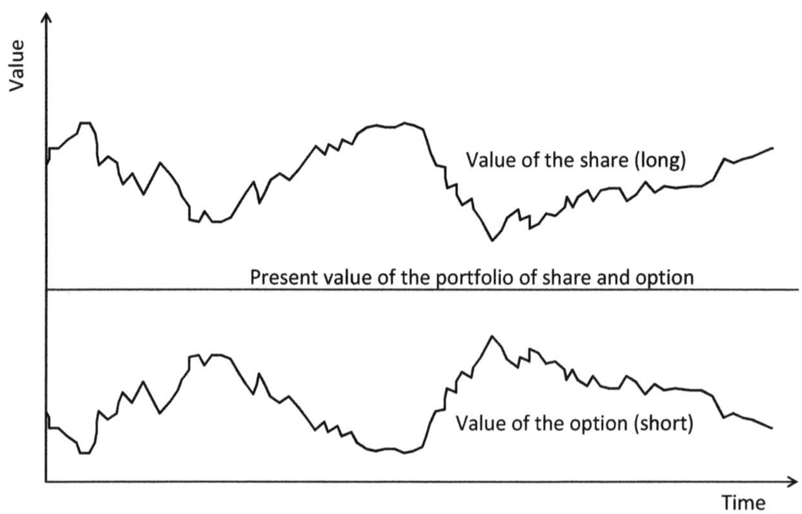

Fig. 2.2 Characteristics of share price changes over time[30]

market", as the famous J.P. Morgan used to say in reply to the question why there is a stock price tumble. It is therefore not sufficient for a reliable modelling

[29] Loistl (1996, p. 328).
[30] Loistl (1996, p. 343).

of prices to rely on prices. Instead, we need to look at the forces that determine prices. This necessity explains the growing interest in modelling the microstructure of the market.

In this book, we rely on Frankfurt's electronic trading system Xetra to analyse the question of the optimal design of a hybrid trading structure by examining various market scenarios with the help of Doubly Stochastic Markov Processes or DSMP for short. DSMP is a high-dimensional Markov model that is capable of structuring and implementing the rules and regulations of any marketplace.[31] The term DSMP was chosen in analogy to Cox's Doubly Stochastic Poisson Processes.[32] The idea of connecting micro- and macrolevels comes from Herman Haken's famous book Synergetics.[33] DSMP's basic catallactic idea consists in the combination of five different aspects:

1. The determination of a marketplace by means of a Markov process with a high-dimensional state space that describes this marketplace.
2. The determination of each feasible activity according to the rules and regulations of the marketplace under consideration and the modification of the state space it generates.
3. The determination of the utility that each activity has for the actor.
4. The connection of each feasible activity with the change of a specific dimension of the state space; for example, an offer to buy the stock j changes the number of offers for that stock j in the marketplace.
5. The determination of the transition rate that changes this specific state dimension takes into account the utility that the action that causes the state space change has for the actor.

The Black and Scholes formula can be derived from two different assumptions. The formula as such was derived several years before the publication of Black and Scholes' famous paper by discounting the value of the option at the time of expiry.[34] The major unsolved issue was the determination of the risky discount rate. We will come back to this question later.

The second assumption refers to a risk-free portfolio thus justifying the application of a risk-free interest rate. This argument has been seen as the major progress

---

[31] The following description follows closely the models already given in Landes and Loistl (1992, pp. 209), Loistl et al (2002, pp. 199), Loistl et al (2004, pp. 17).

[32] See Kingman (2002) for explaining the history of Cox processes.

[33] See Haken (1983a). There is, however, a big difference between the physicists' connection of micro- and macro-level and the adaptation to market problems in economics. In economics there is an interaction among the agents at the micro-level which does not exist at the micro-level in science. All the models in economics borrowed from science ignore this fundamental requirement of catallactics, the exchange by interaction. This was well accepted in the first half of the last century and was honoured by the Nobel prize to von Hayek in 1974. Buchanan (2001) has newly reaffirmed the necessity of catallactics.

[34] See Thorp (1975) mentioning Boness (1964) and Thorp (1969).

for which Black and Scholes have been applauded. The Black and Scholes derivation assumes that the share price S and the time to expiry t determine the price of the call option c in addition to the exercise conditions:

$$c = f(S, t) \tag{2.1}$$

Black and Scholes further assume that the portfolio under consideration consists of q_s shares with a price of S and q_c call options with a price of c. The entire value V_H of this portfolio is therefore given by:

$$V_H = q_s S + q_c c \tag{2.2}$$

This portfolio is called "hedge portfolio", the famous risk-free portfolio. According to (2.2), the value of the hedge-portfolio depends both, on the prices of the shares and options and on the number of shares and options held in the portfolio. The share price may fluctuate over time, but the price of the option is perfectly correlated with the share price.

If both the number of shares and the number of options remain constant, the change in the value of the hedge portfolio can be caused either by a change in the share price dS, which automatically causes a change in the option price, or by the time decay dt. . At a given point of time, i.e. ignoring the time decay, these effects may be expressed by the total differential of (2.2):

$$dV_H = q_s dS + q_c dc \tag{2.3}$$

According to the Black and Scholes formula, the number of shares and options must be selected in such a way that at a certain point in time t, any change in the share value caused by a change in the share price dS is offset by a change in the option value in the portfolio of the same amount but with the opposite sign. We can therefore formulate the condition in absolute terms:

$$|q_s dS| = |q_c dc| \tag{2.4}$$

We assume for ease of reference that the number of shares in the portfolio is not only constant but equal to one: $q_s = 1$. The amount of call options q_c necessary to maintain the hedge portfolio constant can be computed from (2.4).

In general, a risk-free portfolio can be constructed with two securities if their prices are perfectly positively correlated, by holding one security long and the other security short, of course both with the corresponding amounts. As already mentioned, we assume that the price of the call option and the share price are perfectly positively correlated. In the case of the option's hedge portfolio, the share is held long, and the corresponding number of calls is held short.

The marginal change in the portfolio caused by a marginal change in the share price at a time t is given by:

$$\frac{dV_H}{dS} = 1 + q_c\left(\frac{\partial c}{\partial S}\right) \quad \text{with } t = const \tag{2.5}$$

The hedge portfolio may not be affected by any marginal share price change at a given time t:

$$\frac{dV_H}{dS} = 0 \tag{2.6}$$

Combining these conditions, we obtain the number of options necessary to maintain the hedge portfolio q_c:

$$q_c = -\frac{1}{\left(\frac{\partial c}{\partial S}\right)} \tag{2.7}$$

Equation (2.7) is widely known as the hedging principle in option pricing.

As the value of the portfolio remains unchanged, the portfolio may earn a risk-free rate of return. Otherwise, risk-free arbitrage would be possible.

$$\frac{dV_H}{dt} = rV_H \quad \text{or} \quad \frac{dV_H}{V_H} = rdt \tag{2.8}$$

Equations (2.5) and (2.7) make the core assumptions of the Black and Scholes approach explicit: As the share price may fluctuate continuously, the number of options to be held has to be adjusted permanently.

The fluctuating share price will be modelled by means of a stochastic process. The change in the option position required to maintain the risk-free portfolio can be described using the stochastic differential Eqs. (2.9) and (2.10), which are very well known to physicists. The option price will be obtained by integrating the differential Eq. (2.11). Assuming the integration procedure according to Itô and regarding the boundary values (2.12) with X as strike price, the Black Scholes formula (Equ. 2.15) will be obtained. Details see e.g. Loistl[35] or Neftci.[36]

$$\frac{dc}{dt} = rc - rS\frac{\partial c}{\partial S} - \frac{\partial^2 c}{2\partial S^2}\sigma^2 S^2 \tag{2.9}$$

$$dc = \frac{\partial c}{\partial S}dS + \frac{\partial c}{\partial t}dt + \frac{\partial^2 c}{2\partial S^2}\sigma^2 S^2 dt \tag{2.10}$$

[35] Loistl (1996, p. 414).

[36] Neftci (2000, p. 136).

$$c = \int \left[rc - rS\frac{\partial c}{\partial S} - \frac{\partial^2 c}{2\partial S^2}\sigma^2 S^2 \right] dt \tag{2.11}$$

The most important condition for (2.15) to deliver reliable results is that the option must be traded so quickly and in such small units that the share price fluctuations are balanced out in such a way that the risk-free portfolio is maintained all the time.[37] If this condition is not fulfilled, the risks involved are not computable and sometimes not manageable. Warren Buffett explicitly discussed the risks involved.[38]

2.3.2.2 *Discounting the Expected Value of the Option*[39]

In this version, the current option value is equal to the present value (2.14) of the option at the time of expiry (2.13), taking into account the boundary value conditions (2.12). The probability distribution of the share price at the time the option expires is given by a lognormal distribution. With some further assumptions, the option value in $t = 0$ is determined by (2.15), but some parameters have to be interpreted differently. Above all, the discount rate may not be the risk-free rate and the option value is assumed to be equal to the expected value of the option at expiry, see (2.13).

The assumption of a lognormal share price distribution corresponds to the Black and Scholes assumption. At the expiry time T, , the value of the option (WOR) obeys the following boundary conditions with exercise price X[40]:

$$\begin{matrix} A \\ WOR * T \end{matrix} = \begin{cases} x - X, & ifx > X \\ 0, & ifx \leq X \end{cases} \tag{2.12}$$

At time of expiry the expected option value $E[WOR * T]$ is given by

$$\begin{aligned} E[WOR * T] = WORT &= \int_X^\infty (x - X) \cdot f(x)dx \\ &= \int_X^\infty x \cdot f(x)dx - X \cdot \int_X^\infty f(x)dx \end{aligned} \tag{2.13}$$

Discounting at the current time t results in the current value c of the option:

$$c = WORT \cdot e^{-rT} \tag{2.14}$$

37 See above all Kreps (1982).

38 Buffett (2010, pp. 16) and (2009, pp. 17). His evaluation refers to two aspects: Liquidity and the counterparty risk. He avoided both risks by maintaining appropriate liquidity himself, and he avoided counterparty risks by receiving money at the contract's inception.

39 See Thorp (1975,pp. 229), the references mentioned therein and Loistl (1994, pp. 188).

40 See already Thorp (1975, pp. 229), Loistl (1996, p. 194).

By combining these assumptions, the famous Black and Scholes formula will be obtained:

$$c = S \cdot N(d_1) - e^{-rT} X \cdot N(d_2)$$
$$d_1 = \frac{\ln\left(\frac{S}{X}\right) + \left(r + \frac{\sigma^2}{2}\right)T}{\sqrt{T}}$$
$$d_2 = \frac{\ln\left(\frac{S}{X}\right) + \left(r + \frac{\sigma^2}{2}\right)T}{\sigma\sqrt{T}} = d_1 - \sigma\sqrt{T} \tag{2.15}$$

2.3.2.3 Black Scholes Formula is a Convention but not Suitable to Detect Mispriced Investments

The derivation of the option pricing formula according to Black and Scholes "*is based on such simple assumptions – unrealistically simple assumptions*".[41] In spite of these deficiencies within the mathematical community, consensus trumped empirical proof: "*In the end, a theory is accepted not because it is confirmed by conventional empirical tests, but because researchers persuade one another that the theory is correct and relevant.*"[42] As a convention, the Black and Scholes valuation formula has been used since to recognise the value of derivatives, especially options.[43]

Derivatives, or as Buffet refers to them, "weapons of mass destruction" are "marked to model" which Buffet likens to "mark to myth"[44]; thus, creating significant risks for unexperienced investors.

But they did not refrain from investing in derivatives. Buffett invested in mispriced derivatives, as he invests in mispriced securities all the time. He owes his success to his unbeatable capabilities to identify mispriced securities. He calculates the mispricing by his own methods, not by the famous Black Scholes formula and he uses the Black Scholes formula to report the derivatives investments in the annual statements. The application of the Black and Scholes formula for this purpose has been justified to obtain figures by following the common reporting convention, especially to fix the figures of the input variables accordingly, e.g. volatility and interest rate. However, he did not use Black and Scholes pricing as an investment guideline to identify mispriced securities. The identification of mispriced securities using a method that is essentially based on the assumption that there must be no arbitrage opportunities is of course paradoxical.

---

41 Black (1990, p. 11).

42 Black (2009, p. 179).

43 Even Warren Buffett (2009, p. 18) "used Black- Scholes valuation methods" for reporting purposes.

44 Buffet (2003, pp. 13–15).

2.3.2.4 From "Variance" to "Volatility"

The option price calculation is based on the following independent variables

$$c = f(S, K, T, r, \sigma) \text{ and } \sigma^* = f^{-1}(S, K, T, r, c)$$

with

f^{-1} = inverse function of f,
σ = historic volatility,
σ^* = implied volatility,
S = share price,
K = strike price,
T = Time to maturity, and
r = interest rate.

The volatility σ is calculated either as annualised standard deviation of log returns around mean log return or around zero. It was a matter of convenience, if variance or "volatility"—the square root—have been applied.

Ambiguities in determining the figure of "volatility" as independent variable led to a reversal of the question. The market determines the volatility, and the value of the option is derived from this volatility. This so-called "implied volatility" was received with great approval by the market.

The need of the market led further to the introduction of the so-called volatility index, abbreviated "VIX". According to different needs of users, there were different constructions. Details see Fassad and Siriopoulos (2021) and Gunarsson et al. (2024). An important aspect of differentiation is the treatment of stochastic processes. Some approaches focus on changes in the stochastic processes, especially on controlling the variance. The so-called "variance-gamma process" should be mentioned here. The control of the variance follows a gamma distribution.[45] Others take a view of volatility as a futures contract and value it primarily from an arbitrage and fair value perspective, as it is common for futures contracts. The specifics of stochastic processes do not play a decisive role here.[46]

The multitude of applications shows one thing above all with regard to Markowitz' assumption. The market, i.e. the investors, do not avoid variance but have developed this variable into an important building block of risk management.

---

[45] See Madan et al (1998). For the description of a gamma distribution, see chapter 3.4.

[46] See Demeterfi et al (1999), Neuberger (1994), CBOE VIX (2024), and CBOE (2025)

3 Decision-Making with Known Probabilities of Outcome

Abstract

The book follows the basic differentiation between risky actions with known probabilities of the outcome on the one hand and risky actions with unknown probabilities of the outcome on the other. Commonly addressed by the formulation "decision making under risk" and "decision making under uncertainty". Chapter 3 discusses the basic tool to handle decisions under risk: Applying "expected utility" according Daniel Bernoulli's concept. This rule has been operationalized into "mean/variance" rule. According to Markowitz the investor should consider "expected return a desirable thing and variance of return an undesirable thing." The basic description starts with a short history of expected utility and explains, why mean/variance has been overwhelmingly accepted by academics and professionals alike. For those interested, the technicalities of calculating the expected utility for different combinations of probability function and utility functions will be performed. The calculation of expected utility by means of Taylor series expansion will be discussed. The results show that the connection of mean variance decision rule to the Bernoulli expected utility rule is exactly valid in several cases only. Among professionals, the mean variance decision rule has emancipated from Bernoulli. For several utility functions, variance increases the expected value. The connection to absolute and relative risk aversion a la Arrow and Pratt will be discussed.

Keywords

History of mean variance formula • Axioms of Bernoulli • Derivation of mean variance formula from expected utility: explicit analytical integration • Numerical integration • Taylor series expansion • Numerical illustrations of expected utility calculations

O. Loistl et al., *Screen Based Trading and Open Order Book*, New Economic Windows,
https://doi.org/10.1007/978-3-031-99052-6_3

3.1 Decision-Making and Probabilities

3.1.1 The Issue of Modelling Trader Behaviour

The problem of modelling the behaviour of traders is not only freed from the straitjacket of equilibrium, but also from the straitjacket of time series assumptions. Every action of a trader changes the state of nature. Any action creates new trading possibilities and requires new activities of other traders. This is the characteristic of emergence: new trading frames are created by the activities of traders. This contradicts the basic assumption of the time series that all figures originate from the same population and/or that the decision-making frame remains unchanged.

The Logit Choice model requires independence of irrelevant alternative (IIA). This assumption has been seen for a long time as a major restriction to the application of the Logit approach. Landes et al. [1]have shown that the DSMP approach fulfils the IIA requirement. Furthermore, IIA seems in the current discussion not to be as much of a problem as it was considered some years before.

Formally, we assume the stock market to be a time homogenous conservative Markov process $(Z_t)_{t \geq 0}$ in continuous time with values in the discrete countable set Z, the state space. The state vector $z \in Z$, called the market state, is a high-dimensional vector of variables capturing the information attached to the current market status also including variables bearing relevant information of the past[2]: The explicit set of variables might be adjusted to the specific market constellation and computing capacities.

Von Neumann and Morgenstern's publication not only promoted decision-making under risk, but also decision-making under uncertainty. The appropriate research is split into two areas that are separated according to the knowledge of the probability distribution.

Decision-making under the assumption of a known probability distribution could be described as "expected utility according to Bernoulli". If the probability distribution of the outcomes of the scenario is not explicitly known, it is referred to "prospect theory". For the sake of simplicity, we will follow this distinction.

Both areas experienced intensified research in the 1950s and 1960s. Decision-making under risk/uncertainty had a first culmination in 1953 at a meeting in Paris. Among the different proposals the expected utility according to Bernoulli dominated. The details will be explained in the next chapter.

The research of decision-making under uncertainty has not been so simple. The research split in at least two directions: Firstly, human decision-making was investigated in certain test situations. Kahnemann, Tversky and Thaler are prominent examples of this.[3] They accumulated considerable descriptive knowledge

---

[1] Landes et al. (1989a), pp. 53–108.

[2] The explicit decision frame is given in chapter 6.2.

[3] See Thaler (2017). He quotes an impressive list of researchers but does not mention McFadden nor Luce nor Thurstone. These researchers belong obviously to the other (i.e. operational) section of decision-making under uncertainty.

about human behaviour. This expertise found entry into finance under the term "behavioural finance". The other branch tried to cast human decision-making in quantitative terms. A major impetus has been given by Thurstone's proposal, to evaluate an activity not in isolation, but by the comparison to other activities. Further contribution came from Duncan Luce. He proposed, inspired by Thurstone, to evaluate individual activities by the principle of "Independence from Irrelevant Alternatives". By this principle, he was able to structure the evaluation of an alternative by comparison with other alternatives, and he developed a formula.

Suppes (1961) discovered its similarity with entropy nearly at the same time and the practical importance has been discovered by Daniel McFadden. According to his own account, a doctoral student asked for his support. She had to analyse which of the various means of transport passengers would choose. McFadden worked with the student to create an assessment mode of evaluation based on this formula. They hit the passengers' choice quite correctly.

This success induced a chain of application in many business disciplines,[4] but not in finance or economics. The researchers remain loyal to the efficient market hypothesis.

Capital markets are being used to capitalise on technical skills, innovative financing options and, not least, changes in legislation. This time, the trading habits seem to develop and grow beyond the official rulemaking. The SEC proposes supplemental information regarding the definition of "exchange" (2023a). Indeed a "Staff Report on Algorithmic Trading in U.S. Capital Markets" concludes "*Algorithmic trading, including trading that relies on rapid access to and processing of large amounts of market data, is ubiquitous in our equity markets and is increasingly important in our debt markets. Algorithmic trading has brought secondary market participants important benefits such as increased liquidity, cost reduction, and improvements in other measures of liquidity. But advances in technology, and related developments in the provision of and access to market data, have also contributed to the complexity of markets, arguably have contributed to episodes of volatility and dislocation.*" (p. 55).

Trading in the US equity markets today is highly automated and spread even more among different types of trading centres, allowing even more choices about where orders may be routed. The types of trading centres that currently trade NMS (National Market System) stocks are: (1) national securities exchanges operating self-regulatory organisation ("SRO") trading facilities (2) ATSs (Alternative Trading Systems) (NMS Stock ATSs) that trade NMS stock, (3) exchange market makers (4) wholesalers and (5) any other broker-dealer that executes orders internally by trading as principal or crossing orders as agent. In the first quarter of 2023, NMS stocks were traded on 16 national securities exchanges, and off exchange at 33 NMS Stock ATS and at over 220 other Financial Industry Regulatory Authority (FINRA) members. Approximately 56% of NMS share volume

[4] Haghani et al. (2021) counted more than 6000 published applications.

was executed on national securities exchanges.[5] This ample quote indicates that trading on capital markets is changing, and its regulation should be updated.

The quotes indicate that the SEC already takes action to meet that challenge. Due to the complexity of interests and the multiplicity of tools utilised, this change is difficult to cast into rules and regulations. The activities of brokers and dealers are difficult to regulate. They have duties to "maintain an orderly market". It is not possible, to assign their activities precisely as buyers or sellers. Their duty to "maintain an orderly market" also in nonliquid situations in many cases limits their ability to maximize profits. We follow by this reticence Roth and Sotomayor (1992). The authors excluded markets for commodities and for gold, because in these markets an agent could be a buyer at one price and a seller at another price. The market is not "two sided". Such a commingling occurs at NYSE quite frequently. Roth and Sotomayor (1992) have excluded securities markets like NYSE too. Roth (2015) gives a verbal description of "A Game in Milliseconds".

A closer look at the acting traders might change the picture. It's a game where the (external) buyers or sellers are on the odds and the brokers are on the winning side. Brokers exploit their discretionary power. Brokers received that power to maintain an ordinary market in case of lacking liquidity either on buyer's or seller's side. An electronic market might reduce that power.

We will describe rules and regulations of Xetra that is the electronic trading system of Frankfurt Stock Exchange. We have witnessed the development from the very beginning and can therefore follow Walter Eucken's (1989) invitation: "*Put the books aside and observe the reality*"[6] (Preface).

We will demonstrate the variety of issues that can be addressed with this approach. It offers a fairly simple approach for decisions under uncertainty. The "trick" is a pairwise comparison that was suggested by Thurstone almost 100 years ago. Luce put that principle into a formula and McFadden successfully applied this formula to determine an activity to be selected.

A major objection has been the difficulties arising from the adoption of the IIA. This assumption corresponds to Bernoulli's "substitutions principle": The substitution of a single outcome by a lottery is independent of other alternatives. We will show that IIA does not lead to contradictory results in our problem. See chapter 4.3.3.

3.1.2 A Brief History of Decision-Making According to Mean Variance

From the discussion about possible concepts for decision-making under risk, the expected value of utility emerged as the favourite. According to Pressacco and Serafini (2007), de Finetti has promoted the mean variance concept. Not all objections,

---

[5] SEC (2024b), pp. 9.

[6] Eucken (1989), p. IX.

e.g. from Maurice Allais (1979),[7] could be dispelled at the conference in Paris in 1953. In particular, "l'ecôle américaine"—as Allais called it[8]—voted in favour of the expected value of utility. In the same period, Markowitz (1952) developed a quantitative concept for the analytical foundation of portfolio theory and portfolio management based on the mean and variance of ex-post share price and portfolio returns. The acceptance of the concept was promoted by the proof that this mean–variance formula is compatible with the expected value of utility or corresponds to it under certain conditions. Investigation focused on a quadratic utility function and a discrete distribution of returns.

This constellation of compatibility was soon considered insufficient. Empirical studies have mainly focused on continuous distributions of share price returns. In many cases, these did not correspond to a normal distribution. Quadratic utility functions assume a risk attitude that hardly corresponds to real behaviour. Pratt (1964) and Arrow (1965) proposed the indicators "absolute" and "relative" risk aversion. The utility functions compatible with these behaviours were generally more complex than "*mean variance*".

First, the basic technique of the Taylor series for approximating functions and thus also for determining the mean and variance is discussed using the simple constellation "quadratic utility function with discrete probability distribution" already mentioned above. The advanced combinations of utility function types and probability distributions discussed subsequently follow this design principle. They are of central importance in risk decision models.

The transformation of the expected utility value into distribution moments is demonstrated using utility functions of the type "exponential function", "logarithmic function" and "power function". First, the convergence range and its calculation are discussed. Then the important prerequisites for swapping integration and summation for the derivation of the mean–variance formula are explained. The following numerical examples are used to analyse the efficiency of calculating the expected value of utility using the moments of the distribution.

We restrict the analysis to three types of probability distributions: normal distribution, lognormal distribution and gamma distribution, each combined with an exponential utility function. We refrain from analysing logarithmic utility functions and power functions in the interest of concentrating the information. See the numerical examples in Loistl (1976). We can concentrate on the implications of different probability distributions with different "compactness" in the sense of different variance. The speed of convergence depends on this quantity, but not the convergence property per se. However, the discussion of the basic properties of the probabilistic "compactness" is beyond the scope of this study.

---

[7] See Allais (1979).

[8] The discussion is summarized by Allais and Hagen (1979).

The examples show that the various "pitfalls" of the Taylor series approximation can lead to major errors, especially in constellations with infinite limits—the argument should be repeated once again. The usual error estimation in natural science analyses when using Taylor series is regularly missing in economic analyses. Our argument is intended to raise or sharpen awareness of the problem.

Finally, the distinctions between "safety equivalent", "expected utility value" and "stake" are discussed. While the expected utility value has the dimension "utility" according to its name, the certainty equivalent has the dimension "monetary amount" or "safe return". The correspondence with the "stake" depends on the type of utility function.

3.2 Calculation of the Expected Value of the Utility

3.2.1 Bernoulli Principle: the Axioms

The Bernoulli Principle states that individual alternatives are interchangeable, because their evaluation is completely independent of other alternatives that are also available. If A_1 is preferred to A_2, then the following must apply with equal probability p

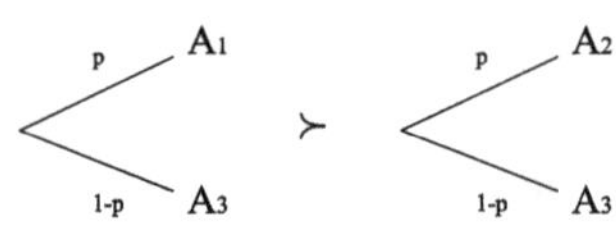

in case of $A_1 \sim A_2$ the following must apply $\sim$

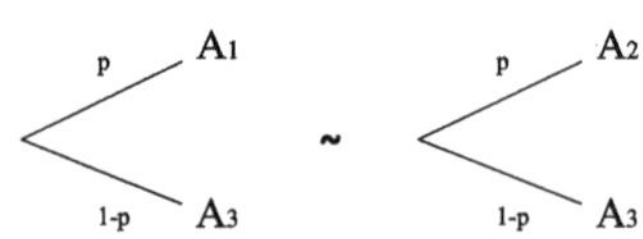

In addition, the following relationships apply

(a) if

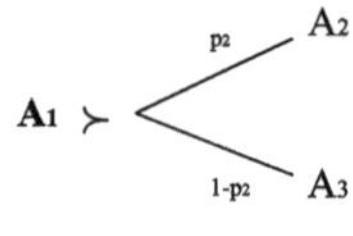

Since A_1 is preferred to the (A_2A_3) lottery with probabilities p_2 and $1 - p_2$, the following applies:

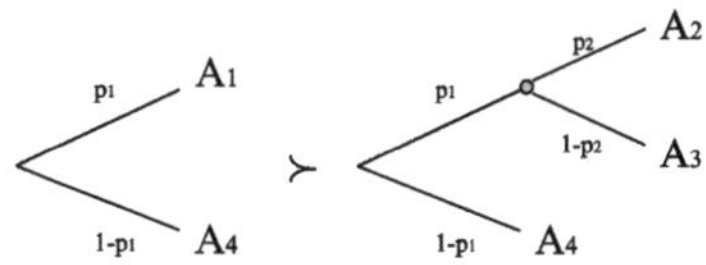

In addition, the following relationships apply

(b) if

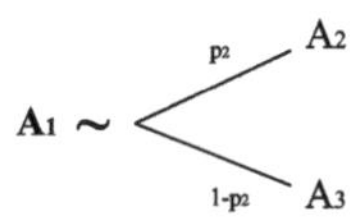

due to the indifference between A_1 and the A_2, A_3 lottery with the probabilities p_2 and $(1 - p_2)$ can be substituted:

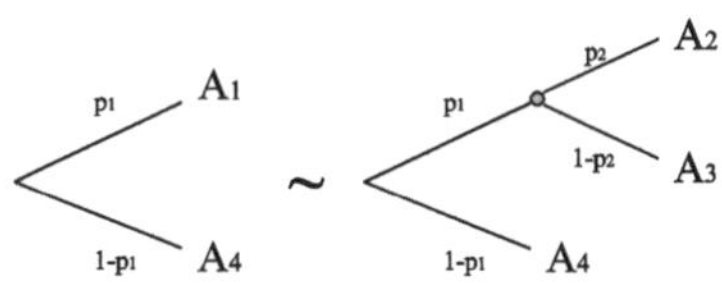

A_1 can be substituted by the lottery with the values A_2 and A_3. The evaluation of the individual alternatives is independent of the other choices. This situation is therefore referred to as the axiom of substitution as well as the axiom of independence.

The substitution theorem.[9]

[9] Counterexample from Allais (1979), p. 27.

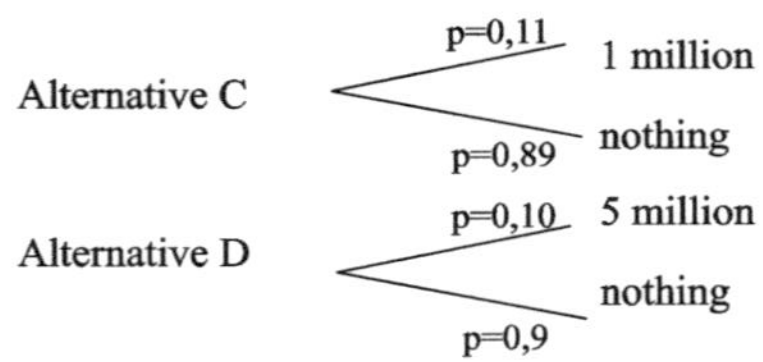	For many people, it seems sensible to choose alternative A in Situation I and alternative D in situation II. In situation I, the certainty of winning 1 million carries more weight than the prospect of winning 5 million. It is associated with the risk of receiving nothing at all
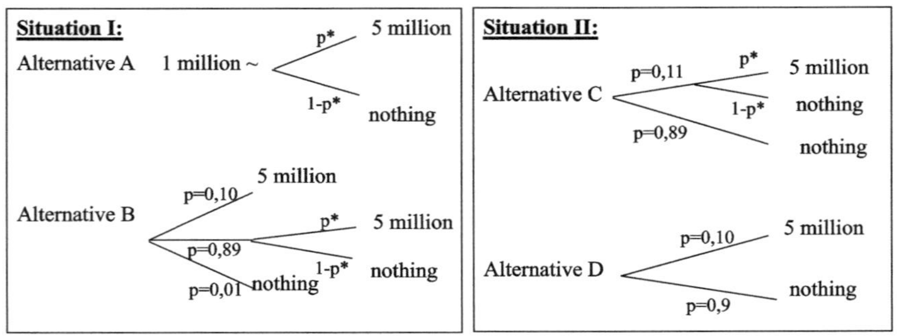	In Situation II, on the other hand, the only slightly higher probability of winning weighs less heavily than the prospect of winning the considerably higher sum of 5 million instead of 1 million. However, this assessment is not consistent according to the substitution principle

The contradiction can be shown as follows:

We are looking for the indifference probability p^*, which indicates the probability of winning 5 million in the standard lottery, so that the standard lottery "5 million or nothing" is estimated to be equal to the certain amount of 1 million. So, we get:

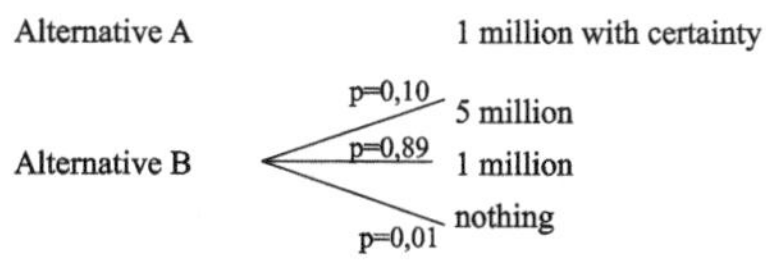

According to our assumption: A > B and D > C.

From this follows for the probabilities: $p^* > 0.10 + 0.89\,p^*$ and $0.10 > 0.11\,p^*$

Multiplying and rearranging the results in.

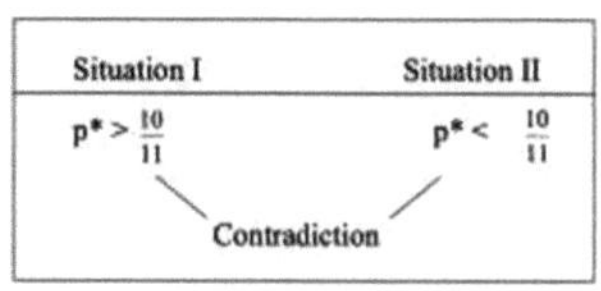

The following figure shows the consistency or inconsistency of Bernoulli's theory based on empirical surveys of students:

	Schematic	
	A > B	A < B
C > D	Bernoulli	**Anti-Bernoulli**
C < D	**Anti-Bernoulli**	Bernoulli

	Survey * share in %	
	A > B	A < B
C > D	0	**0**
C < D	**60–75**	40–25

Most respondents (approx. 60–75%) voted against the substitution or independence axiom.

3.2.2 Bernoulli Principle: the Constructive Formulas

The expected value of the utility $E[U(x)]$ is defined as

$$E[U(x)] = \int_{-\infty}^{+\infty} U(x) \cdot f(x)dx \tag{3.1}$$

$$E[U(x)] = \sum_{i=1}^{n} U(x_i)p_i \tag{3.2}$$

with x =Continuous realisation of the random variable 'wealth of the decision-maker' X or 'return on investment'

x_i =Discrete realisation of the random variable 'decision maker's wealth' X or 'return on investment'.

$U(x)$ = Utility function of the decision maker.
$f(x)$ = Density function of the random variable X
p_i = Discrete probability for the realisation of x_i
n = Number of possible discrete realisations.

We will explicitly integrate an exponential utility function in combination with the following probability distributions.

Normal distribution with exponential utility function

$$U(x) = 1{,}000\left(1 - e^{-bx}\right)f(x) = \frac{1}{\sqrt{2\pi} \cdot s} e^{-\frac{(x-\overline{x})^2}{2s^2}} \tag{3.3}$$

For the expected utility value $E[U(x)]$ the solution of the integral is

$$E[U(x)] = 1{,}000\left(1 - e^{\left(-b\overline{x} + \frac{b^2 s^2}{2}\right)}\right) \tag{3.4}$$

Gamma distribution with exponential utility function:

$$E[U(x)] = 1{,}000\left(1 - \int_{0}^{\infty} e^{-bx} \cdot \frac{1}{\Gamma(\alpha)} \cdot \beta^{\alpha} \cdot x^{\alpha-1} \cdot e^{-\beta x}\right)dx \tag{3.5}$$

The integral can be solved analytically. We obtain:

$$E[U(x)] = 1{,}000\left(1 - \left(\frac{\beta}{\beta + b}\right)^{\alpha}\right) 0 < x < \infty \tag{3.6}$$

For the lognormal distribution, there is currently no analytical solution of the integral according to (3.1). The listed lognormal distribution expected utility values were calculated using numerical integration.

In (3.1), a one-dimensional random variable is assumed whose density function $f(x)$ is known. In portfolio theory, the sum of the random returns of all securities is of central importance as a random variable, weighted by the respective share values. At the heart of the utility theory approach is the determination of the utility-optimal shares of the individual securities. A key problem is determining the probability distribution of the overall portfolio return. In the case of a normal distribution, the type of distribution is known, and operational statements can be derived. In other cases, the random variable of the weighted sum of the random individual returns is no longer so easy to determine. However, Stein's lemma has brought a considerable improvement in the determination of multivariate distributions.[10] The possibilities of using Taylor approximations to achieve further improvements in the efficiency of Stein's Lemma have not yet been explored completely.[11]

In the following analysis, we will not deal with the possibilities/limitations of the Taylor series for multidimensional probability distributions or utility functions. Since Markowitz, the entire distribution function of the portfolio return is regularly not considered, but only the mean, variances and covariances of the individual securities. From these figures the mean and variance of the total portfolio return can be determined without major difficulties.[12]

3.3 Calculation via Taylor Series-Expansion

3.3.1 Taylor Approximations Applied to Quadratic Utility Functions

The function value $U(X_i)$, which belongs to the argument x_i, is to be determined with the aid of a Taylor expansion around the mean value $\overline{x} = 6$ by successive approximation with the aid of the derivatives.

Function and derivatives

$$U(x) = 2x - \frac{x^2}{5};\ U\prime(x) = 2 - \frac{2x}{5};\ U''(x) = -\frac{2}{5} \tag{3.7}$$

1. Approximation based on the mean value

[10] See in particular Adcock (2014), Adcock and Shutes (2012), Adcock et al. (2012), Landsman and Neslehova (2008).

[11] See Meckes (2009).

[12] For professionals, the portfolio performance according to mean variance and covariances/correlations is currently decisive. Expected utility functions do not play a major role in this context. See the excellent presentation in Fischer/Wermers (2013).

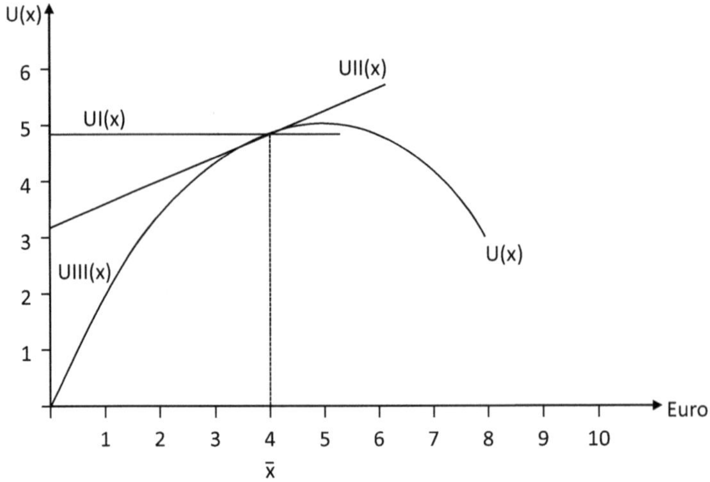

Fig. 3.1 Function curves of the successive Taylor approximations

$$U_I(x) = 2(\overline{x}) - \frac{(\overline{x})^2}{5} = 4.8 \tag{3.8}$$

2. Approximation with consideration of the first derivative

$$U_{II}(x) = U_I(x) + U\prime(\overline{x})(x - \overline{x}) = 4.8 + \left(-\frac{8}{5} + \frac{2x}{5}\right) = 3.2 + \frac{2x}{5} \tag{3.9}$$

3. Approximation with consideration of the second derivative (Fig. 3.1)

$$U_{III}(x) = U(x) + U''(\overline{x})\frac{(x - \overline{x})^2}{2} = 2x - \frac{x^2}{5} = U(x) \tag{3.10}$$

UI: Function curve with Taylor-approximation I.
UII: Function curve with Taylor-approximation II.
UIII: Function curve with Taylor-approximation III.

3.3.2 Expected Utility Value as a Function of the Central Moments of Probability Distributions

Discrete Probability Distribution.

In general, every (whole rational) polynomial of the n-th degree

$$P = \sum_{t=0}^{n} a_t \cdot x^t \tag{3.11}$$

can be represented exactly by a Taylor-expansion of the n-th degree.

$$\sum_{t=0}^{n} a_t \cdot x^t = \sum_{t=0}^{n} \frac{U^{(t)}(\overline{x})(x-\overline{x})^t}{t!} \tag{3.12}$$

with $U^{(j)}$ = j-th derivation of the utility function.

The expected value of the utility can be represented as a function of the moments of the probability distribution using the Taylor expansion. For the sake of simplicity, only two values x_1 and x_2 with the discrete probabilities p_1 and p_2 are assumed.

Using the Taylor approximation to degree n, we obtain for the two values x_1 and x_2 respectively:

$$U(x_1) = \sum_{j=0}^{n} \frac{U^{(j)}(\overline{x})}{j!}(x_1-\overline{x})^j \tag{3.13}$$

$$U(x_2) = \sum_{j=0}^{n} \frac{U^{(j)}(\overline{x})}{j!}(x_2-\overline{x})^j \tag{3.14}$$

Equations (3.13) and (3.14) assume that the function $U(x)$ can be represented by a Taylor series of order n.

The following applies to the expected value of the utility according to (3.2)

$$E[U(x)] = U(x_1) \cdot p_1 + U(x_2) \cdot p_2 \tag{3.15}$$

If we insert the corresponding expressions of the Taylor expansion (3.13) and (3.14) for $U(x_1)$, $U(x_2)$ and multiply the two sums by p_1 and p_2 respectively, we obtain

$$E[U(x)] = \left(\sum_{j=0}^{n} \frac{U^j(\overline{x})}{j!}(x_1-\overline{x})^j\right) \cdot p_1 + \left(\sum_{j=0}^{n} \frac{U^j(\overline{x})}{j!}(x_2-\overline{x})^j\right) \cdot p_2 \tag{3.16}$$

Performing the multiplication with p_1, p_2 and a rearrangement leads to expressions of the moments of the probability distribution.[13] The derivation for mean and variance is explicitly carried out by the following equation

$$E[U(x)] = U(\overline{x}) \cdot (p_1 + p_2) + U\prime(\overline{x}) \cdot \left[x_1 p_1 + x_2 p_2 - \overline{x}(p_1 + p_2)\right] + \frac{U''(\overline{x})}{2!} \cdot \left[(x_1 - \overline{x})^2 \cdot p_1 + (x_2 - \overline{x})^2 \cdot p_2\right] \tag{3.17}$$

The expression in [] in the second part of (3.17) is equal to the variance.

3.3.3 Expected Utility Value and Continuous Distribution Moments

3.3.3.1 Calculation with Finite Integration Limits and Polynomial Utility Function

In the case of finite integration limits and polynomial utility functions, the results of the discrete case can be transferred immediately.[14]

$$E[U(x)] = \int_A^B f(x) \left(\sum_{j=1}^{n} \frac{U^{(j)}(\overline{x})}{j!} (x - \overline{x})^j \right) dx \tag{3.18}$$

With a finite summation limit $n < \infty$ and a finite integration interval $-\infty < A < B < \infty$, the order of integration and summation can be reversed. We then obtain:

$$E[U(x)] = \sum_{j=0}^{n} \frac{U^{(j)}(\overline{x})}{j!} \int_A^B (x - \overline{x})^j f(x) dx \tag{3.19}$$

---

[13] It applies:

$$U\prime(x) \cdot (x_1 p_1 + x_2 p_2) - \overline{x} \cdot (p_1 + p_2) = 0$$

$$U\prime(x) \cdot (x_1 p_1 + x_2 p_2 - \overline{x}) = 0$$

(Note:

$$x_1 p_1 + x_2 p_2 = \overline{x}$$

).

therefore

$U\prime(x) \cdot (\overline{x} - \overline{x}) = 0$

$(x_1 - \overline{x})^2 \cdot p_1 + (x_2 - \overline{x})^2 \cdot p_2 = \sum_{i=1}^{2} (x_i - \overline{x})^2 \cdot p_i = \sigma^2$

and therefore generally:

$E[U(x)] = U(\overline{x}) + \sum_{j=2}^{n} U^{(j)}(\overline{x}) \cdot \sum_{i=1}^{m} (x_i - \overline{x})^j \cdot p_i \cdot \frac{1}{j!}$

[14] The prerequisite is, of course, that the radius of convergence of the utility function covers the range of possible realisations of the random variable.

The expressions under the integral are equal to the central moments of the distribution. Consequently, with finite summation and integration limits, the expected value of the utility can be represented as a function of the central moments of the probability distribution.

3.3.3.2 General Assumptions When Swapping Integration and Summation

In the general case, however, some conditions that are not self-evident must be checked. If they are not fulfilled, the calculation will be incorrect.

Two main points need to be checked:

- Does the radius of convergence of the Taylor expansion of the utility function cover the realisation area of the random variable?
- Is it possible to swap integration and summation?

3.3.3.3 Convergence Issues

Arbitrary functions can be represented by an infinite Taylor expansion for arguments within the specific radius of convergence. The radius of convergence of the function $U(m)$ can be determined as follows: We define the j-th derivative for a development around the value m as

$$\frac{U^{(j)}(m)}{j!} = a_j \tag{3.20}$$

The following theorem now applies to the radius of convergence of the Taylor expansion:

The Taylor expansion of the function value $U(y)$ around the value m converges if $|y - m|$ is less than the limit of $|a_j/a_{j+1}|$. It diverges if $|y - m|$ is greater than the limit of $|a_j/a_{j+1}|$.[15]

The following applies to selected function types (Table 3.1).[16]

Logarithmic and potential utility functions can therefore be approximated by a Taylor series developed in a possibly very narrow range only. The range depends on the value by which the function is developed. If you want to focus on the central moments—as is usual in portfolio theory—then you must develop around the mean value (Fig. 3.2).

---

[15] There are numerous complicated formulas for estimating convergence. To determine the radius of convergence of the Taylor series of the functions under consideration, the above formulation of the d'Alembert criterion should be appropriate. The frequently used formula for estimating the Lagrange residual does not provide "practicable" results for all function types in all areas. For example, it is only of limited use for the estimation of logarithmic functions. This limitation is obviously overlooked by Sinn (1980), p. 118. The correct radius of convergence can already be found in Tsiang (1972), p. 360.

[16] See Loistl (2015), p. 678, Platanakis et al. (2017), p. 7.

Table 3.1 Utility functions and convergence range

Function type	Convergence range
Finite polynomial	$-\infty < x < +\infty$
Exponential function	$-\infty < x < +\infty$
Logarithmic function	$0 \leq x \leq 2m$
Power function	$0 \leq x \leq 2m$

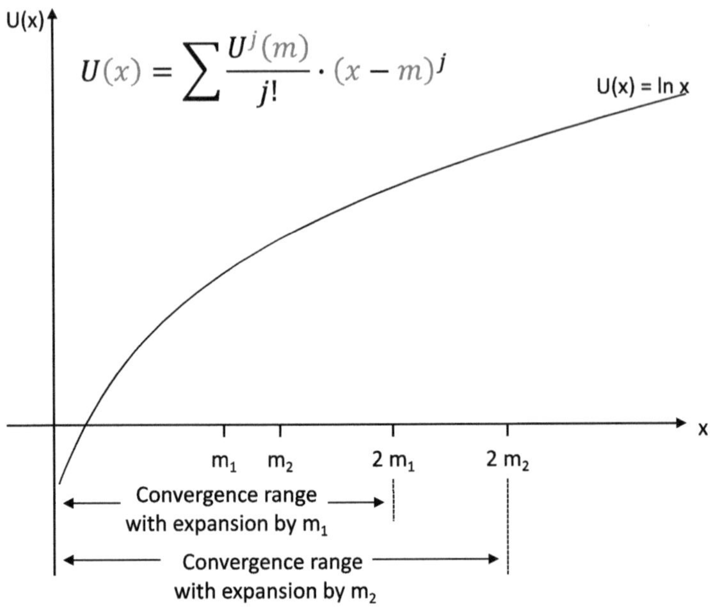

Fig. 3.2 Convergence of the Taylor expansion in the case of a logarithmic function with different convergence ranges due to different mean values

As far as the possible realisations of the uncertain prospect lie within the convergence range, an exact representation of the function value is possible by a Taylor development and thus the exact calculation is not questioned, at least from this side.

3.4 Numerical Examples

3.4.1 Parameters of the Probability Function

The same mean values and variances are assumed for all three probability distribution types: $\overline{x}_I = 10, \sigma_I^2 = 82, \overline{x}_{II} = 15, \sigma_{II}^2 = 261$

Table 3.2 Parameters of the distribution types

Parameters of the analysed distributions							
Gamma distributions				Lognormal distributions			
α		β		μ		σ	
I	II	I	II	I	II	I	II
1.219512	0.862069	0.12195	0.057471	2.003167	2.322996	0.773845	0.877558

The function parameters α and β must be defined accordingly for the gamma distribution. The first two moments are determined according to the equation:

$$\overline{x} = \frac{\alpha}{\beta}, \sigma^2 = \frac{\alpha}{\beta^2} \tag{3.21}$$

From this we obtain both parameters for both gamma distributions, shown in Table 3.2. The gamma distribution is characterised by the parameters derived from the moments. In the lognormal distribution, the (logarithmic) mean and the (logarithmic) variance are directly included in the density function.

The numerical values of the exponential utility function are taken from Loistl (1976):

$$U(x) = 1{,}000\left(1 - e^{-0.05x}\right)$$

The step-by-step approximation in Table 3.3[17] reveals the convergence behaviour of the Taylor approximation.

In both headers, the probability distributions are first systematised according to mean–variance. Type I have the pair (10, 82), type II the pair (15, 261). In row two, the three probability distributions are systematised separately according to the parameter pairs. The third line contains the expected utility values, characterised by the header element $E[U(x)]$. In the following row, only the first column $U(x) moment$ is labelled, the remaining fields are empty. The following rows contain the Taylor approximation values. The respective header column indicates the approximate utility values obtained with a Taylor expansion up to the second, third and fourth moments. For the normal distribution, the field of the third moment is empty. Normal distributions are known to be symmetrical with the third moment equal to zero.

The accuracy of the mean–variance rule is determined by comparing the $E[U(x)]$ values in the first row with those in the third row, starting with $U''(x)$.

[17] Data for normal and lognormal distributions taken from Loistl (1976), p. 908, Tables 4 and 5. The formulas for the moments of the lognormal distribution are taken from Aitchison and Brown (1957), p. 8. The formulas for the moments of the gamma distribution are taken from Rinne (1997), p. 349.

Table 3.3 Values of the Taylor series approximation up to the 4th moment (curvature)

	Distribution Type I:			Distribution Type II:		
	Normal	Lognormal	Gamma	Normal	Lognormal	Gamma
$E(x)$	10	10	10	15	15	15
$Var(x)$	82	82	82	161	261	261
$E[U(x)]$	328	348	342	345	437	417
$CE(x)$	7.9499	8.5542	8.3760	8.3710	11.4895	17.4933
$U(x)moment$						
$U''(x)$	331	331	332	373	374	375
$U'''(x)$	-	364	349	-	559	465
$U''''(x)$	328	332	342	348	116	382

For a normal distribution with mean 10 and variance 82, the "true" expected utility value is 328, the approximation using the mean–variance rule is 331—a comparatively good approximation. The approximation by the third moment is omitted. The approximation by the fourth moment then already leads to the exact expected utility value. The development of the approximation is similar for normal distribution II, whose values are in the fourth number column. The true expected utility value is 345. The mean–variance rule yields 373. The approximation by the fourth moment is considerable, even though the difference is greater than with normal distribution I. Overall, it can be stated that the Taylor series converges for normal distributions and exponential utility functions. The speed of convergence obviously also depends on the "compactness".

The approximation behaviour of the gamma distributions is similar. The mean–variance approximation of the "more compact" distribution I is comparatively close to the true expected utility value: 332 vs. 342. Obviously, the approximation oscillates: the third "approximation" fails considerably at 349. The fourth approximation hits the expected utility value exactly. The convergence behaviour is similar for distribution II, although the differences are larger: The expected utility value is 417, the mean–variance approximation with 375 hardly deserves this characterisation. The approximations of the third moment with 465 and the fourth moment with 382 oscillate decreasingly around the expected utility value. Overall, convergence is theoretically guaranteed, although the approximation will take several more terms. The compactness argument is: Larger variance requires slower convergence, possibly oscillating.

The approximation is different for the lognormal distribution. We know from the preliminary theoretical considerations that the Taylor series does not converge. The true expected utility values are 348 (distribution I) and 437 (distribution II). The mean–variance approximations are 331 (distribution I) and 374(distribution II). The two following Taylor series approximations of the third and fourth moments are 364 (distribution I) and 332 (distribution I) and 559 (distribution II) and 116 (distribution II) respectively. An approximation with decreasing difference does not occur; the opposite is the case.

The equation for expected utility with gamma distribution and exponential utility function is described in chapter 3.4.4.3.

$$E[U(x)] = 1{,}000 \cdot \left(1 - \frac{\beta^{\alpha}}{\beta + b^{\alpha}}\right) \tag{3.22}$$

The figures are given in Table 3.3 last row. Mean variance approximation $U''(x) = 375$ is not good, the following approximations $U'''(x)$ and $U''''(x)$ indicate that the successive approximations come closer to the true expected utility value, however oscillating.

3.4.2 Risk Aversion: Several Formulas

The following characterisations result from the first and second derivatives of the utility function:

1. $U\prime(x)$ Marginal utility—for economic reasons the following assumptions apply:
a. $U\prime(x) > 0$ Unlimited needs (non-saturation)
b. $U\prime(x) < 0$ Unrealistic, additional available units reduce the utility
2. $U''(x)$ Change in marginal utility
a. $U''(x) > 0$ Risk-taking—applies to gamblers
b. $U''(x) < 0$ Risk-averse—normal case for financial considerations

Criteria for the risk aversion can be classified into an **Absolute Risk Aversion ($\mathbf{RA_A}$)**, that eliminates the influence of a linear transformation of the utility function with

$$RA_A = \frac{-U''(x)}{U\prime(x)} \tag{3.23}$$

whereby the following applies

$$U_1(x) = C_1 \cdot U(x) + C_0$$

$$U_1\prime(x) = C_1 \cdot U\prime(x)$$

$$U_1''(x) = C_1 \cdot U''(x)$$

or a **Relative Risk Aversion ($\mathbf{RA_R}$)** that measures the elasticity of marginal utility

$$RA_R = \frac{-x \cdot U''(x)}{U\prime(x)} = x \cdot RA_A$$

The absolute risk aversion $\mathrm{RA_A}$, based on a utility function $U(x) = \sqrt{x}$ is calculated as follows:

$$U\prime(x) = \frac{1}{2}x^{-0.5}$$

$$U''(x) = -\frac{1}{4}x^{-1.5}$$

$$RA_A = \frac{0.25x^{-1.5}}{0.5x^{-0.5}} = \frac{0.25}{0.5}x^{-1} = \frac{1}{2}x^{-1}$$

whereas the relative risk aversion RA_R, based on a utility function $U(x) = \ln x$ is calculated as follows:

$$U\prime(x) = \frac{1}{x}$$

$$U''(x) = -\frac{1}{x^2}$$

$$RA_A = \frac{x^{-2}}{x^{-1}} = \frac{1}{x}$$

$$RA_R = x \cdot x^{-1} = 1$$

Further examples of different utility functions.

1. Quadratic utility function $U(x) = x - \frac{x^2}{1{,}000}$ with a relevant realisation range $0 < x < 500$

The following applies for the four criteria:

$U'(x) = 1 - \frac{2x}{1{,}000} = 1 - \frac{x}{500} > 0,\ if\ 0 < x < 500$, positive marginal utility

$U''(x) = -\frac{1}{500} < 0$,diminishing marginal utility

$RA_A = \frac{1}{500-x}, \frac{dRA_A}{dx} = \frac{1}{(500-x)^2} > 0$,increasing absolute RA

$RA_R = \frac{x}{500-x}, \frac{dRA_R}{dx} = \frac{500}{(500-x)^2} > 0$,increasing relative RA

2. Exponential utility function $U(x) = 1{,}000\left(1 - e^{-0.05x}\right)$

The following applies to the four criteria:

$U'(x) > 0$ positive marginal utility
$U''(x) < 0$ decreasing marginal utility
$RA_A = 0.05$ constant absolute RA
$RA_R = 0.05x$ increasing relative RA

3. Potential utility function $U(x) = \begin{matrix} 2{,}000x^{0.5} & for x > 0 \\ 0 & for x = 0 \\ -500x^2 & for x < 0 \end{matrix}$

for $U(x) > 0$ applies

$U'(x) = 1{,}000x^{-0.5} > 0$ positive marginal utility

$U''(x) = -500x^{-1.5} < 0$ decreasing marginal utility

$RA_A = \frac{1}{2}x^{-1}$ decreasing absolute RA

$RA_R = \frac{1}{2}$ constant relative RA, elasticity of marginal utility equals 0.5

4. Logarithmic utility function $U(x) = 1{,}000 \ln x, \textit{whereas} x > 0$

The following applies to the four criteria:

$U'(x) = \frac{1{,}000}{x} > 0$ positive marginal utility

$U''(x) = \frac{-1{,}000}{x^2} < 0$ decreasing marginal utility

$RA_A = \frac{1}{x}$ decreasing absolute RA

$RA_R = 1$ constant relative RA, elasticity of marginal utility equals 1

3.4.3 Certainty Equivalent: The Basis of the Mean–Variance Formula

3.4.3.1 Comparing Buying and Selling Lottery Tickets

Calculating with certainty equivalents instead of the expected utility value has several advantages (Fig. 3.3):

On the one hand, one operates with the dimension of monetary amounts instead of utility amounts. The certainty equivalents can therefore also be compared intersubjectively and can be added together without changing the scale or dimension.

On the other hand, when calculating with certainty equivalents, the differentiation of the original cash flows according to the respective risk and the allocation of companies to respective risk classes becomes unnecessary, because the cash flows from a company have already been transformed into adequate secure cash flows according to the respective risk attitudes of the investors, as expressed in their utility functions.

In particular, the discount rate is also adjusted to the respective risk class. The hypothesis of a "safe interest rate" thus becomes superfluous.

Calculating the certainty equivalent from the expected value of the utility ensures that the certainty equivalent derived in this way has a sound basis in terms of decision theory and is not determined by a blanket or global risk discount.

If one assumes an equilibrium on the capital market, where supply and demand should meet and balance each other out, then one must consider that the certainty equivalent is the selling price of a lottery or generally of an uncertain prospectus,

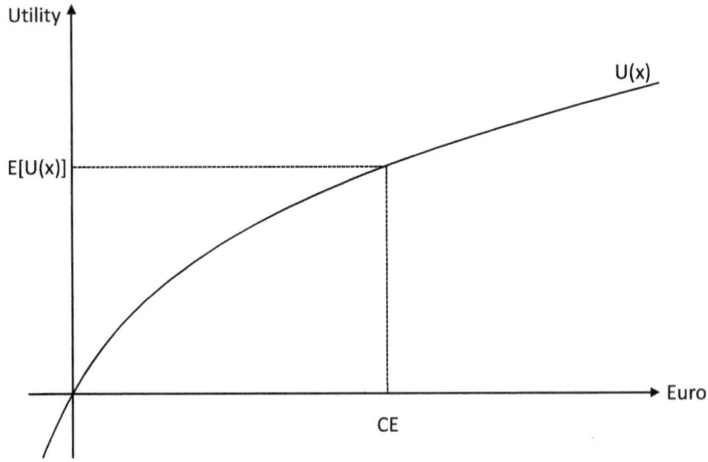

Fig. 3.3 Relationship between certainty equivalent, expected utility value and real monetary amounts

whereas the purchase price corresponds to the stake Y.[18] It is calculated according to the equation.

$$E\big[U(x-y)\big] = U(0) \tag{3.24}$$

It corresponds to the amount to be subtracted from each value so that the expected utility value has a certainty equivalent of zero.

In the case of an exponential utility function, both values are the same; in the case of a logarithmic or quadratic function, they are different.

When buying an uncertain prospectus, e.g. a security, the seller's certainty equivalent and the buyer's stake must therefore correspond.

If we restrict ourselves to exponential utility functions and normal distribution or obtain the following equation determining Certainty Equivalent CE. The following applies in this case:

$$e^{(-aCE)} = e^{\left(-a\mu+\frac{a^2\sigma^2}{2}\right)} \tag{3.25}$$

and therefore

$$CE = \mu - \frac{a\sigma^2}{2} \tag{3.26}$$

The famous mean–variance formula is equal to the CE with the expected utility itself.

[18] Cf. e.g. Schneeweiß (1967), pp. 42, pp. 85; Raiffa (1970), pp. 89, pp. 200, Myerson (2015), p. 10.

3.4.3.2 Examples Buying Price Formulas

The relationships between the certainty equivalent and the stake are demonstrated using the quadratic and exponential utility function. The realisations of the prospects to be evaluated should be subject to a normal distribution with expected value $\overline{x} = 10$ and $s^2 = 82$.

We obtain the following results for the two different utility functions.

1. Quadratic utility function

$$U(x) = x - \frac{x^2}{100}$$

The expected value of the utility is obtained according to the above equations

$$E[U(x)] = 13.75$$

The result for the certainty equivalent is then

$$CE = 16.46$$

For the stake Y, the following equation is obtained according to the above equation

$$U(0) = E[U(x - Y)]$$

$$0 = \int_{-\infty}^{+\infty} \left(x - Y - \frac{(x - Y)^2}{100} \right) f(x)dx$$

Here $f(x)$ denotes the density function of the normal distribution with the above parameters. If you solve for y, you get $Y = 17.70$

2. Exponential utility function

$$U(x) = 1{,}000\left(1 - e^{-0,.05x}\right)$$

The expected value of the utility is calculated according to the equation given above

$$E[U(x)] = 512.64$$

The certainty equivalent as the sales price of the lottery is calculated as follow:

$$CE = 14.375$$

The following equation applies to calculate the buying price of a good or the buying price of a lottery ticket, the stake Y.

$$U(0) = \int_{-\infty}^{+\infty} 1{,}000\left(1 - e^{-0.05(x-Y)}\right) f(x)dx$$

If $f(x)$ denotes the density function of the normal distribution with parameters from above, you get:

$$Y = 14.375$$

3.4.3.3 Solving the Expected Utility Integral Explicitly

The directly integrable cases a)-c) discussed below can be traced back to the following integral[19]:

$$\int_{-\infty}^{+\infty} e^{-px^2+qx}dx = e^{\frac{q^2}{4p}} \cdot \sqrt{\frac{\pi}{p}} (p > 0) \tag{3.27}$$

The following cases can be solved:

1. Normal distribution with exponential utility function

$$U(x) = 1{,}000\left(1 - e^{-bx}\right); f(x) = \frac{1}{\sqrt{2\pi} \cdot s} e^{-\frac{(x-\overline{x})^2}{2s^2}}$$

If you set

$\overline{x}$ = Expected value of X, s^2 = Variance of X.
$p = \frac{1}{2s^2}$; $q = \frac{\overline{x}-bs^2}{s^2}$, you get $E[U(x)] = 1{,}000\left(1 - exp\left(-b\overline{x} + \frac{b^2 s^2}{2}\right)\right)$

2. Lognormal distribution with potential utility function

$$U(x) = \frac{x^c}{c}; f(x) = \frac{1}{x\sigma\sqrt{2\pi}} \cdot e^{-\frac{(\ln x-\mu)^2}{2\sigma^2}} \quad 0 < x < \infty$$

μ = Expected value of $\ln x$
σ^2= Variance of $\ln x$
If you set $z = \ln x$; $q = \frac{\mu + c\sigma^2}{2\sigma^2}$,you get:

[19] Gradsteyn and Ryzhik (2007), p. 337, Nr.3.323.2.10.

3. Lognormal distribution with logarithmic utility function

$$U(x) = \ln x 0 < x < \infty$$

with $z = \ln x$ you get

$$E[U(x)] = \int_0^{+\infty} z \frac{1}{\sigma\sqrt{2\pi}} e^{\frac{(z-\mu)^2}{2\sigma^2}} \cdot dz = \mu$$

The Certainty Equivalent *CE* is usually determined according to the form[20]

$$U(CE) = E[U(x)]$$

and for the different distribution types a) to c) you get the following results:

$$CE = \overline{x} - bs^2$$
$$CE = e^{\left(\mu + \frac{cs^2}{2}\right)}$$
$$CE = e^{\mu}$$

4. Gamma distribution and exponential utility function:
   Preliminary remark: Why gamma distribution?

Gamma distributions are predestined for modelling market activity at the micro level, i.e. for the occurrence time point of buy and sell orders and the transformation of the orders in prices. These questions were neglected for a long time. Beja and Hakansson (1979) already posed the question of how to model the transformation of orders into prices in the 1970s. The mainstream consistently ignored this essential task at the time, probably also because data about the path from "orders to prices" was difficult to obtain. In the meantime, the data situation has improved significantly. We can therefore expect progress in the analysis of this arguably central economic issue, not least in view of these detailed data collections. Then the economist's metaphor quoted by Daniel McFadden: "economists know the price of everything and the value of nothing" can also be invalidated.[21] What is urgently needed now are approaches for modelling events at the micro level, e.g. via the arrival and matching of orders. To model these events, one must have the exact time points of submission: Because one can match only orders that are already placed at the trading venue. Merging orders into transaction prices is

---

[20] Schneeweiß (1967), p. 85.

[21] McFadden (1999), p. 75 alludes with this metaphor to Oscar Wilde's characterisation of a cynic (in Lady Windermere's Fan). The rigid disregard for real conditions in the models does indeed suggest a cynical attitude instead of a search for truth. Cf. also the numerous examples in McFadden, l.c.

then not a question of time series analysis, but of arrival priority: Matching of order follows the price time priority rule. These vital circumstances have not been regarded previous models. However, we now need concepts that transparently represent the arrival of orders, the prioritisation of orders and the merging of buy and sell orders to fairly determine transaction prices. This requires probability distributions to analyse the occurrence of events. The gamma distribution is the basic distribution for analysing event arrivals. It is indeed time to use methods that correspond to real market events, especially beyond the analysis of ex-post time series data. The central question is why people decide to place buy or sell orders and how to model these decision-making processes. A technical, downstream question is the transformation of these orders into prices.

The integral of expected utility values (3.1) can be solved analytically and therefore the correct comparison values are easy to determine. We then do not need to resort to numerical integration to determine them. An essential part of the gamma probability distribution is the gamma function that gives the probability distribution its name:

$$\Gamma(\alpha) = \int_0^{\infty} y^{\alpha-1} \cdot e^{-y} dy \alpha \in (0, \infty) \tag{3.28}$$

If we make a variable substitution in (3.28) according to the equation $y = bx$ we obtain the gamma distribution. If a random variable X follows a gamma distribution with the parameters α and β, then the density function is given as

$$\mathrm{f}(x) = \frac{1}{\Gamma(\alpha)} \cdot \beta^{\alpha} \cdot x^{\alpha-1} \cdot e^{-\beta x} x \in (0, \infty) \tag{3.29}$$

The parameters of the gamma distribution are $\alpha \in (0, \infty)$ and $\beta \in (0, \infty)$, they stand for:

$\alpha \widehat{=}$ Time period until the n-th event occurs

$\beta \widehat{=}$ Average event rate per time unit.

If a random variable X follows a gamma distribution with the parameters a and b, then the distribution function is given by:

$$\mathrm{F}(x) = \frac{\Gamma(\alpha, \beta x)}{\Gamma(\alpha)} x \in (0, \infty) \tag{3.30}$$

with $\Gamma(\alpha) = \int_0^{\infty} x^{\alpha-1} \cdot e^{-x} dx =$ gamma function, see (3.28)

$$\Gamma(\alpha, \beta x) = \int_0^{\beta x} t^{\alpha-1} \cdot e^{-t} dt = lowerincompletegammafunction. \tag{3.31}$$

If a random variable X follows a gamma distribution with the parameters a and b, then according to Eq. (3.29) the expected value m_1 and variance m_2 are given as:

(see Fisz (1962) p. 136; Rinne (1997), p. 349).

$$E[X] = \frac{1}{\beta}\alpha \tag{3.32}$$

$$V[X] = \frac{1}{\beta^2}\alpha \tag{3.33}$$

The central moments m_3, m_4 are calculated as follows: (Rinne (1997), p. 349)[22]:

$$m_3 = 2\beta^{-3} \tag{3.34}$$

$$m_4 = \beta^{-4} \cdot \left(6\alpha + 4\alpha^2\right) \tag{3.35}$$

The exponential utility function is defined according to the previous uses as

$$U(x) = 1{,}000\left(1 - e^{-bx}\right) \tag{3.36}$$

with $b=$ risk aversion coefficient.

The expected value of the utility $E[U(x)]$ is according to the usual formula

$$E[U(x)] = \int_0^\infty U(x) \cdot f(x)dx \tag{3.37}$$

defined in the present case as

$$= 1{,}000\left(1 - \int_0^\infty e^{-bx} \cdot \frac{1}{\Gamma(\alpha)} \cdot \beta^\alpha \cdot x^{\alpha-1} \cdot e^{-\beta x}\right)dx \tag{3.38}$$

$$= 1{,}000\left(1 - \frac{\beta^\alpha}{\Gamma(\alpha)}\right) \cdot \int_0^\infty x^{\alpha-1} \cdot e^{-(\beta+b)x}dx \tag{3.39}$$

Let us set $v = x \cdot (\beta + b)$ and $dx = \frac{dv}{\beta+b}$ we obtain

$$= 1{,}000\left(1 - \frac{\beta^\alpha}{\Gamma(\alpha)}\right) \cdot \int_0^\infty v^{\alpha-1} \cdot e^{-v} \cdot \frac{1}{(\beta+b)^\alpha}dv \tag{3.40}$$

Considering the definition of the gamma function according to (3.28) we obtain:

$$E[U(x)] = 1{,}000\left(1 - \frac{\beta^\alpha}{(\beta+b)^\alpha}\right) \tag{3.41}$$

[22] Wikipedia-Wolfram Mathworld provides different definitions for the moments m_3 und m_4. We follow Rinne.

References

For case a) Schneeweiß (1967) derived a closed integration as a solution to a differential equation as part of the proof that the expected value or expected value approach is consistent with Bernoulli's principle for the combination mentioned. Feldstein (1968)[23] discusses indifference curves for the lognormal distribution-logarithmic utility function but does not calculate the Combination's expected utility.

For the combination "gamma distribution exponential utility function" Bierwag (1974) published an analytical solution of the expected utility value integral. A comparison with our results is difficult due to different definition of initial variables.

[23] Feldstein (1968), p. 7.

Performance of Real Trading Venues 4

Abstract

This chapter introduces the real behaviour at trading venues. The real or digital locations where traders place orders and other traders accept that orders. The matching of two fitting orders generates a transaction and produces a price. The last mile of a trading process cannot be studied by investigating time series of prices. Prices are the final product of the trading process. We propose an innovative description of order's placing and matching. At the end of that chapter is a short comparison of mean variance modelling versus real decision making: the one developed to handle decisions under risk und the other developed to handle decisions under uncertainty. We vote for the decision-making under uncertainty and explain the tool proposed in the next chapter.

Keywords

Trading as contracting of orders • Organisation of true trading venue • Functioning of open order book • Identification of order types on true microdata • Numerical examples • Market's microstructure • Order types and trading strategies

4.1 Overview

4.1.1 Meeting Place for Buyers and Sellers

We follow Buchanan (1975, p. 229): "Economics comes closer to a science of contract than a science of choice" and learned his experience alike: "a formal mathematics of human interaction can possible become even more challenging" Buchanan (2001, p. 31). According to our experience, a science of choice is an important part of a science of contract. It has to regard the circumstances to contract a deal. Each trader makes his own choice: to place, accept or withdraw

O. Loistl et al., *Screen Based Trading and Open Order Book*, New Economic Windows,
https://doi.org/10.1007/978-3-031-99052-6_4

an order. But every trader must consider the possibilities and intentions of other traders, which influence their order decisions. The science of contract comprises a science of choice and the traders' interactions.

The most important aspects are price, quantity and quality. The specific procedures may differ in different markets, but the fundamentals are similar. The core business of any market is to facilitate the interactions of buyers and sellers to exchanges goods and money—and to exchange messages. These "features" cannot be modelled by investigating time series, not by price time series and not even by additionally investigating time series of orders. Such an attempt is comparable to a weather forecast in which only time series of the temperature are extrapolated. The weather forecast is based on a comprehensive integrated assessment of all weather-determining forces on a causal basis. Successful investors rely on much more data than ex-post share prices: "There's no data like more data" is the maxim of a successful player in this field.[1]

In a first step, we model the electronic trading venue of the Frankfurt Stock Exchange, Xetra. It was developed in the 1980ies and is now used successfully on several stock exchanges on several continents. The advantage of an electronic trading venue is the clearcut application of its rules and regulations. The implementation of Xetra performance is therefore quite simple: you have to implement the rules and regulations of Xetra. The basic version leaves no room for discretionary brokers who pursue their own interests.

The rules on stock exchanges are designed to speed up the trades. There can be differences between trading on a trading floor managed by human brokers on the one hand and a computerised trading floor on the other. Indeed, trading managed by human brokers gives these brokers a great deal of discretion to bridge potential liquidity gaps between buyers and sellers, especially in rapidly changing situations. But these brokers are not allowed to pursue their own interests by taking their own positions. They are obliged to maintain an "orderly market" (in the US). Frankfurt's Xetra, has installed so-called "designated sponsors" that are similarly obliged to provide liquidity.[2] Our approach will not cover "designated sponsors", as these are used for non-liquid shares, and we concentrate on the liquid stocks in the DAX.

We should bear in mind that prices are generated by matching individual orders to buy respective to sell a specific quantity of securities for/within a specified price/range. The submission of individual buy-respective sell-orders depends on the utility/value any person achieves by selling/buying the asset under consideration. Consequently, trading is mainly motivated by perceived differences between observed prices and assessed values. Orders express traders' willingness to buy respective the willingness to sell. The following figure sketches the dependencies.

---

[1] Mercer's maxim is quoted by Zuckerman (2019, p. 221).

[2] See Deutsche Börse (2023).

4.1.2 Activities of the Traders: Information Processing and Order Selection

Harold L. Vogel (2018) illustrates the real performance at an exchange by the famous cartoon of Kevin KAL Kallaugher at the beginning of his book. The cartoon illustrates a normal day at the stock exchange with excited and agitated traders and other visitors. The major difference to computerised trading results from the presence of traders at the floor in the cartoon. They can watch each other and process the information provided by their talks and their behavioural attitudes.

At computerised trading venues, traders cannot observe each other immediately but receive information mainly via the open order book. They can watch on screen the orders that other traders submit, withdraw, resubmit and they can observe how orders are matched to generate trades and prices alike. The quantitative formulas reproducing what is happening are given in Chapter 6. The formulas describe the cartoon's excited actions of human beings. In the end, the formulas must describe the performance of the market at the micro level. Traders who expect the highest profits or benefits will be most excited and try to complete their trades as quick as possible. Therefore, the action promising the highest utility has the shortest reaction time. According to DSMP, the highest action promising the highest profit or utility implies the shortest reaction time.

Discrete Choice is appropriate to handle issues of organised complexity. It has been used successfully for some time in areas such as marketing, transport and environmental issues. The evaluation of specific individual activities is the core issue of discrete choice and the reason we use this approach.

4.1.3 Algorithmic Trading Patterns in Xetra Orders

4.1.3.1 Introduction

Algorithmic trading has become a standard technique in most investment firms. Another term is "high frequency trading", hft for short. Nasdaq estimated that 50 per cent of stock trading volume in the US is currently driven by computer-backed high frequency trading.[3] Investigating algorithmic trading should therefore primarily rely on individual limit orders, collected in the limit open order book, LOB.[4] Having collected this data we can investigate individual activities and traders' reactions alike. Investigating reactions and interactions must rely on individual events, i.e. in our case, on the orders' submission, matching with an opposite order or its cancellation. Short roundtrip times in combination with low latency algorithms offer ideal trading conditions for automated systems, enabling them to adjust to new conditions in sub-second range. As these response times are key in the analysis of algorithmic trades, we take advantage of the high precision of time stamps in

---

[3] Nasdaq.com/glossary/H/high-frequency-trading.

[4] Deutsche Bundesbank: Bedeutung und Wirkung des Hochfrequenzhandels am deutschen Kapitalmarkt, Monatsbericht Oktober (2016, pp. 38–61).

our data set. These time stamps of order events are recorded with a precision of 1/100 of a second. Thus, using this data set, we can carry out detailed lifetime studies and search for algorithms using lifetime deviations in the sub-second range. Time-stamped orders and prices make possible the observation of reactions of traders on the release of price sensitive information. Furthermore, it can be shown what can be expected: Traders react to price sensitive information by adjusting orders. The adjustment of prices therefore follows from the adjustment of orders. Without adjustment of orders, an adjustment of prices cannot occur. But not every adjustment of an order generates an adjustment of prices. This differentiation can be observed by observing both, buy and sell orders. The transitional analysis of orders, the so-called "duration" in the sense of lifetime, is only possible if both, times of submission and time of expiry, are recorded.

Considering the diversity of trading forms, a diversity of models is to be expected. Moreover, the model's form under consideration depends on the availability of data. The first big differentiation regards the involvement of human activities. Does the model assume that the data is generated in one way or the other by human actions and are the human actions implemented, or is the model directed towards the recognition of pattern inherent in the data. The latter is AI's basic philosophy. The principle leads to tremendous results. Both, the amount of training data and the computing power determine AI's performance.

The basic requirement has been to model the motives of the traders as the driving force. Luce proposed to reduce the dependence of the decision-making process on external circumstances by extending the decision-making idea, already proposed by Thurstone. The comparative judgement of desirability helps to reduce the influence of these side circumstances, and he proposed the irrelevance from independent alternatives. That seemed to be a very courageous step, and it proved to be very useful.

Regarding the data, it is obvious that human decisions do not produce prices on markets, but human actions manifest themselves in the placing of orders. It is not sufficient to model the pattern of orders, but the decisive aspect is modelling the decision procedure to place orders. If this core aspect is not included in the market's performance, then the causal structure is not completely captured.

Many of the currently published investigations of orders do not regard the decision procedure of order submission but start with already placed orders.[5] However, a market's decisive function is the matching of orders placed by human beings and the matching of opposite orders.[6]

[5] See Zhang et al. (2022, 2021), Manahov et al. (2018), Bleher et al. (2021), Sirignano (2019), Dalko and Wang (2020).

[6] Details see Deutsche Börse (2024, p. 42).

4.1.3.2 The Frankfurt Stock Exchange and the Data Set

Introduction

Deutsche Börse AG runs the Frankfurt Stock Exchange (FWB). It is by far the most important among the seven German stock exchanges. By Xetra, electronic trading is organised as a combination of auctions and continuous trading.[7] While many of the DAX-40 stocks are also listed on other exchanges, most of the trading for these stocks happens on the Xetra system that offers remote access.

The functioning of order driven markets is explained in Deutsche Börse (2024) and Francioni and Schwartz (2017). It is a mixture of auction and continuous trading. Our model simulates the continuous trading variant. Matching of opposite orders follows the price time priority principle.[8]

Order Types

The Xetra system offers the indication of trading interest by many order types. Two basic order types are admitted for price determination in the various trading forms:

1. **Market orders** are unlimited bid/ask orders. They are to be executed at the next price determined.
2. **Limit orders** are bid/ask orders, which are to be executed at their specified limit or better. Depending on the order types, orders can have further specific execution conditions, validity constraints, and trading restrictions.[9] This first trading model variant refers to limit orders. If the limit orders can be viewed by all traders, then we have a limit open order book, LOB.

Order Event Codes

The tables and figures in this book were generated using a database that recorded all order book entries occurring in the 6 trading days in the time from Wednesday 5th to Wednesday January 12th of 2005. It consists of 5,014,200 database entries that record changes in the electronic limit order book of Xetra. A database entry is generated whenever an order is entered into the system, partially executed, fully executed, cancelled, modified, automatically entered or automatically cancelled. Each such order entry is time-stamped as soon as it is entered into the Xetra order book software. These timestamps feature a precision of 1/100s. The matching algorithm relies on these timestamps to execute trades according to the price-time priority rules given in the Xetra market model. The entries of the database under consideration consist of different event types.

Table 4.1 lists the different types of codes and frequencies:

[7] Details see Deutsche Börse (2024).

[8] Details see Deutsche Börse (2024, p. 21).

[9] Deutsche Börse (2024, p. 10).

Table 4.1 Frequency of different events in the database along with their event code found in the time from January 5th to January 12th of 2005

Event type	Event code	Absolute frequency	% Entry	% Termination
Order entry	1	2,284,628	99.98%	
Order modification	2	36,165		
Order cancellation	3	1,626,896		70.15%
Order filled completely	4	675,232		29.12%
Order partially filled	5	373,760		
Order deleted automatically	6	16,597		0.72%
Technical Entry	101	461	0.02%	
Technical Cancellation	103	461		0.02%

A total of 5,014,200 database entries were examined. Absolute count data are given in the middle column, while the two rightmost columns list the percentage of orders started/ended via each respective event code.

1. Due to the restriction of the dataset to a certain observation period, there were some orders, where the order entry was not observable in the data set. Similarly, there were orders without a suitable end of code 3, 4, 6 or 103. This is the reason why the sum of order entries (codes 1 and code 101 add up to 2,284,628 + 461 = 2,285,089) does not match the sum of order terminations (codes 3, 4, 6 and 103 add up to 1,626,896 + 675,232 + 16,597 + 461 = 2,319,186).
2. Percentage of orders, that are entered via a 1 resp. 101 code. 100% corresponds to all order entry events in the database.
3. Percentage of orders terminated via a 3, 4, 6 resp. 103 event. 100% corresponds to all order terminating events in the database.

Order Event Sequences

Every new order submission generates an event with event code 1. Cancellation generates an event with event code 3. Full execution generates an event with event code 4. Therefore orders, that are entered into the system and then deleted again without any executions generate event code sequences characterised by 1–3. These orders are often termed no-fill deletion orders. Orders that are entered into the system and then filled in a single transaction generate event code sequence 1–4. These orders are usually termed one-fill completed orders. Many orders also feature events of partial executions each generating event code 5. This leads to sequences of type 1–5–5-... –5–3. The last event code 3 indicates that the remaining part of the order has been cancelled. In the sequence 1–5–5-... –5–4 the last event code indicates that the remaining part of the order has been executed entirely. These orders are also of interest, but do not get a special name here. The number of order modifications characterised by code 2 event is rather small. It does not even add up to a single percentage point. This fact indicates that the primary method of

Table 4.2 Example of 1–5-5–3 order sequence[10]

Modification timestamp	Event code	Buy sell	Limit	Price	Size
2005–01–05 09:51:27.87	1	S	35.00	0.00	20,000
2005–01–05 13:11:55.05	5	S	35.00	35.00	2,485
2005–01–05 16:27:13.58	5	S	35.00	35.00	377
2005–01–05 16:27:16.11	3	S	35.00	0.00	17,138

changing existing orders is obviously to cancel the old order and re-submit another one. An example given in the following Table 4.2 illustrates a 1–5–5–3 order.

Further data fields omitted in this table entail the order expiry date, auction trade flag, order type, order restriction, trade restriction, order entry time stamp, order number and ISIN code.

The order is inserted with a volume of 20,000 at time 09:51:27.87. Partial execution with a size of 2,485 reduces the available volume to 20,000–2,485 = 17,515 at time 13:11:55.05 and then another partial execution of 377 units leads to 20,000–2,485–377 = 17,138 remaining units from 16:27:13.58 on. At 16:27:16.11 the remaining volume of 17,138 units is cancelled altogether. Most orders belong to the 1–3, 1–4, 1–5–4 and 1–5–3 type. Table 4.3 shows the frequencies of the most common sequence codes in conjunction with different order types.

Order types and the sequence codes most frequently generated by them.

1. The letters L/M/I/T correspond to limit, market, iceberg and market-to-limit order types respectively.
2. Market orders are not executed immediately when submitted with restriction to auction phases or during the call phase of the auction. This fact allows for cancellation of market orders. The 1–3 market order sequences found above are of exactly this origin.

Table 4.4 exhibits the frequency of each order type in combination with order restrictions.

Percentage of the money volume and number of orders belonging to each category are shown above.

- Restriction ‘F’ means Fill-Or-Kill, ‘I’ means Immediate-or-Cancel and ‘S’ means Triggered-Stop-Order.
- The left part of the table shows the relative frequency of each order type entered into the Xetra system in conjunction with each order restriction. 100 percent corresponds to all orders submitted. Thus, in the left part of the table all orders are counted, regardless of whether they are executed or cancelled. The total percentage figures do not sum up to 100% due to rounding effects.

[10] Source: Prix et al. (2007), Kopp et al. (2008).

Table 4.3 Event code sequences for order types and order restrictions in the Xetra order book

Order type/Sequence combinations	Absolute freq	% of Order type	% of all entries
L- with seq. 1–3	1,480,911	67.29%	64.82%
L- with seq. 1–4	436,451	19.83%	19.10%
L- with seq. 1–5-4	77,919	3.54%	3.41%
L- with seq. 1–5–3	41,502	1.89%	1.82%
LI with seq. 1–4	34,347	1.56%	1.50%
L- with seq. 1	27,406	1.25%	1.20%
L- with seq. 1–5–5–4	24,430	1.11%	1.07%
(Other)	77,902	3.54%	3.41%
Total	**2,200,868**	**100%**	**96.33%**
M- with seq. 1–4	44,794	75.84%	1.96%
M- with seq. 1–5–4	4,397	7.44%	0.19%
M- with seq. 1–3	4,290	7.26%	0.19%
MS with seq. 1–4	3,321	5.62%	0.15%
M- with seq. 1–5–5–4	800	1.35%	0.04%
MI with seq. 1–4	514	0.87%	0.02%
MS with seq. 1–5–4	220	0.37%	0.01%
(Other)	726	1.23%	0.03%
Total	**59,062**	**100%**	**2.59%**
I- with seq. 1–3	13,258	62.69%	0.58%
I- with seq. 1–5–3	702	3.32%	0.03%
I- with seq. 1	543	2.57%	0.02%
I- with seq. 1–5–5–3	432	2.04%	0.02%
I- with seq. 1–4	428	2.02%	0.02%
I- with seq. 1–5–5–5–3	345	1.63%	0.02%
I- with seq. 1–5–5–5-5–3	289	1.37%	0.01%
(Other)	5,151	24.36%	0.23%
Total	**21,148**	**100%**	**0.93%**
T- with seq. 1–3	2,729	76.87%	0.12%
T- with seq. 1–4	797	22.45%	0.03%
T- with seq. 1–5–4	19	0.54%	0.00%
T- with seq. 1–5–5–4	3	0.08%	0.00%
T- with seq. 1–5–5–5-4	1	0.03%	0.00%
T- with seq. 1–5–5–5–5–4	1	0.03%	0.00%
Total	**3,550**	**100%**	**0.15%**

Table 4.4 Importance of different order types concerning number of orders and money volume traded

	number of orders submitted				money volume traded			
Restriction	Limit	Market	MtL	Iceberg	Limit	Market	MtL	Iceberg
none	93.96%	2.40%	0.16%	0.93%	80.08%	1.32%	0.13%	4.24%
F	0.01%	0.00%	0.00%	0.00%	0.14%	0.20%	0.00%	0.00%
I	2.34%	0.03%	0.00%	0.00%	0.02%	0.00%	0.00%	0.00%
S	0.03%	0.16%	0.00%	0.00%	4.83%	0.03%	0.00%	0.00%

- The right part of the table shows the relative amount of money volume traded using each order type in conjunction with each order restriction. Money volume was computed using the size of the execution in shares times the price of the transaction per share. Thus, if the price is better than a possible limit supplied, the transaction price was used for the computation. The cancelled part of any order is disregarded in this part of the table. 100 percent in the right part of the table corresponds to the total money volume traded on Xetra in the observation period. The total percentage figures do not sum up to 100% due to rounding effects.

Tables 4.3 and 4.4 indicate that limit orders play the most important role in Xetra in terms of number of orders entered into the system as well as concerning traded volumes. The dominance of limit orders is greater when comparing the number of orders. This is due to the fact that the typical volume of limit orders is lower than that of iceberg orders or market orders. Iceberg orders are an instrument typically used to trade larger volumes with a single order. In the money volume part of the table, the iceberg orders do show up considerably stronger than in the pure order count part. In this paper we are investigating limit orders only.

More Actively and Less Actively Traded Stocks in the Sample

We use the actual trades' money volume as a proxy for liquidity of each stock in the DAX-30. The results and a ranking according to this measure are given in Table 4.5.

ESMA Guideline Limit Order Book

ESMA guidelines propose the following system for the limit order book entries:

- New/Cancellation/Modification of Orders[11]
- Additional Limit Price
- Classification of an Iceberg Limit Order
- Peg (or Pegged) Orders[12]

[11] ESMA (2015, p. 231).

[12] Order's limit is linked to another market figure, e.g. index quotation.

Table 4.5 Ranking of the DAX-30 stocks according to money volume traded during the trading days from January 5th to January 12th of 2005

	money volume					order counts		
stock	insertions in €	(partial) exec. in EUR	% of total	cancels in €	% of total	# insertions	# (partial) exec	# cancels
DTE	11,828,478,731	4,943,385,187	41.79%	6,709,010,564	56.72%	102,992	66,925	60,236
SAP	9,736,429,511	3,590,803,808	36.88%	6,133,401,159	62.99%	128,310	72,740	82,167
DBK	9,469,106,165	3,427,840,346	36.20%	5,997,248,669	63.33%	121,055	60,878	83,319
SIE	9,617,142,107	2,983,210,594	31.02%	6,517,991,136	67.77%	117,034	62,447	75,561
ALV	8,790,277,310	2,420,874,661	27.54%	6,365,267,254	72.41%	139,377	53,282	107,569
RWE	5,681,840,719	2,059,831,162	36.25%	3,568,859,575	62.81%	92,385	54,657	57,242
EOA	7,223,954,037	2,023,701,781	28.01%	5,121,734,538	70.90%	101,513	46,768	70,762
DCX	6,127,425,933	1,887,165,222	30.80%	4,258,908,966	69.51%	106,081	46,882	78,365
MUV2	6,704,429,897	1,727,628,726	25.77%	5,003,312,853	74.63%	126,827	40,623	102,038
BAS	5,417,235,455	1,559,059,342	28.78%	3,806,098,197	70.26%	101,962	41,656	73,566
BAY	4,331,672,091	1,499,615,910	34.62%	2,800,234,703	64.65%	88,208	44,242	59,384
HVM	3,809,997,784	1,440,028,234	37.80%	2,420,967,668	63.54%	73,804	35,883	53,476
VOW	3,790,013,654	1,404,451,392	37.06%	2,532,581,837	66.82%	72,255	41,303	51,283
SCH	3,220,077,589	1,169,923,324	36.33%	2,005,412,669	62.28%	59,785	34,784	36,808
IFX	2,307,849,938	1,051,246,991	45.55%	1,259,620,703	54.58%	60,000	35,302	38,333
BMW	3,514,440,533	1,017,405,425	28.95%	2,603,134,296	74.07%	85,254	31,886	68,350
MEO	3,051,119,590	961,073,566	31.50%	2,033,491,197	66.65%	75,733	30,020	55,788
CBK	2,983,413,630	957,340,370	32.09%	2,070,980,883	69.42%	71,676	32,220	54,939
TKA	1,803,884,997	599,383,000	33.23%	1,148,294,495	63.66%	49,433	25,196	33,266

(continued)

Table 4.5 (continued)

	money volume					order counts		
stock	insertions in €	(partial) exec. in EUR	% of total	cancels in €	% of total	# insertions	# (partial) exec	# cancels
MAN	2,369,511,487	542,591,278	22.90%	1,789,611,094	75.53%	45,841	19,812	33,763
CON	2,066,085,303	505,688,538	24.48%	1,519,165,870	73.53%	56,939	21,832	42,015
DPW	1,812,172,774	481,907,183	26.59%	1,314,871,778	72.56%	51,807	21,389	37,590
ADS	1,770,215,224	447,125,622	25.26%	1,286,488,383	72.67%	56,950	17,964	44,821
DB1	1,416,524,808	422,635,469	29.84%	945,572,830	66.75%	34,948	14,174	25,332
LHA	1,177,439,125	397,502,755	33.76%	737,285,375	62.62%	42,659	19,028	30,512
ALT	1,246,653,282	327,284,804	26.25%	884,871,110	70.98%	45,370	18,590	32,164
TUI	1,372,789,752	325,475,811	23.71%	1,024,373,231	74.62%	43,419	18,139	32,086
HEN3	1,300,108,649	307,276,160	23.63%	958,371,953	73.71%	54,805	14,370	44,954
LIN	1,239,932,379	303,736,968	24.50%	893,918,504	72.09%	48,285	15,698	38,181
FME	785,318,869	168,525,398	21.46%	582,477,219	74.17%	30,382	10,302	23,026
Total/ Average	125,965,541,324	40,953,719,025	30.75%	84,293,558,706	68.21%	2,285,089	1,048,992	1,626,896

- Classification of a Stop Order
- Routed Orders[13]
- Classification of Strategy Orders[14]
- Priority Changing[15]
- Trading Phases[16]

4.1.3.3 Analysis of No-Fill Deletion Order Lifetimes

Summary Statistics

Table 4.6 provides a detailed picture of the lifetimes of no-fill deletion orders (i.e. orders coded with '1–3') as described in chapter 4.1.3.2.3. These no-fill deletion orders embody approx. 65% of all order insertions.

Summary statistics of the no-fill-deletion order lifetimes for each stock as well as for the pool of all DAX-30 stocks together are given in the middle columns. All lifetimes were measured in seconds and recorded for orders placed in the time from January 5th to January 12th of 2005. Total number of observations for each stock is given in the rightmost column.

The lifetimes of the no-fill-deletion orders exhibit a skewed shape. We will investigate this shape further in chapter 4.1.3.3. The table indicates that the other DAX-30 companies are more or less in the same range. An interesting fact is that the mode value for the no-fill deletion order lifetime of almost all DAX-30 stocks is in the very narrow range of 2.02 to 2.04 with the only exceptions of Adidas-Salomon, Münch. Rückvers. and Schering (values of 60.01, 0.99 and 60.00). This pattern might be a first indicator of many orders being timed by software programs supporting the human trader or by fully automated trading programs. The total number of no-fill deletion orders for each stock and the size for the entire DAX-30 pool is given in the rightmost column. For comparison and since one-fill-completion orders amount to more than 22% of all orders, Table 4.7 shows the lifetime distribution of those orders.

Summary statistics for the pool of all DAX-30 stocks is given in the middle columns. All lifetimes were measured in seconds and recorded for orders placed in the time from January 5th to January 12th of 2005. The total number of observations for each stock is given in the rightmost column.

A Brief Introduction to Kernel Density Estimates

Like the widely known histograms used to visualise a density function, it is possible to picture the approximate density function in a slightly more accurate way that avoids the blurring effect of the histogram classes. Thus, alternative methods, such as the general kernel density estimation, may give a clearer and more precise picture of any density distribution. To illustrate this procedure more closely, we

[13] Investor prescribes the routing course.

[14] What if scenarios especially relevant in option trading.

[15] Circumstances under which the priority changes, e.g. time priority instead of the common price time priority.

[16] Placing an order at a determined trading phase, e.g. auction phase or continuous trading.

Table 4.6 Summary statistics of the lifetimes of all no-fill deletion orders

Stock name	Min	1st Q	Mode	Median	Mean	3rd Q,	Max	N
DT.TELEKOM	0.07	5.23	2.03	24.09	679.10	106.90	627,500.00	56,039
SAP	0.06	2.96	2.02	11.94	375.40	55.00	620,400.00	75,786
DEUTSCHE BANK	0.06	4.53	2.02	14.69	266.20	55.10	514,300.00	75,891
SIEMENS	0.07	3.16	2.03	12.43	360.80	54.95	584,700.00	70,202
ALLIANZ	0.05	2.98	2.02	11.16	278.00	46.38	521,400.00	99,937
RWE	0.06	4.67	2.02	22.65	471.80	80.56	532,600.00	52,059
E.ON	0.08	3.50	2.02	14.86	297.50	59.95	629,100.00	64,980
DAIMLERCHRYSLER	0.07	4.33	2.02	17.70	338.00	62.09	625,400.00	70,683
MUENCH.RUECKVERS	0.07	4.08	0.99	12.46	240.60	39.59	526,200.00	96,736
BASF	0.07	4.52	2.02	18.29	321.30	60.10	625,600.00	69,632
BAYER	0.07	4.87	2.03	24.14	474.80	88.65	519,900.00	55,017
BAY.HYPO-VEREINSBK	0.07	6.97	2.03	27.90	437.00	93.74	527,500.00	47,848
VOLKSWAGEN	0.08	5.39	2.02	29.54	469.50	95.98	538,300.00	43,147
SCHERING	0.07	7.10	60.00	38.70	407.30	109.70	529,100.00	34,242
INFINEON TECH	0.08	6.84	2.03	33.06	1,098.00	135.30	622,600.00	34,370
BAY.MOTOREN WERKE	0.06	4.60	2.02	18.04	406.50	60.20	585,800.00	60,642
METRO	0.06	8.65	2.03	24.09	265.10	69.38	610,500.00	52,951
COMMERZBANK	0.06	4.76	2.02	20.80	469.50	80.47	433,700.00	48,861
THYSSENKRUPP	0.08	5.21	2.03	25.46	836.10	108.60	623,800.00	31,008
MAN	0.07	7.59	2.02	34.72	425.80	119.10	584,000.00	31,024
CONTINENTAL	0.06	7.05	2.02	27.91	351.40	86.08	457,300.00	39,803

(continued)

Table 4.6 (continued)

Stock name	Min	1st Q	Mode	Median	Mean	3rd Q,	Max	N
DEUTSCHE POST	0.07	5.33	2.03	27.14	474.20	110.00	434,800.00	35,130
ADIDAS-SALOMON	0.07	3.89	60.01	19.41	265.00	67.06	535,800.00	42,332
DEUTSCHE BOERSE	0.07	4.58	2.03	28.14	307.90	112.10	94,650.00	23,820
LUFTHANSA	0.06	6.48	2.04	34.68	721.20	132.00	534,900.00	27,915
ALTANA	0.07	5.82	2.02	33.49	307.60	119.10	432,700.00	30,451
TUI	0.07	5.50	2.02	26.30	433.10	103.00	625,600.00	29,488
HENKEL	0.06	4.65	2.03	18.17	192.10	60.23	273,500.00	43,433
LINDE	0.07	7.45	2.03	26.54	277.00	84.96	200,200.00	35,791
FRESEN.MED.CARE	0.07	4.59	2.03	36.81	364.80	132.70	229,800.00	22,066
DAX-30 POOL	**0.05**	**4.58**	**2.02**	**19.50**	**393.50**	**69.38**	**629,100.00**	**1,501,284**

Table 4.7 Summary statistics of the lifetimes of all the one-fill completed orders of all 30 DAX stock

Stock name	Min	1st Q	Mode	Median	Mean	3rd Q,	Max	N
All one-fill-completions	0.00	0.00	0.00	0.00	714.40	24.20	635,900.00	521,251
One-fill-completions with lifetime > 0	0.01	6.80	0.85	28.62	1,523.00	116.90	635,900.00	244,495

plot the same distribution (no-fill deletion order lifetimes to 197.5s) using both methods:

Intuitively, kernel density estimates can be understood as histograms with infinitely fine classes smoothed by moving averages. Thus, the classes do not water down the structure of the data. Formally, kernel density estimates are functions of the form

$$f(x) = \frac{1}{n}\sum_{i'=1}^{n} K\left(\frac{x - x_i}{h}\right) \tag{4.1}$$

where K is the kernel function. For all plots in this paper, Gaussian kernels were used, i.e. all kernel density plots use the equation

$$f(x) = \frac{1}{n}\sum_{i'=1}^{n} K\left(\frac{x - x_i}{h}\right), \textit{where} K(u) = \frac{1}{\sqrt{2\pi}}\left(-\frac{1}{2}u^2\right) \tag{4.2}$$

The smaller the range of the moving average, the more detailed the picture you get. For an extensive comparison of the properties of different kernels see Hwang et al. (1994).

The No-Fill-Deletion Order Lifetime Distribution

The plot in Fig. 4.4 investigates the distribution of the lifetime of no-fill-deletion orders. To give a precise picture, we differentiate 4 different time scales. We apply the kernel density estimation procedure to characterise the lifetime frequency.

The kernel bandwidth used, and number of orders contained in each interval are indicated below each of the four diagrams. The spikes in the plot and the overall shape of the plot reveal a pattern that to our knowledge has not yet been discovered: cancellations occur predominantly after some very ‘special’ lifetimes: At 1s and 2s, there is a local maximum. After 30s, 60s, 120s and 180s there are more such local maxima. Less obvious are the weaker spikes at exactly 4, 5 and 6s. These overall patterns are valid for most of the individual stocks. Figure 4.5 below illustrates the remarkable similarity in cancellation patterns for the four most actively traded, and the five least actively traded stocks given for the range of 0–67.5s.

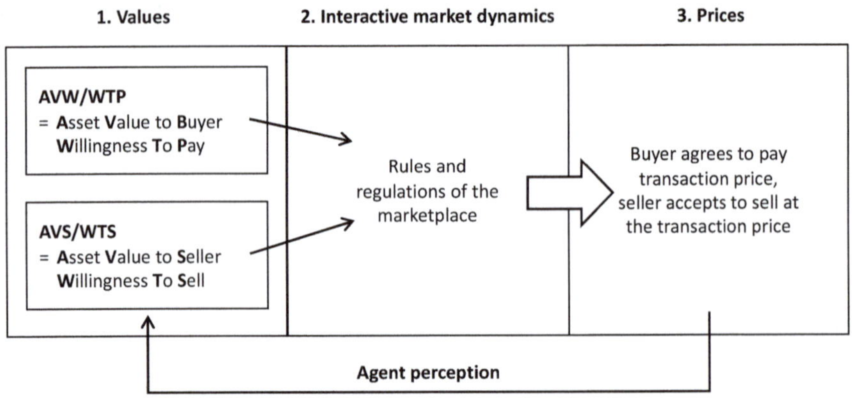

Fig. 4.1 Emergence of prices from values/orders by market dynamics

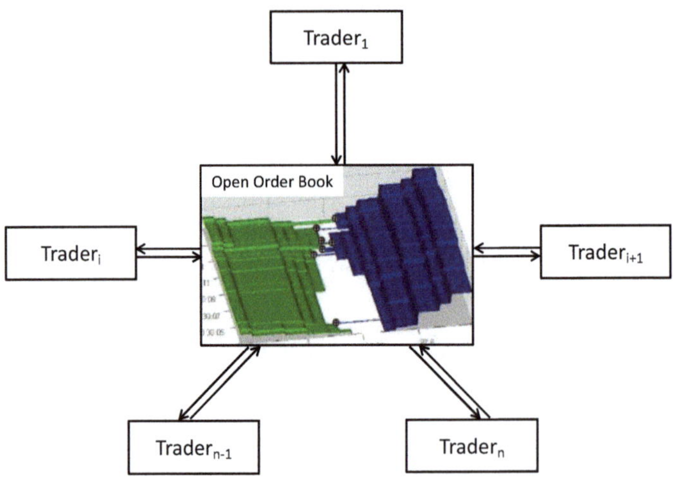

Fig. 4.2 Network structure of trading venues under Xetra

For the stock TUI, the peak at 60s is not observable. The pattern of no-fill-deletion order lifetimes is present throughout the daily trading time. Figure 4.6 illustrates the observed no-fill-deletion order lifetimes for different time tracking subsets.

The intervals in Fig. 4.6 correspond to the time windows from start of trading at 9:00 to 12:00, from 12:00 to 15:00 and from 15:00 till the closing auction at 17:30. The one-fill-completed orders with a lifetime greater than zero are not terminated by cancellation or execution. The execution of orders is beyond their control and therefore not subject to the peaking of the lifetimes at the end of each update cycle.

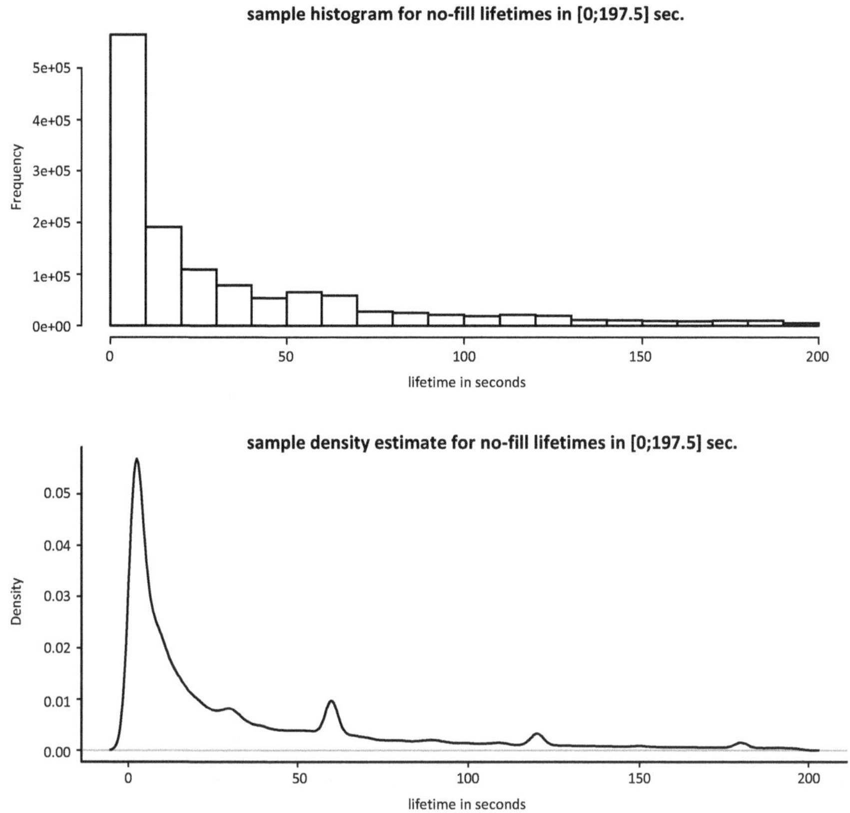

Fig. 4.3 Histogram and kernel density estimate for the same distribution

Investigation of Lifetime Peaks at Multiples of 60 Seconds

Example of Automated Order Placements—Constant Initial Cushion Orders

A closer look at no-fill deletion orders (i.e. orders with sequence code '1–3') with lifetimes close to the lifetime peaks shown in Fig. 4.4 gives the following picture. The peaks at multiples of 60s can be explained (at least partly) by sequences of orders which we term constant-initial-cushion (CIC) orders. The orders of such a sequence have the following properties. A CIC order sequence consists of both, bids and asks, i.e. of order placements on both sides of the market, where the bids and asks to have the same order size. The name 'CIC orders' is motivated by the observed order limits. All bids (asks) of such a CIC order sequence have the same constant cushion at insertion (constant-initial-cushion), where cushion is defined as

$$cushion = \begin{cases} best\ \ bid\ - bid\ \ order\ \ limit\ \ for\ \ a\ \ bid \\ ask\ limit\ - best\ \ aks\ \ limits\ \ or\ \ an\, ask \end{cases} \tag{4.3}$$

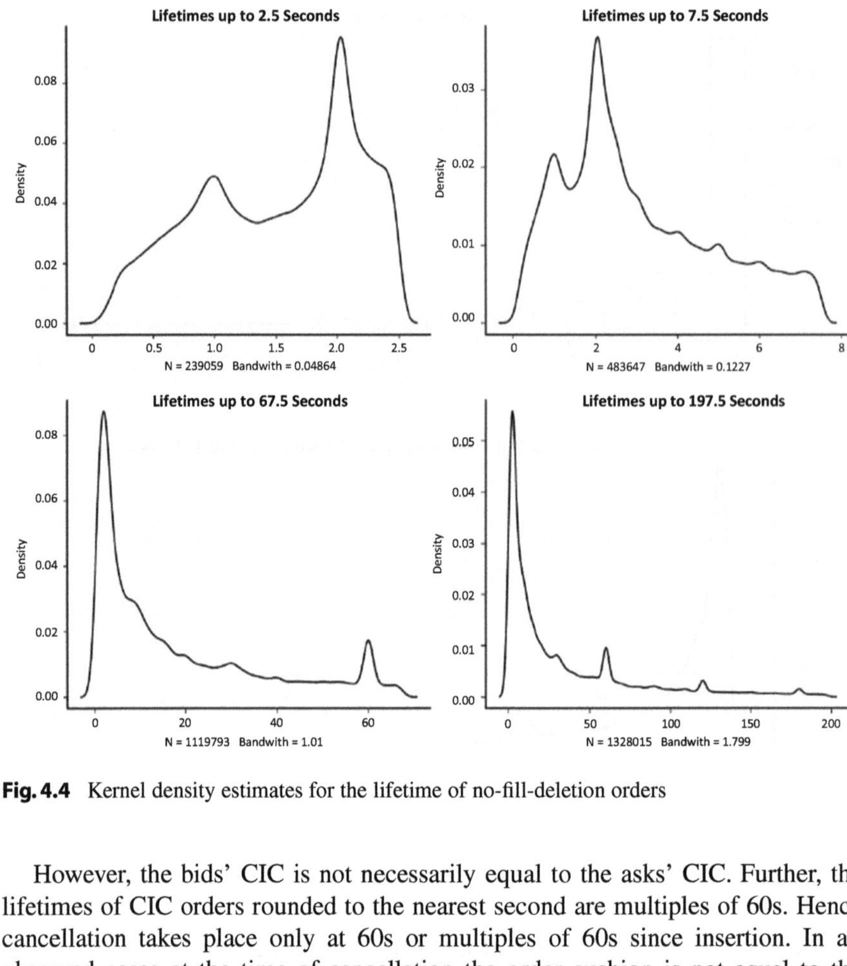

Fig. 4.4 Kernel density estimates for the lifetime of no-fill-deletion orders

However, the bids' CIC is not necessarily equal to the asks' CIC. Further, the lifetimes of CIC orders rounded to the nearest second are multiples of 60s. Hence cancellation takes place only at 60s or multiples of 60s since insertion. In all observed cases at the time of cancellation the order cushion is not equal to the CIC. Furthermore, for each CIC order with rounded lifetime equal to $l*60$ seconds with $l \geq 2,\ l \in \mathbb{N}$ the following can be said. In all observed cases, the observed cushions at 1. 60, …,(l − 1). 60s since insertion are equal to the CIC. The observed cushions at any other point of time during the lifetime of a CIC order are not necessarily equal to the CIC. After a CIC order is cancelled (except for the last bid and ask cancellation in a sequence) a new CIC order is inserted. If a CIC bid (ask) is cancelled another CIC bid (ask) is inserted at a limit equal to $bestbid - CIC(bestask + CIC)$.

If the best bid (thin straight line) or best ask (thin dashed line) changes such that the inserted bid or ask (thick lines) has no longer the CIC at multiples of 60s since insertion, the corresponding order is deleted and a new order is inserted at the CIC. Obviously, deletion only occurs at order lifetimes of multiples of 60s since insertion.

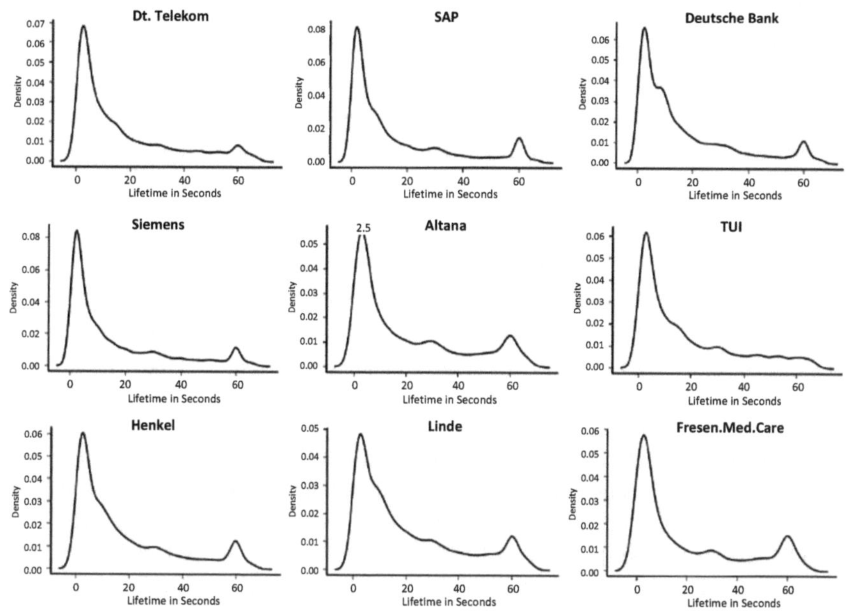

Fig. 4.5 Kernel density estimates for the lifetime of no-fill-deletion orders in the interval [0;67.5] seconds for the most actively traded (DTE, SAP, DBK, SIE, ALT) and the four least actively traded (TUI, HEN3, LIN, FME) stocks

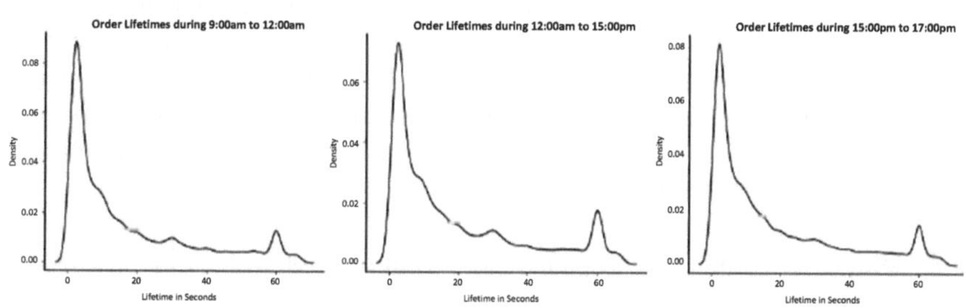

Fig. 4.6 Kernel density estimates for the lifetime of no-fill-deletion orders in the interval [0;67.5] recorded during different times of day for all DAX-30 stocks

Table 4.8 and Fig. 4.7 illustrate a part of a sequence of CIC orders observed for SAP AG on 5th January 2005 between 13:51:36 and 13:55:36. At 13:51:36.00 (at 13:51:35.96) a CIC ask (a CIC bid) was inserted with an order size of 1,200 shares and CIC of 26 cent. At the time of these insertions the best bid and best ask were 129.87 and 129.90, respectively. 60s later at around 13:52:36 the best bid was still at 129.87, while the best ask had moved up to 130.01. Therefore, the cushion of the CIC bid remained at 26 cents, while the cushion of the CIC ask decreased to 15 cents. Consequently, the CIC ask was deleted and a new CIC ask was inserted

Table 4.8 Sample CIC orders placed on January 6th, 2005, for SAP

Time at Insertion (hh:mm:ss.cs)	Lifetime (sec.)	Limit (Euro)	BestBid (Euro)	BestAsk (Euro)	CIC (Euro)	Size	(B)id/(A)sk
13:51:36.00	60.05	130.16	129.87	129.90	0.26	1200	A
13:52:36.05	60.03	130.27	129.87	130.01	0.26	1200	A
13:53:36.08	59.91	130.32	129.90	130.06	0.26	1200	A
13:54:35.99	60.17	130.28	129.90	130.02	0.26	1200	A
13:55:36.16	59.96	130.20	129.87	129.94	0.26	1200	A
13:51:35.96	120.07	129.61	129.87	129.90	0.26	1200	B
13:53:36.03	120.12	129.64	129.90	130.06	0.26	1200	B
13:55:36.15	59.95	129.61	129.87	129.94	0.26	1200	B

at limit 130.01 + 0.26 = 130.27. The deleted CIC ask had a lifetime of 60.05s. Approx. 60s later the cushion of both the CIC bid and ask had changed due to the moving best offers. The CIC ask at 130.27 (CIC bid at 129.61) was deleted and a new CIC ask at 130.06 + 0.26 = 130.32 (a new CIC bid at 129.90 -0.26 = 129.64) was inserted. The deleted ask (bid) had a lifetime of 60.03s (120.07s). Hence, the lifetimes of the CIC orders depended on the variability of the best bid and ask (see Fig. 4.7). The lifetimes of the CIC orders shown in Table 4.8 and Fig. 4.7 varied around 60 and around 120s. As the best ask showed higher variation than the best bid in this period (see Fig. 4.7), we observe 5 insertions on the ask side and only 3 on the bid side.

In Table 4.8 CIC orders are illustrated for only small snapshot of 5 min. For identifying all CIC order sequences for a stock, we define explicit filtering criteria. To avoid data snooping, we used data from 8 to 15th of December 2004 to get the defining criteria for CIC orders and applied them to investigating data spanning the period between 5 and 12th of January 2005. The applied filtering criteria for identifying CIC order sequences are given as follows.

1. All orders in a CIC order sequence are no-fill-deletion orders, i.e. orders with sequence code '1–3'.
2. A sequence of CIC orders consists of bids and asks. Whenever a bid in this sequence is valid in the order book, an ask of this sequence also must be valid in the order book and vice versa.
3. A sequence includes at least 3 orders (i.e. one bid and two asks, or two bids and one ask). Hence, the number of orders in a sequence $N \geq 3$.
4. All bids and asks in a sequence of CIC orders fulfil the following criteria.
   a. The bids' and asks' cushions at insertion are constant. The bids' cushion at insertion is not necessarily equal to the asks' cushion at insertion.
   b. The bids' and asks' volumes are constant. The bids' volume is equal to the asks' volume.
   c. The lifetimes of the bids and asks rounded to the nearest second are equal to 60s or a multiple of 60s.

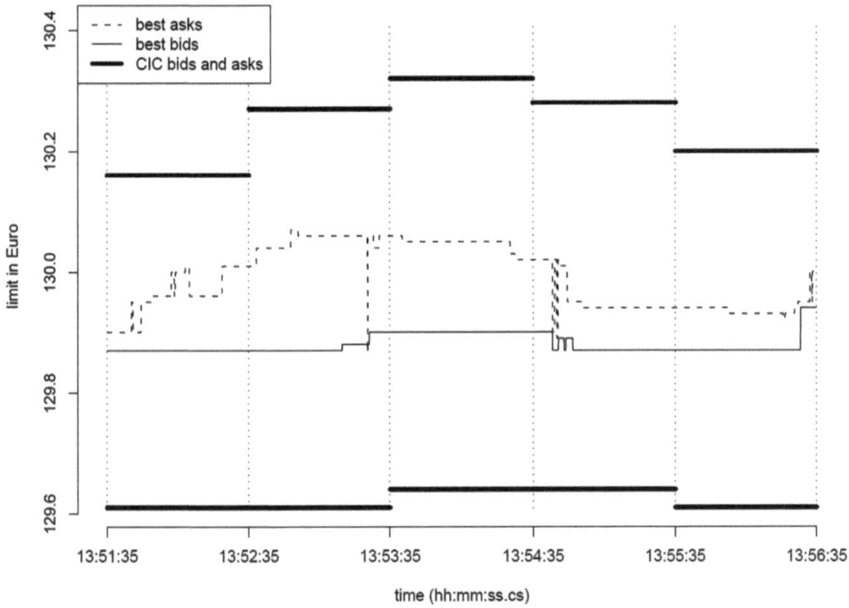

Fig. 4.7 CIC orders for SAP AG on 5th January 2005 between 13:51:35 and 13:56:35 with lifetimes of multiples of 60s (dotted lines)

The result of the application of these filtering criteria to order book data for SAP AG between 5 and 12th of January 2005 is given in Table 4.9. As shown in Table 4.9, we identified 14 sequences of CIC orders, where the cushions and order sizes of CIC orders for different CIC order sequences varied. Between 5 and 12th of January 2005 the order size varied between 1,000 and 2,200 for SAP. The CIC ranged between 16 and 27 cents for the CIC bids and between 25 and 55 cents for the CIC asks for SAP. The maximum lifetime of a CIC order was 840.23 s. For all CIC orders we find rounded lifetimes of 60s and multiples thereof.

A possible explanation for these observations of CIC order sequences may be that an automated order placement system updates CIC orders at intervals of 60s by cancellation and subsequent insertion such that the orders' cushions fulfil the properties described above. A further look at the order book suggests that the intra-day change of the order volume or cushions for the CIC orders is because of order matching of a CIC bid or ask. At the end of each of the indicated periods (excluding end of day periods) shown in Table 4.9 we find executed orders each with insertion time equal to the deletion time of the last observed CIC order in the corresponding sequence. Further, each of these executed orders has the same cushion and order size as the last deleted CIC order of the corresponding sequence. However, the data set does not allow us to identify the order submitting trader. Therefore, we cannot make a definite statement about these suggestions. In the next chapter, we further substantiate our explanations by investigating all 30 DAX stock for occurrences of CIC order sequences.

Table 4.9 All CIC orders placed between 5 and 12th of January 2005 for SAP

Period			CIC		Size	Lifetime			Number N
Day (dd-mm-yyyy)	Begin (bh:mm:ss.cs)	End (bh:mm:ss.cs)	Bid (Euro)	Ask (Euro)		Min. (sec.)	Median (sec.)	Max (sec.)	
05–01–2005	10:00:34.86	14:00:35.73	0.26	0.26	1900	59.68	60.04	419.99	298
05–01–2005	14:14:35.67	14:38:35.89	0.18	0.49	1200	59.84	59.99	120.06	27
05–01–2005	14:45:35.99	15:47:36.33	0.26	0.26	1900	59.86	60.04	299.88	91
05–01–2005	15:53:36.41	15:58:36.47	0.26	0.26	1000	59.90	60.02	60.08	10
05–01–2005	16:05:36.68	16:36:36.50	0.16	0.55	1100	59.72	60.02	239.52	24
05–01–2005	17:15:36.91	17:26:36.88	0.18	0.49	1300	59.86	60.06	119.90	15
06–01–2005	10:02:34.68	17:28:37.30	0.26	0.26	1200	59.70	60.06	419.84	580
07–01–2005	10:00:35.33	14:28:36.72	0.27	0.27	2200	59.72	60.03	840.23	340
07–01–2005	14:51:36.95	17:28:37.64	0.26	0.26	1700	59.68	60.01	239.60	181
10–01–2005	10:01:35.52	17:27:37.91	0.28	0.27	1100	59.74	60.06	360.08	567
11–01–2005	11:36:13.38	16:00:15.14	0.26	0.26	1700	59.78	60.04	300.03	354
11–01–2005	16:27:15.50	17:27:15.93	0.26	0.26	1000	59.73	60.02	120.30	61
12–01–2005	10:05:35.66	15:47:38.22	0.25	0.25	1700	59.61	60.04	480.19	422
12–01–2005	16:01:38.02	17:27:38.23	0.25	0.25	1600	59.64	60.01	120.18	136

CIC Order Statistics for All DAX 30 Products

Table 4.10 shows footprints of CIC order insertions for almost all DAX 30 stocks. The cushion ratio shown in Table 4.10 expressing the cushion as percentage of the median price observed between 5 and 12th of January is around 0.2%. A lower bound for the bid and ask cushion is observed at 4 cents for most of the DAX stocks. The existence of an absolute lower bound on the cushion would explain high cushion ratios for stocks with low median prices such as Lufthansa and Infineon. Based on this observation, one can approximate the cushion for each stock by max (0.2% Median Price, 0.04). For Deutsche Börse, Thyssen Krupp and TUI the rows in Table 4.10 are empty, because CIC orders are not identifiable for any of the three companies. This observation is consistent with the result reported in Fig. 4.5, where for TUI no significant lifetime peaks for 60s could be found. The lifetime distribution of Deutsche Börse AG and Thyssen Krupp, which are not plotted here, exhibit similar lifetime distributions lacking significant peaks at multiples of 60s. The volumes of the CIC orders are multiples of 100 shares. Stocks with cushion equal to 4 cents have the highest maximum volumes ranging between 12,500 and 15,000 stocks. The maximum volume of 15,000 stocks was observed for Deutsche Telekom, Bay. Hypo Vereinsbank and Infineon. Comparing the median CIC order volume to the median order volume of all no-fill deletion orders shows a higher average volume for CIC orders. The maximum lifetime of CIC observed ranges between 540s to 5,220s. The overall maximum lifetime of 5,220 was observed for Infineon for both the CIC bid and ask inserted at 12:46:35 and cancelled at 14:18:35 on the 5th of January 2005. During this period in which also the intraday auction took place (see chapter 2.1) the best bid and ask remained the same. The stocks with CIC order cushion equal to 4 cent have all median lifetime at around 120s. Infineon has even median lifetime of 179.89s. The column Money volume in Table 4.10 shows that CIC orders represent between 4.3 and 18.4% of all no-fill-deletion orders observed between 5 and 12th January 2005.

Motivation for CIC Order Placement Strategy

We want to conclude with some thoughts regarding the motivation for submitting and cancelling these CIC orders. The explanation of the motivation is complicated by the fact that our data set only identifies the orders placed into the order book, but not the trader who enters the orders. Hence, we do not know whether two different orders were placed by the same trader or not. The observation of CIC order sequences can be interpreted as fishing for profitable round–trip trades. The CIC orders on both sides of the order book indicate that the CIC strategy assumes a scenario with prices just fluctuating around a mean without exhibiting trends. The stock is purchased if the price decreases such that the deviation from the average price is larger or equal to the CIC order cushion. The stock is sold if the price moves above the average price by the amount of the CIC order cushion. Such a strategy is profitable in a volatile market, but not in a trend market. The profitability of this strategy depends on the CIC order volume and the cushion for CIC bid and ask. The higher the cushion the higher the profitability, but the lower the chance of realisation. In addition, the determination of the cushion at insertion

Table 4.10 CIC orders for all DAX30 stocks between 5 and 12th of January 2005

	Cushion	Avg. Price	Cushion Avg. Price	Lifetime (in seconds)			Size			Order count		Money volume	
				Min	Mode	Max	Min	Mode	Max	Abs	Frac	Abs	Frac
	(€)	(€)	(%)								(%)		(%)
DTE	0.04	16.48	0.2	60	60	2940	5000	9600	15,000	745	1.3	150,163,345	2.5
SAP	0.26	129.84	0.2	60	60	840	500	1700	2200	2937	3.7	591,816,334	10.6
DBK	0.13	66.23	0.2	60	60	780	1000	3800	4300	1622	2.0	343,483,744	6.5
SIE	0.12	62.06	0.2	60	60	840	2000	2400	4800	1498	2.0	273,398,822	4.6
ALV	0.19	96.23	0.2	60	60	540	100	1600	2700	3649	3.5	562,927,448	9.6
RWE	0.09	42.85	0.2	60	60	900	100	6300	6300	1267	2.3	265,575,457	8.1
EOA	0.13	66.99	0.2	60	60	960	2300	2300	4900	1737	2.5	340,863,284	7.3
DCX	0.07	35.71	0.2	60	60	1140	4300	6700	8300	1967	2.6	439,349,415	11.4
MUV2	0.19	92.42	0.2	60	60	1080	1300	2300	2300	1288	1.3	217,210,579	4.7
BAS	0.11	52.26	0.2	60	60	660	2300	3000	3900	1783	2.5	291,205,997	8.4
BAY	0.05	24.02	0.2	60	60	2160	5200	6700	8100	1726	3.0	290,945,789	11.8
HVM	0.04	17.00	0.2	60	60	4200	5300	6600	15,560	577	1.1	62,192,520.6	2.9
VOW	0.07	35.73	0.2	60	60	1200	600	5400	5500	1522	3.1	263,128,385	11.3
SCH	0.11	54.48	0.2	60	60	1260	1300	2700	4700	2149	6.0	246,424,472	14.1
IFX	0.04	7.79	0.5	60	60	5520	8000	15,000	15,000	679	1.9	62,984,586	5.8
BMW	0.07	34.29	0.2	60	60	1980	4500	4600	7900	1613	2.4	305,461,820	12.8
MEO	0.08	41.00	0.2	60	60	2220	1800	3200	3600	1209	2.2	141,716,192	7.5
CBK	0.04	16.00	0.2	60	60	2700	400	8300	8700	602	1.1	73,558,230	4
TKA	–	–	–	–	–	–	–	–	–	–	–	–	–

(continued)

Table 4.10 (continued)

	Cushion	Avg. Price	Cushion Avg. Price	Lifetime (in seconds)			Size			Order count		Money volume	
				Min	Mode	Max	Min	Mode	Max	Abs	Frac	Abs	Frac
MAN	0.06	29.34	0.2	60	60	1500	1000	2100	2400	1393	4.3	60,930,622	3.6
CON	0.10	48.39	0.2	60	60	1080	1300	1700	2700	1439	3.5	138,479,424	9.9
DPW	0.04	16.93	0.2	60	60	2520	900	5600	13,800	1137	3.1	176,887,988	14.8
ADS	0.24	117.96	0.2	60	60	1800	100	100	1400	3050	7.0	154,558,164	13.2
DB1	–	–	–	–	–	–	–	–	–	–	–	–	–
LHA	0.04	10.64	0.4	60	60	2760	700	8500	11,000	1045	3.6	99,854,331	15.7
ALT	0.09	45.28	0.2	60	60	2400	100	1400	1600	1500	4.8	82,628,914	10.1
TUI	–	–	–	–	–	–	–	–	–	–	–	–	–
HEN3	0.13	66.15	0.2	60	60	2220	600	900	1200	865	2.0	44,269,749	5.0
LIN	0.10	48.14	0.2	60	60	2100	900	1200	1600	1618	4.3	89,179,307	10.9
FME	0.12	58.09	0.2	60	60	1800	300	600	900	1983	9.0	62,146,240	11.8

Stocks are ordered according to traded money volume

Table 4.11 Illustration of price slippage

Modification timestamp	Event code	Order type	Buy sell	Price	Size
2005–01-11 13:02:56.76	1	M	S	0.00	14,900
2005–01-11 13:02:56.76	5	M	S	95.24	420
2005–01-11 13:02:56.76	5	M	S	95.23	1,200
2005–01-11 13:02:56.76	5	M	S	95.22	2,489
2005–01-11 13:02:56.76	4	M	S	95.21	10,791

must also consider possible triggering of volatility breaks due to excessive price deviations (for details on volatility breaks in the Xetra market model see Deutsche Börse AG (2004)). In the following, these basic considerations are supported by an investigation of the liquidity demand observed in the German order book between 5 and 12th of January 2005. To compare the liquidity provided by CIC orders to the liquidity demand we define price slippage for highly aggressive orders which accept existing orders leading to an immediate trade. We use a narrow definition of slippage by defining slippage as the difference between the highest and the lowest transaction price achieved when executing the order. In more details, given the transaction prices $p_1^j, \ldots, p_N^j$ of the transactions triggered by the accepting order j, the slippage for this accepting order j is defined as

$$slippage_j = \max_{i=1,\ldots,N}\left(p_i^j\right) \cdots \min_{i=1,\ldots,N}\left(p_i^j\right) \tag{4.4}$$

A sample order with price slippage is given in Table 4.11. In this example, the price slippage is 95.24 – 95.21 = 0.03.

A 1–5-5–5-4. market order for the stock Allianz is shown above. The prices achieved in the transaction vary from 95.24 to 95.21.

In the case of an ask acceptance the minimum transaction price $\min_{i=1,\ldots,N}\left(p_i^j\right)$ is equal to the best ask observed immediately before the acceptance. In case of a bid acceptance the maximum transaction price $\max_{i=1,\ldots,N}\left(p_i^j\right)$ is equal to the best bid observed immediately before the acceptance. Therefore, the definition of slippage can be reformulated as

$$slippage_j = \begin{cases} \max_{i=1,\ldots,N}\left(p_i^j\right) - \textit{best ask before acceptance for an ask acceptance } j \\ \textit{best bid acceptance} - \min_{i=1,\ldots,N}\left(p_i^j\right) \textit{ for a bid acceptance } j \end{cases} \tag{4.5}$$

Hence, we do not use the mid limit (calculated as average of best bid and ask) as reference quantity but the corresponding best offer. This view reflects the view taken by the CIC order placement strategy which takes the best bid and ask as reference for the determination of the order limit.

Table 4.12 plots the slippage for SAP between 5 and 12th of January 2005. For each slippage ranging between 0 and 35 cent the money volume traded on both sides of the market in the period of consideration is plotted. The row with slippage equal to 0 cents reads as follows. A money volume of 733,719,000 (720,040,000) was traded on the bid (ask) side with slippage of 0 cent. This amounts to 86.53 (84.03) percent of all matched bid (ask) money volumes for SAP during the period covered by the data. The row with slippage equal to 25 cents has the following interpretation. 122,000 (1,878,000) were traded with slippage equal to or larger than 25 cents. Hence, if CIC orders were inserted at bid and ask CIC of 25 cent with sufficient size and had always price-time-priority, then 122,000 (1,878,000) of CIC bids (asks) would have been traded. At a cushion of 16 cent 1,192,000 (3,395,000) of CIC bids (CIC asks) would have been traded. As the cushion of CIC orders for SAP ranged between 16 and 55 cents with median at 26 cent (see Tables 4.9, 4.12) indicates plenty of trading opportunities for this CIC strategy.

Table 4.13 gives an overall picture of the chance of realisation of CIC orders for all 30 DAX stocks. For each stock the money volume matched by orders with (a) slippage equal to zero and with (b) slippage equal to or greater than the median CIC of the observed CIC orders is shown. Seller and buyer-initiated trades are differentiated. The great majority of trades had slippage of 0.00. The amount of money volume traded with slippage equal to 0.00 ranges between 98.99 (97.68) percent for Deutsche Telekom and 86.53 (84.03) percent for SAP of the total traded seller initiated (buyer initiated) money volume. For SAP, for instance, we notice that bid (ask) money volume of 109,000 (1,384,000) were matched by orders with slippage equal to or larger than the median bid and ask CIC of 26 cent. It is also observable that the median bid (ask) CIC is not lower than the maximum bid (ask) slippage for all stocks observed between 5 and 12th of January 2005. As the CIC may vary over the day and from one day to the next with CIC being lower than the median cushion (see, e.g., Table 4.9), trading opportunities may also exist for those stocks. However, the detection of such algorithmic trades may lead to imitation and a race for liquidity demand, i.e. fight for the most aggressive orders with high slippage. For instance, if an imitating trader placed other CIC orders at a cushion of one cent lower than the cushion of the observed CIC orders, he or she would snatch liquidity demand from under the observed CIC order inserter's nose.

For each slippage the money volume traded at that slippage is recorded. All observations were made from 5 to 12th of January 2005, for the stock SAP AG.

Distribution of Constant Initial Cushion Orders Lifetimes

The lifetimes of CIC orders reported in the previous section are not exactly equal to multiples of 60s but vary within a range of one hundredth of a second. Figure 4.8 shows the observed lifetimes of CIC orders plotted as histogram and fitted to normal distributions with sample means equal to 60.01 and 120.01s and sample standard deviation of about 0.11 and 0.12s, respectively.

Both lifetime distributions deviate from the Gaussian distribution and are leptokurtic. For both distributions the Kolmogorov–Smirnov test rejects the normality

Table 4.12 Amount of Money Volume traded at different depths between 5 and 12th of January 2005 for SAP

Price slippage	Matched Bid Money Volume				Matched Ask Money Volume			
(Euro)	Abs. ('000 Euro)	Rel. (%)	Cumul. ('000 Euro)	Rel (%)	Abs. ('000 Euro)	Rel. (%)	Cumul. ('000 Euro)	Rel (%)
0.00	733,719	86.53	847,983	100.00	720,040	84.03	856,932	100.00
0.01	50,113	5.91	114,264	13.47	57,738	6.74	136,891	15.97
0.02	20,994	2.48	64,152	7.57	26,084	3.04	79,153	9.24
0.03	11,780	1.39	43,157	5.09	12,880	1.50	53,069	6.19
0.04	8,217	0.97	31,377	3.70	10,548	1.23	40,189	4.69
0.05	7,621	0.90	23,160	2.73	10,266	1.20	29,641	3.46
0.06	3,179	0.37	15,538	1.83	3,333	0.39	19,375	2.26
0.07	2,895	0.34	12,360	1.46	3,311	0.39	16,042	1.87
0.08	1,950	0.23	9,465	1.12	1,506	0.18	12,731	1.49
0.09	1,856	0.22	7,515	0.89	2,151	0.26	11,225	1.31
0.10	1,454	0.17	5,659	0.67	2,173	0.25	8,973	1.05
0.11	1,325	0.16	4,205	0.50	1,386	0.16	6,800	0.79
0.12	590	0.07	2,880	0.34	300	0.04	5,414	0.63
0.13	166	0.02	2,290	0.27	635	0.07	5,114	0.60
0.14	129	0.02	2,124	0.25	230	0.03	4,479	0.52
0.15	803	0.09	1,995	0.24	854	0.10	4,249	0.50
0.16	21	0.00	1,192	0.14	297	0.03	3,395	0.40
0.17	267	0.03	1,170	0.14	121	0.01	3,098	0.36
0.18	153	0.02	903	0.11	139	0.02	2,977	0.35
0.19	106	0.01	751	0.09	151	0.02	2,839	0.33
0.20	351	0.04	644	0.08	98	0.01	2,688	0.31
0.21	133	0.02	294	0.03	–	–	–	–
0.22	20	0.00	161	0.02	196	0.02	2,590	0.30
0.23	17	0.00	141	0.02	506	0.06	2,394	0.28
0.24	2	0.00	124	0.01	10	0.00	1,888	0.22
0.25	13	0.00	122	0.01	493	0.06	1,878	0.22
0.26	–	–	–	–	46	0.01	1,384	0.16
0.27	–	–	–	–	137	0.02	1,338	0.16
0.28	–	–	–	–	917	0.11	1,201	0.14
0.29	–	–	–	–	62	0.01	284	0.03
0.30	–	–	–	–	105	0.01	223	0.03
0.32	88	0.01	109	0.01	–	–	–	–

(continued)

Table 4.12 (continued)

Price slippage	Matched Bid Money Volume				Matched Ask Money Volume			
(Euro)	Abs. ('000 Euro)	Rel. (%)	Cumul. ('000 Euro)	Rel (%)	Abs. ('000 Euro)	Rel. (%)	Cumul. ('000 Euro)	Rel (%)
0.34	–	–	–	–	41	0.00	117	0.01
0.35	21	0.00	21	0.00	77	0.01	77	0.01

hypothesis at the 1 per cent significance level. The peak around, e.g., 60s lifetimes for CIC orders might lead to the conclusion that computer software updates orders on a basis of 60s lifetime. However, periodic updates inside the exchange might not explain the fluctuations around the order lifetime of 60s. A factor that might cause the fluctuations within a few hundredths of a second around 60s is the electronic network connecting the exchange with exchange members. We assume that all signals are generated inside the exchange member group. If we assume that the signals are transmitted through an electronic network and might have to travel longer distances, then this might explain some of the order lifetimes' fluctuations. The diagram below illustrates the argument.

A real-time data feed provided by the exchange (or other companies specialising in data-providing) is transmitting input to the exchange member. The exchange member reacts and enters a new order at time T1. The signal travels through the network layer and arrives at a time T2. The time spent on the way to the exchange might be subject to possible network delays. The time stamp on the order is generated in the exchange and therefore already carries the delay that has occurred from T1 to T2. After a fixed time interval, like 60s, counting from time T1, the exchange member updates its positions. Let's assume that it decides to cancel the order. A signal is then emitted at time T3. The signal again travels through the network layer and arrives at time T4 in the exchange. Another time stamp is recorded at arrival. This time stamp again already contains the delay that occurred between T3 and T4. If the network speed is not constant, but subject to perturbations, then this would generate variation in the order lifetime from T2 to T4. It is a well-known fact among network specialists that latency distribution of network traffic usually exhibits Gaussian similar shape. There are papers documenting that even very few participants in the network are usually sufficient for the network traffic time distribution to exhibit Gaussian features Meent et al. (2006). Deviations of the network traffic distribution from Gaussianity is treated, for instance, in Zhigang et al. (2002). Hence, the delays might be a simple consequence of communication via electronic network media. Such a conclusion suggests further investigations of the electronic infrastructure of a marketplace and the remote market participants might be necessary, as this might be of relevance with respect to best execution issues.

Table 4.13 Percentage of Total Matched Money Volume at different trade slippages for buyer and seller-initiated trades between 5 and 12th of January 2005 for all DAX30 stocks. Stocks are ordered according to the traded money volume for each stock

	Total money volume matched by zero slippage orders				Bid CIC (BCIC)	Bid Slippage (BS)	Bid Money Volume Matched by Orders with BS > = BCIC		Ask CIC (ACIC)	Ask Slippage (AS)	Ask Money Volume Matched by Orders with AS > = ACIC	
	Bid Abs. ('000 Euro)	Bid Rel. (%)	Ask Abs ('000 Euro)	Ask Rel. (%)	Median (Euro)	Max. (Euro)	Abs. ('000 Euro)	Rel. (%)	Median (Euro)	Max. (Euro)	Abs ('0'00 Euro)	Rel. (%)
Dt. Telekom	1,113,578	98.99	1,203,600	97.68	0.04	0.02	0	0.00	0.04	0.02	0	0.00
SAP	733,719	86.53	720,040	84.03	0.26	0.35	109	0.01	0.26	0.35	1,384	0.16
Deutsche Bank	698,109	89.01	758,876	90.79	0.13	0.11	0	0.00	0.13	0.16	135	0.02
Siemens	629,025	91.36	652,542	89.93	0.12	0.08	0	0.00	0.12	0.23	443	0.06
Allianz	454,538	88.96	525,366	85.28	0.19	0.23	1,113	0.22	0.19	1.04	2,500	0.41
RWE	493,865	90.25	406,656	91.57	0.09	0.08	0	0.00	0.09	0.08	0	0.00
E.ON	418,362	87.99	426,587	89.44	0.13	0.18	501	0.11	0.13	0.11	0	0.00
DaimlerChrysler	414,266	93.24	409,357	92.48	0.07	0.07	36	0.01	0.07	0.09	663	0.15
Münch.Rückvers	352,506	89.97	362,653	88.53	0.19	0.13	0	0.00	0.18	0.23	289	0.07
BASF	317,073	91.90	344,747	90.28	0.11	0.20	38	0.01	0.10	0.10	132	0.03
Bayer	319,895	95.03	340,663	93.78	0.05	0.05	55	0.02	0.05	0.04	0	0.00
Bay.Hypo-Vereinsbk	340,336	93.31	326,027	95.47	0.04	0.09	3,844	1.05	0.04	0.04	8	0.00
Volkswagen	322,593	92.87	317,895	93.22	0.07	0.11	152	0.04	0.07	0.18	1,693	0.50
Schering	272,369	93.70	231,830	88.16	0.11	0.09	0	0.00	0.11	0.10	0	0.00
Infineon Tech	236,572	98.83	247,441	97.38	0.04	0.02	0	0.00	0.04	0.02	–	–

(continued)

Table 4.13 (continued)

	Total money volume matched by zero slippage orders				Bid CIC (BCIC)	Bid Slippage (BS)	Bid Money Volume Matched by Orders with BS > = BCIC		Ask CIC (ACIC)	Ask Slippage (AS)	Ask Money Volume Matched by Orders with AS > = ACIC	
	Bid Abs. ('000 Euro)	Bid Rel. (%)	Ask Abs ('000 Euro)	Ask Rel. (%)	Median (Euro)	Max. (Euro)	Abs. ('000 Euro)	Rel. (%)	Median (Euro)	Max. (Euro)	Abs ('0'00 Euro)	Rel. (%)
Bay.Motoren Werke	227,900	93.11	217,481	92.28	0.07	0.13	103	0.04	0.07	0.07	19	0.01
Metro	224,767	94.49	202,919	89.58	0.08	0.12	77	0.03	0.08	0.15	669	0.30
Commerzbank	239,726	95.71	204,733	95.78	0.04	0.03	0	0.00	0.04	0.09	45!	0.21
Thyssenkrupp	133,645	96.65	133,160	91.40	–	0.04	–	–		0.04	–	–
MAN	120,533	93.10	114,082	91.24	0.06	0.10	271	0.21	0.06	0.06	22	0.02
Continental	119,351	92.97	99.330	91.68	0.10	0.10	173	0.14	0.10	0.20	93	0.09
Deutsche Post	104,995	96.51	115 214	96.07	0.04	0.03	0	0.00	0.04	0.04	113	0.09
Adidas-Salomon	88,472	90.44	96.132	86.18	0.24	0.23	0	0.00	0.24	0.19	0	0.00
Deutsche Börse	86,344	94.11	107.106	95.49	–	0.08	–	–	–	0.28	–	–
Lufthansa	97,030	96.55	84,391	96.28	0.04	0.04	21	0.02	0.04	0.05	32	0.04
Altana	58,730	92.49	81,893	90.72	0.10	0.19	50	0.08	0.09	0.30	171	0.19
TUI	72,358	94.15	75,616	91.34	–	0.09	–	–	–	0.07	–	–
Henkel	68,351	87.37	61,378	92.70	0.13	0.59	1,337	1.71	0.13	0.20	3	0.00

(continued)

Table 4.13 (continued)

	Total money volume matched by zero slippage orders				Bid CIC (BCIC)	Bid Slippage (BS)	Bid Money Volume Matched by Orders with BS > = BCIC		Ask CIC (ACIC)	Ask Slippage (AS)	Ask Money Volume Matched by Orders with AS > = ACIC	
	Bid Abs. ('000 Euro)	Bid Rel. (%)	Ask Abs ('000 Euro)	Ask Rel. (%)	Median (Euro)	Max. (Euro)	Abs. ('000 Euro)	Rel. (%)	Median (Euro)	Max. (Euro)	Abs ('0'00 Euro)	Rel. (%)
Linde	67,573	89.85	64,400	91.87	0.10	0.17	39	0.05	0.10	0.17	266	0.38
Fresen.Med.Care	34,285	90.69	38,664	91.18	0.12	0.12	8	0.02	0.12	0.18	46	0.11

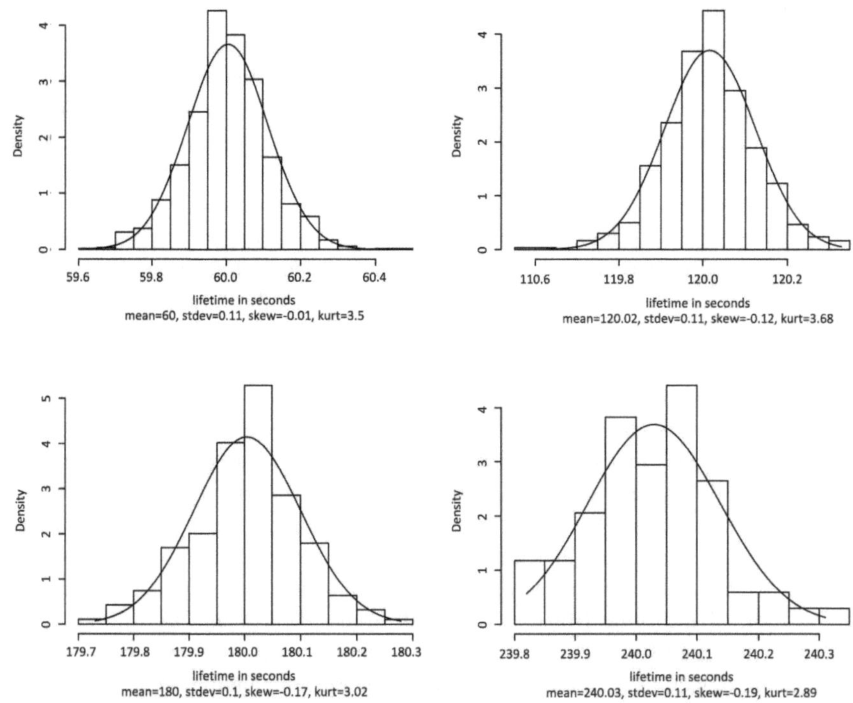

Fig. 4.8 Lifetime distribution of observed CIC quotes for Allianz AG placed between 5 and 12th of January 2005 (histogram). The thick line represents the normal distribution with estimated parameters for mean and standard deviation (stdev). Sample kurtosis (kurt) and skewness (skew) are stated

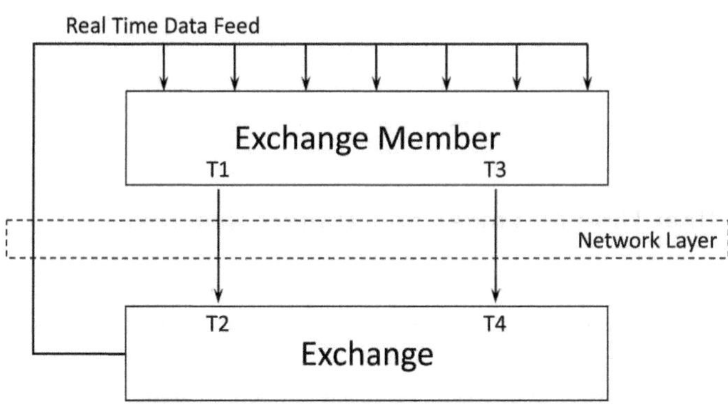

Fig. 4.9 Illustration of the communication between the exchange and exchange members

4.1.3.4 Summary

Our findings indicate the existence of previously undiscovered patterns in the structure of the order book when investigating the second and sub-second range of no-fill-deletion lifetimes. Bearing in mind that this range is nowadays the time frame professional traders and algorithm designers must cope with we investigate these patterns on an order-by-order basis, i.e. by analysing relevant orders and the corresponding detailed order event entries in the order book. In more detail, we analyse all no-fill-deletion orders with lifetimes equal to multiples of 60s and detect sequences of orders which we term constant-initial-cushion (CIC) orders. The distance at insertion of a CIC bid (ask) limit to the best bid (ask) limit—termed constant-initial-cushion—is about 0.2% of the median price for most of the 30 DAX stocks. To avoid data snooping, we analysed data from 8 to 15th of December 2004 to get the defining criteria for CIC orders and applied these criteria for filtering and investigating data spanning the period between 5 and 12th of January 2005. Our investigation leads us to evidence of activities of automatons trading on the buy and sell side, seemingly fishing for round trip trade opportunities. A first check of the round-trip hypothesis is provided by the fact that the slippage generated by the execution of accepting orders goes beyond the CIC at least in several situations. However, in most of all trades the slippage in the Xetra order book of Deutsche Börse AG is 0.00. Some 90% of all DAX-30 accepting orders—measured by trading volume—are executed without any slippage at all. Hence, the detection of such algorithmic order placements may lead to imitation of this observed order placement strategy and consequently a race for the rare, most aggressive orders in the order book. This illustrates the importance of camouflaging applied algorithmic trading strategies. A further observation is that the lifetimes of CIC orders are not exactly equal to multiples of 60s but vary in the range of a few hundredth of a second. This might give an indication of the influence of variations in the speed of the electronic network connecting the exchange with exchange members. Such a conclusion suggests to further investigate the electronic infrastructure of a marketplace and the remote market participants, as this might be of relevance with respect to best execution issues.

4.1.4 Real Time Messages and Traders Reaction

In this chapter, we focus on the interesting case of the release of (unscheduled) company-specific messages routed in real-time to the trading screens. The influence of this real-time information flow on trading behaviour is investigated using tick-by-tick order book data. Professional screen traders persistently monitor the actual market climate and observe incoming information and other traders' behaviour in a real-time manner. If and how traders react to real-time information flows is an actual issue of high practical relevance. Of course, a quick change of data frame, of the order book, requires instantaneous monitoring and fast adjustment decisions. One of the most important recent developments in stock exchanges information management systems is the real-time provision of full-displayed order book data to market participants. This evolution, which also represents an improvement in market transparency, offers considerably more detailed real-time order book information to stock market participants than ever before.

To really understand the numerous market phenomena or so-called market anomalies documented in the financial literature, it is important to investigate data about individual behaviour see Thaler (1999), which has not been available until recently. How traders act, i.e. which orders they place, accept, or cancel is documented in the order book. The order data set we apply allows us to track each single order and, therefore, constitutes an ideal laboratory for studying individual behaviour. MIFID's updating to MIFID III is in preparation.[17] Regardless the new rules, ESMA, European Securities and Markets Authority,[18] addresses in its reporting rules the handling of orders, not only prices. SEC (2023a) and (2023b), which require the documentation of best execution from order data, underline the importance of investigating order book data.

Besides stock returns, bid-ask spreads, and depths of the order book, we study whether traders imitate in their decisions to buy or to sell individual securities. Various stories about herding exist and, in our opinion, the reasons might be that existing empirical studies focus almost exclusively on the investigation of price time-series. Moreover, most studies rely on data of low frequency like quarterly, monthly, or daily stock prices or holdings of stocks. Hence, actions that occur at shorter time intervals cannot be captured. Furthermore, empirical studies usually investigate the behaviour of a specific group of market participants (institutions, fund managers, individual investors, etc.) and in most cases, datasets about the trading activities of professional market participants are applied. In our opinion, the reason might be that existing empirical studies mentioned focus almost exclusively on the investigation of price time series.

However, even regarding order time series per se does not provide a comprehensive understanding of market's performance. The knowledge of market microstructure performance is only complete when the investigation of order marching is included. The Nobel Prize awarded to Alvin E. Roth proves this fact conclusively.[19]

Therefore, we propose to study individual behaviour from order book data, from submission until matching or cancellation. We are in the position to investigate time stamped tick by tick data of orders. We can therefore investigate the fate of any individual order. It is obviously difficult to understand such investigations by researchers that are used to a bunch of time series data only. These are accessible by the common statistical figures like mean variance, etc., but these figures do not allow the investigation of individual orders. Furthermore, empirical studies usually investigate the behaviour of a specific group of market participants (institutions, fund managers, individual investors, etc.) and in most cases, datasets

[17] See ESMA (2024).
[18] ESMA (2017).
[19] Roth (2018) and Roth (2015).

about the trading activities of professional market participants are applied. Most studies investigate professionals' investment behaviour only. Also, professionals tend to herd, but probably to a smaller extent than individual investors, who are often supposed to play a key role in 'misbehaving' markets.

Our empirical analysis is based on (1) reconstructed order book data of highly liquid securities that are part of the German DAX-30 stock index, and (2) real-time company-specific messages from the Reuters Alert information system during the period 6–13 December 2006. We argue that herding is most likely captured empirically as an intraday phenomenon when traders react to new information by changing their positions. Therefore, we emphasise the importance of investigating herd behaviour on the micro-level of order flows during the trading session. Focusing on trading behaviour around the time of company-specific news release offers some additional insights into market participants' instantaneous order reactions and to their tendency to behave convergent in their decisions to buy or to sell.

4.2 Information and Traders' Behaviour

In order to study traders' reaction to the real-time information flow, we investigate log-returns, relative bid-ask spreads, ask (bid) side depths, and total order book depths.

4.2.1 Event Data[20]

The event data set comprises company-specific messages publicly released over the Reuters system during the trading session, which we obtain from the Reuters Alert system. Each message is time-stamped according to the minute of the day the news is released in the system and contains detailed information about the message. The exact documentation of release time and news content allows us to examine the first release[21] of a particular piece of information. Reuters Alert also offers a filtering system, which we use to extract company-specific news only.[22]

Moreover, we only consider messages in English released during 10:00–17:00 o'clock and further exclude all messages that do not have an informational essence on the level of individual securities. Concerning the latter, we classify objectively by studying whether the name of the stock shows up in a message body. If a message fulfils these two criteria, it is included into the sample. The removement of

[20] Details see chapter 1.1. We are grateful to Deutsche Börse for providing the data for research purposes.

[21] Most messages in the Alert system show up in English and German, but usually the message in English is released before the equivalent message in German shows up.

[22] The other categories are general, political, market, economic, industrial, corporate, all alerts.

index-related news items from the information flow obviates the intraday seasonality influencing these index-related messages. Moreover, we concentrate on the impact of explicitly firm-specific news items on trading in the particular security the message is released for.

The company-specific alert system comprises all important aspects relevant for a security's value (company news or independent press, interviews, analyst opinions, competitors and sectors), and further represents the information flow observed by traders on the screens.

4.2.2 Empirical Results

In a first step, we study common patterns in order submission behaviour on the level of individual securities. For this purpose, the order flow is analysed by grouping each observed order activity, i.e. event types "insertion" or "cancellation", according to its aggressiveness. We classify aggressiveness by order size, order position, and the way the order constitutes liquidity. Order size can be low, medium, or high, and is grouped according to the 1/3 and the 2/3 quantile. Orders can be immediately marketable (market orders), or can be positioned within the spread area, or deep, deeper, deepest in the order book. Again, we group by the 1/3 and 2/3 quantile of observed money-volume at which the order is inserted. Orders are further differentiated as liquidity-providing insertions, liquidity-demanding insertions, or (liquidity-withdrawing) cancellations. We divide the days into subsequent time intervals of two minutes and for each interval we count the number of occurrences in the different categories.

Apparently, there is considerable systematics in order submissions in individual securities. In liquidity-providing insertions, one systematic factor explains more than 60% of the variation across different order book areas. The influence of latent factors determining the submission of liquidity-withdrawing cancellations is also considerable. On average over all stocks, more than 50% (70%) of the variation is explained by the first (the second and the first) systematic factor in cancellation behaviour. Liquidity-demanding insertions in individual securities are driven by two latent factors that count for more than 0% of the submission of liquidity-demanding insertions across different order book regions.

4.2.3 Company-Specific Messages and Individual Stocks[23]

We investigate an event-period of 40 min around the exact point in time the message showed up in the Reuters system, starting ten minutes before the minute the message is publicly released, and ending 30 min after.

[23] Previous version has been presented in Kopp, Loistl et al. (2008).

In order to test for statistical significance in differences between event and non-event periods we use a dummy variable regression model. We calculate the extent of news impact by the difference in time- and stock-specific averages between event and non-event periods. $\mu_{\%}(\sigma_{\%})$ gives the percentage deviation of event and non-event periods arithmetic means (standard deviations).

The table gives the news impact based on comparing event and non-event periods' means μ and standard deviations $\sigma_{\%}$ (in per cent for log-returns and relative spreads; in absolute values for the herding ratio), and statistical significance, i.e. the p-value, for an event period of 40 min.

Table 4.14 gives the news impact for log-return Φ_{it}^{R}, relative bid-ask spread Φ_{it}^{S} and herding ratio Φ_{it}^{H}, based on comparing event and non-event periods' means and standard deviations. The relation of information disclosure on security returns

Table 4.14 News impact in individual stocks

	Excess Bid Volume 8_i^B			Excess Ask Volume 8_i^A			Excess Ask Volume 8_i^D		
	μ_{abs}	σ_{abs}	p	μ_{abs}	σ_{abs}	p	μ_{abs}	σ_{abs}	p
Adidas	−72	−83.00	0.0884	89	−96	0.8483	−0.0700	0.05	0.0001
Allianz	−101	761.00	0.3310	−553	582	0.0102	0.0800	0.00	0.0001
BASF	51	−50.00	0.1460	122	−85	0.7617	0.0000	0.04	0.5395
Bay.Motoren Werke	−99	−93.00	0.0001	1047	−89	0.0282	0.0400	−0.04	0.0001
Bayer	−57	−59.00	0.0001	1374	−93	0.0555	0.0700	−0.05	0.0001
Commerzbank	−97	−98.00	0.0278	981	−97	0.0759	−0.1900	−0.16	0.0001
Continental	−66	−80.00	0.1102	−7,791	−88	0.0125	0.1500	−0.08	0.0001
Daimlerchrysler	−93	−90.00	0.0001	−81	−88	0.3709	−0.0200	−0.06	0.0002
Deutsche Bank	−93	−93.00	0.0001	−437	−94	0.0170	0.0100	−0.01	0.0001
Deutsche Börse	−85	656.00	0.3679	−640	529	0.1023	0.0600	−0.05	0.0001
Deutsche Post	−113	−86.00	0.0038	1,179	−91	0.0008	0.2500	−0.38	0.0001
Dt. Telekom	499	98.00	0.0001	−17,975	−75	0.0001	0.2500	0.04	0.0001
E.ON	−94	−93.00	0.0001	−696	−36	0.0001	0.0800	−0.09	0.0001
Linde	−101	−98.00	0.2174	−84	−97	0.9219	0.0400	−0.14	0.0026
Lufthansa	−99	−94.00	0.0001	−2	−91	0.9880	0.1100	0.05	0.0001
MAN	−36,320	15.00	0.0001	−1,513	−87	0.0002	0.0300	0.04	0.0001
Metro	−69	−78.00	0.1489	−25,221	−91	0.0001	−0.3300	−0.09	0.0001
Münch.Rückvers	−98	−98.00	0.3903	2,032	−77	0.4380	0.0100	−0.18	0.5803
RWE	−97	−94.00	0.0007	343	−94	0.6966	−0.0500	−0.04	0.0001
SAP	1,436	−49.00	0.0001	1,589	−96	0.5283	0.0100	−0.02	0.0261
Siemens	−102	−97.00	0.0001	102	−95	0.8099	0.2000	0.01	0.0001
Thyssenkrupp	−76	−79.00	0.0001	−1,076	−85	0.0001	−0.0600	−0.06	0.0001
TUI	−105	−94.00	0.0001	1	−96	0.9953	−0.2700	0.03	0.0001
Volkswagen	1.718	39.00	0.0001	−399	15	0.0010	−0.0400	−0.06	0.0001

is given in the left column. For log-returns, news impact is significant above 5% (1%) in 15 (14) out of 25 cases. And for the major part of the securities investigated, incoming company- specific messages reduce the log-return considerably. Liquidity measured by the relative bid-ask spread also strongly reacts to the real-time information flow, although the reaction is significant for less stocks than in the case of log-returns. However, whether the spread widens or reduces depends on the stock investigated. Concerning the extent of herding, we find highly significant (absolute) differences between event and non-event periods. For 23 out of 25 securities, the difference is significant above 0.05. This finding supports our expectation that real-time company-specific messages should influence trading behaviour in individual stocks. On average, buying (selling) pressures are more severe during event periods. Traders process the information routed on the trading screens by changing their positions, leading to imbalanced limit order books. Hence, traders in fact herd in their decisions to buy or sell stocks. The magnitude of these imbalances is considerably higher around the time of company-specific news release.

As already indicated by the results for the herding ratio, the reaction of order flows to company-specific real-time news arrival is impressive. The bid (ask) side reaction is significant for 23 (22) out of 25 securities. However, there is no obvious systematic pattern that would hold across stocks. The total liquidity provided by limit order in the securities' order books is strongly influenced by the release of company-specific messages. For any stock, the reaction is significant above 0.05. In most cases, order book depth (based on all limit orders on bid and ask side of the book) falls during event periods. For earnings announcements, the literature most often documents reduced liquidity around the time of release.

The finding that the real-time flow of company-specific messages is a catalyst for trading in individual stocks contradicts the standard approach, which argues that earnings and dividend announcements constitute the only source of relevant information. Traders in fact actively monitor the company-specific information flow routed in real-time to the trading screens. The reactions to the real-time information flow of company-specific messages are significant and considerable.

4.2.4 Conclusion

We show that traders actively monitor the company-specific information flow and process the information provided by updating or revising their order activities. During event periods, liquidity in the security the message is released for is significantly and considerably lower than during non-event periods. Furthermore, also returns reduce. Most interesting, we show that event periods are characterised by a higher degree of money-volume imbalance. If company-specific news is released in the Reuters system, traders tend to herd on a particular side of the order book, which causes higher imbalance between bid and ask side. From investigating the traders' reaction to company-specific messages we find evidence of herding to a side of the order book. Therefore, earnings and dividend announcements are not the only source of relevant information.

Also, on the market level we detect significant and substantial reactions to the type of information disclosure studied in this paper. As on the level of individual securities, returns are lower, and liquidity deteriorates around the time of message release. Moreover, we show that individual stocks' excess returns show strong co-variation in the cross-section.

The first systematic factor in excess returns explains around two-thirds of the variation on the level of individual stocks, and its influence is weaker during event-periods.

News impact on market-wide herding is also significant. The frequency of herd behaviour is 47% higher when company-specific news is published. However, the commonalities in the imbalances are rather low overall, which speaks in favour of the finding that imbalances are a rather idiosyncratic phenomenon. Furthermore, we find that liquidity on ask or bid side is (on average) significantly lower during event periods, which is in a line with the findings for earnings or dividend announcements in the existing literature.

4.3 Modelling Agents' Performance on Markets and Complexities

4.3.1 Modelling Agents' Actions and Interactions on Markets

The history of market microstructure modelling has been affected by two different branches of discussion. One is the application of stochastic processes to describe time series of share price relationships, the other is the investigation of buying and selling motivation, i.e. how people act in markets. We start by a short summary of the statistical modelling feature. Human actions are the ultimate cause of the performance of markets. These approaches neglect the fact, that prices are generated by matching orders and orders are placed by human agents. Our goal is to model how human agents make markets work.

This approach is a major step forward in the sense that the differentiation between prices and orders is introduced. However, a further step must be gone to modelling the stock exchange performance. Prices are generated by matching buy and sell orders, i.e. an order submitted to the exchange matches an already existing order exhibiting the appropriate price and quantity limit. The limit order can be modelled by means of a Poisson process. A major issue that has to be settled further is modelling the factors or forces that determine the orders. We have already concluded that the limit orders indicate the traders' willingness to buy or to sell. The appropriate approach to model such behavioural attitudes is provided by the discrete choice approach. See Train (2003) and Wertenbroch and Skiera (2002). The motivation is provided by the stochastic utility for buying or selling certain quantities of stocks at a given limit. The stochastic utility function has to imitate "*[…] the process by which securities markets translate investors' latent demands into realised prices and volumes [...]*" Madhavan and Panchapagesan (2000, p. 627); "*how investors' latent or hidden demands are ultimately translated into prices and volumes*" Madhavan (2002, p. 28). "*Asset prices evolve in markets*" O'Hara (2003, p. 1335).

To image the real microstructure of the stock markets, the first step is the differentiation between prices and orders. The price quotations observed on the markets are just the tip of the iceberg of economic activity on the stock exchange. Disregarding the motivation and activity beyond the surface of quoted prices and orders might result in confusion when observing the events at the trading screen. Talking about screen fighting may not lead to the impression that these fights do not follow rational rules. For instance, it might be confusing to an external observer unfamiliar with the internal rationality that about 67% of Xetra orders are cancelled, partly within seconds and then resubmitted with another limit. An important question is therefore how beliefs about values are converted into orders and how these orders are matched to generate prices.

4.3.2 Basic Requirements of the Individual Choice Behaviour Model

We start by explaining the basic postulate of individual choice behaviour that a decision frame should fulfil the famous postulate of "Independence from Irrelevant Alternatives". In discussing this postulate, we also explain other rules and investigate cases that do or do not fulfil these requirements. We transfer the abstract postulates of the quantitative decision-making scenario into our concrete trading scenario. We fulfil those requirements that Duncan Luce labels "Achill's heel".

> All of our procedures for data collection and analysis require the experimenter to make explicit decisions a certain action did or did not occur, and all of our choice theories – including this one- begin with the assumption that we have a mathematically well-defined set, the elements of which can be identified with the choice alternatives. How these sets come to be defined for organisms, how these may or may not change with experience, how to detect such changes, etc., are questions that have received but little illumination so far.[24]

Basically, our decision-making scenario fulfils these postulates. A trader confines the relevant set of shares he intends to investigate a priori and then decides the portfolio selection. The number of shares may consist of an index such as the DAX, Dow Jones or S&P 500.[25] An index with the fixed number of shares is

[24] Luce (2005, p. 3).

[25] At the time, we got the complete tick by tick data, the data file comprised the shares' performance of 30 stock. In between the number of stocks in the DAX has been increased to 40. But changing number of stocks does not interfere our basic message. It is directed towards the performance of orders of individual stocks, not towards the whole bunch.

appropriate to explain the specifics of the Independence from Irrelevant Alternatives. The portfolio selection procedure among the, e.g. DAX stocks is not affected if another stock is listed on the stock exchange but is not included in the DAX. The contractual agreement among investor and portfolio manager may provide in the contract that trading is restricted to the set of 30 DAX stocks. But of course, the evaluation of any of the remaining DAX stocks has to be renewed, when one of the DAX stocks will be replaced by a stock outside the DAX set. In this case the IIA property is violated. It is obvious that the calculation of the portfolio selection must be repeated.

Similarly, the portfolio selection must be renewed, when another element of the decision frame changes. A trader reviews his portfolio composition and his investment strategy when he got aware that there occurred a change of an orderbook insertion.

There are more important requirements. Submitting an order changes the orderbook, matching of orders changes the order book adequately. A new price is quoted and the volume of shares to be transferred is notified. In our datafile, these accounting activities are recorded. The probabilities of carrying out any of these actions are provided by the transition probabilities, if the actions' consequences are precisely determined. This is the case with an open order book just described. In the case of a complex activity with ambiguous consequences, the transition probabilities must be calculated separately, however complicated this may be. In any case, we have a balanced situation: if the specific consequences of an action are explicitly known, the probability of change of the element under consideration can be derived from this. If theses consequences are diffuse and cannot be adequately described, the transition probabilities must be calculated.

The open electronic order book changes according to the action taken. If an opposite order with matching conditions has already been placed, the orders match, generate a transaction and the order book changes accordingly. A new price will be notified and the sets of buy and sell orders will be reduced alike. The books of buyer and seller adjust accordingly, the buyer receives shares and transfers money, and the seller gets money and transfers shares. These are not just pure accounting activities, but represent the "last mile" of the trading event.

In case of a non-electronic market, the consequences of placing an order are not so obvious. There is no open order book contrary to an electronic market. The order will be submitted to a broker. A broker has a lot of discretionary power as to how he deals with this order. He is obliged to "maintain an orderly market". The transaction price must reflect the market situation. In fulfilling this obligation, he can fulfil the order himself, or he can transfer the order to another broker. These blurred constellation on the capital markets induced game theorists to restrain from trying to develop a model to analyse the matching conditions on the capital markets, as they had done for many other market constellations. See Roth and Sotomayor (1992).

4.3.3 Independence from Irrelevant Alternatives Relevance for Trading

The relevance of IIA, a major objection to discrete choice, to our approach needs to be discussed. We will show that this basic assumption in our model is consistent with our approach.

Let's start with the basics, the logit approach implies the independence from the IIA property. IIA refers to the issue of framing.[26] A decision is influenced by the circumstances surrounding the decision problem. With regard to our problem, we need to clarify which shares influence the portfolio decision. We assume that the investor selects his portfolio from the shares in the index only, in our case, from the DAX. However, our results are relevant for the selection of portfolios that are restricted to other indices or exchange traded funds that are subject to other restriction. The investor has made the basic decision that the shares outside the selected index are not relevant for his portfolio selection. With this explanation in mind, we will discuss the explanations of two experts: Firstly, Duncan Luce's description that relies on probability. We will provide the formal description in detail in the next chapter. But let us quote this expert: "*The heart of the axiom is the assumption that when, for whatever reason, the restaurant has only entrees S the probability of selecting roast beef is the same as the conditional probability of selecting it when the whole menu is available.*"[27]

Before explaining the quantitative model, we will discuss whether Train's basic assumptions are fulfilled in our case[28]:

> ***Firstly***, *the alternatives within the decision-relevant set must be mutually standalone and independent.*
> ***Secondly***, *the set of alternatives must include all possible alternative actions the agent will evaluate*
> ***Thirdly***, *the set of alternatives must be finite.*

The alternatives consist of the orders prescribed by the exchange. For the sake of trading speed, the trader can indicate his willingness to buy or sell in a well-tested manner only. His intention is vested in an order form prescribed by the management of the trading venue. Of course, the management strives to offer order forms that fulfil the needs of the traders. But contrary to a bazaar, both, buyers and sellers, can transact on a manner that is in accordance with the rules of the exchange, offering a well described ad finite number of alternative order forms.

The activities are also restricted to orders regarding the share included in the index, as already mentioned. Trading opportunities on shares outside the defined

---

[26] Discussed by McFadden (1999).
[27] Luce (2005, p. 7).
[28] See Train (2003, p. 15). Conditions given by formula provides Luce (2005, p. 5) or Das and Singh (2020, p. 193).

set of shares do not have an impact on the portfolio selection decision of traders/investors. Of course, the investor will review his decision from time to time on the selection of securities to include in his portfolio. In practice, there usually is a separation between research, portfolio selection and trading. We will combine the frame of order placement with the Markov process frame. The action taken changes precisely one element of the Markov process and the probability to take that specific action provides also the transition probability of that specific Markov process under consideration. That connection depends on the precise description of the consequences an action generates. In other cases, the transition probabilities must be calculated using a master equation.

4.4 Organised Complexity to Model Interactions of Traders

4.4.1 Varying Complexities Require Different Probability Capabilities

Colander et al. "*emphasize complexity as a defining factor of the new work at the edge of economics*".[29] Colander (2000) already addresses the issue of complexity: "*The movement of economics away from deductive principles*" is "*based on an evolving belief that complexity science was the appropriate domain for economics.* ".[30] With regard to Weaver's definition, Colander refers obviously to "*organised complexity*". In a recent paper Colander explicitly mentions, "*Hayek also recognizes that "organised complexity*" is dependent on the "*manner in which the individual elements are connected with each other*".[31]

The identification of different forms of complexity, introduced by Warren Weaver some 80 years ago and taken up again more recently, could help to sharpen the core question we want to address.

Warren Weaver differentiates the problem according to "complexity" on one axis and "randomness" on the other (see Fig. 4.10). Weaver identifies three different areas: Problems with low complexity and absence of randomness are problems with **organised simplicity**, located **in the left lower corner**. Problems with high degree of complexity and high degree of randomness are problems of **disorganised complexity, located in the right upper corner**. In the **middle region** are located problems of **organised complexity**. We refer to the graphical illustration provided by George Klir (2006) in Fig. 4.10.

Klir identifies deficits in the formal statistical methods to tackle problems of organised complexity. He proposed a research program called Generalised Information Theory to develop the methods to handle these problems appropriately. We

[29] Colander et al. (2004, p. 18).

[30] Colander (2000, p. 128).

[31] Colander (2008, p. 14).

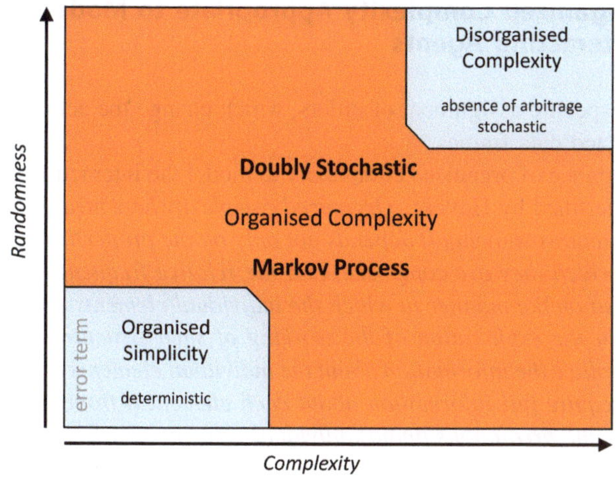

Fig. 4.10 Different forms of complexity[32]

adjusted Klir's figure to illustrate our issue by inserting some additional descriptions to explain the different forms of complexity models in capital markets (see Fig. 4.11).

As the additional insertion on the randomness axis indicates, the error term in statistical optimisation problems may embody randomness in problems of organised simplicity. Risky assets are in most of the cases treated by means of the expected value of utility, represented by means and variance of activities' outcome. It is an open question if such models should be classified as problems of "organised simplicity" or of "disorganised complexity". The subsumption into "organised complexity" seems not convincing. These models are not dealing with actions and interactions at the level of individual agents and of discrete choice among individual activities including randomness. The term complexity has been used differently to Weaver's definition.

Axtell's (2005) "degree of complexity" discussion might not be mixed with Weaver's differentiation in organised and disorganised complexity. Laughlin (2006) characterises "*complexity theory, a branch of mathematics born in the 1970's that subsumes the topics of chaos, fractals, and cellular automata*".[33] Warren Weaver's differentiations are appropriate to sharpen the issue under consideration. David Luckham's Complex Event Processing (2002) refers obviously to organised complexity.

---

[32] Adapted from Klir (2006, p. 4), who provides a graphic interpretation of Weaver (1948).

[33] Laughlin (2006, p. 131).

4.4.2 Organised Complexity Appropriate to Model Interacting Agents

IIA requires specific assignment of orders, which change the actions of the traders in the connected data frames.

The importance of organised complexity to model the interactions among agents has been underlined by Hayek: "*Organized complexity here means that the character of the structures showing it depends not only on the properties of the individual elements of which they are composed, and the relative frequency with which they occur, but also on the manner in which the individual elements are connected with each other. In the explanation of the working of such structures we can for this reason not replace the information about the individual elements by statistical information but require full information about each element if from our theory we are to derive specific predictions about individual elements. Without such information about the individual elements, we shall be confined to what on another occasion I have called mere pattern predictions—predictions of some of the general attributes of the structures that will form themselves but not containing specific statements about the individual elements of which the structures will be made up.*"[34]

The question where the so-called "*agent-based models of financial markets*"[35] fit into this complexity system also remains unanswered.

The claimed information quality of equilibrium prices has been questioned for many years: "*Like most things of great value, they are for practical purposes impossibly hard to get... If prices are the language of the market, orders are the messages whereby participants convey their preferences for possible trades.*"[36]

The authors determine "*any rule that converts orders into trades and (possible new), prices as market mechanism. The market mechanism, then, is a procedure which uses orders as inputs and generates as its output trades and (possible new) prices.*"[37]

In reality, prices are generated by matching orders that are placed by acting agents. Thus, the focus should be on investigating the factors determining the order-placing and order-accepting decision. We need to look at the order book, not just the prices.

This specification requirement becomes even more important as there are several trading facilities where the agents can submit their orders for execution. The issue of best execution is a hot issue at the moment with respect to MiFID, the "Markets in Financial Instruments Directive".

Furthermore, agents act on a case-by-case basis..."*instead of globally optimal decisions, purposive agents act relatively myopically and seek local optima, at best, probably preferring robust and resilient solutions to optimal ones, and certainly so*

---

[34] Hayek (1974, p. 2).
[35] Axtell (2007, p. 113).
[36] Beja/Hakansson (1979, p. 145).
[37] Beja/Hakansson (1979, p. 145).

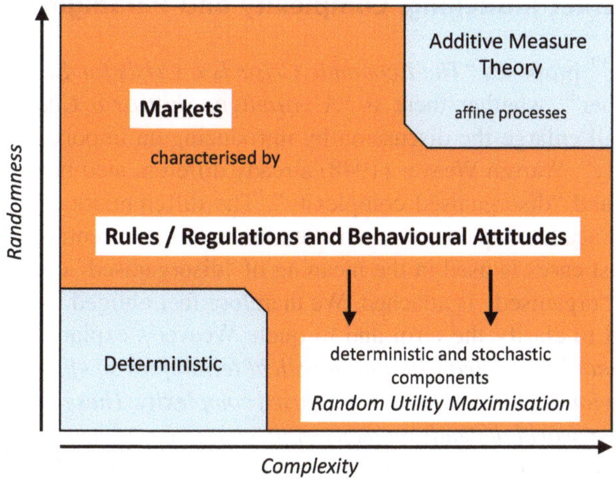

Fig. 4.11 Stochastic issues of capital markets

in environments where it is costly to switch between (brittle), policies in response to exogenous events".[38]

Figure 4.11 illustrates the connections of complexities and market modelling. The predominant approaches to date refer either to organised simplicity in the bottom left-hand corner or to disorganised complexity in the top right-hand corner. Organised simplicity is characterised by low complexity and low randomness. Randomness is represented mainly by an error term. Market models that represent disorganised complexity are characterised by probabilistic models based on additive measure theory. This category also includes models that deal with so-called affine processes. The criteria for describing economic activities of disorganised complexity are mainly statistical variables such as mean and variance and higher moments as well as the criteria derived from their combination such as covariances. The important section in between, covered by organised complexity, has not been investigated too much. Klir refers to this not yet investigated field of problems and proposes a new research program that deals, e.g. explicitly with probability theoretical models applying non-additive measure theory. He breaks fresh ground regarding probability theory to developing tools that are capable of tackling issues at the core of economics. They are probably not only at the core of economics, but also capable of tackling until now unsolved questions in science. These questions have been articulated by Weaver (1948), but quite recently by Laughlin (2006), referring to the issue of emergence in science.

[38] Axtell (2007, p. 114).

4.4.3 Market Modelling, Complexity and Paradigm Shifts

Alan Kirman[39] proposes "*The Economic Crisis is a Crisis for Economic Theory*". He asks further[40] whether there is "*A paradigm Shift or a Change in Perspective*"? We shall enlarge the discussion by introducing an important differentiation of "complexity". Warren Weaver (1948) already differentiated between "organised complexity" and "disorganised complexity". The differentiation is at the core of our book. But academia paid not much attention to this differentiation. Today, complexity in most cases is used in the meaning of "disorganised" complexity, even if the adjective "organised" is attached. We therefore feel obliged to avoid misunderstandings and to clarify the term and to quote Weaver's explanation: "*These new problems cannot be handled with the statistical techniques so effectively describing average behaviour in problems of disorganised complexity. These new problems, and the future of the world depends on many of them, requires science to make a...great advance, an advance that must be even greater than the nineteenth-century conquest of problems of simplicity or the twentieth-century victory over problems of disorganised complexity. Science* ***must, over the next 50 years, learn to deal with these problems of organised complexity***".[41] (Emphasis authors).

Regarding the discussion in economics and finance, we are in delay to implement that differentiation. But there is hope that big data and big computer combined with the results of prospect theory and quantitative psychology, will make up for the delay. The solution we propose implements organised complexity consequently. Interactions among individual agents require the realistic modelling of each individual agent. We have to model the basics of the real world as they are. "*We have to put the books aside and see the world as it is. We have to turn from the authorities to the facts.*" (Walter Eucken (1989), Vorwort).

Accordingly, we have explicitly modelled the possible activity of each agent between which she can choose and her holding of shares of that corporations admitted to trading on the trading venue under consideration. Furthermore, to provide a real picture of the trading venue under consideration, we need to consider the orders placed for any security and identify the traders who placed that orders. To organise the sequence of serving the orders, we rely on time stamped orders. Serving the orders follows basically the principle of "first come, first serve". In most trading venues this is concretised by the "price time priority rule". We apply that rule in modelling the trading. Accordingly, all data we apply are time stamped up to 1/100s. Time is very important to decide the matching of orders. We rely on an innovative relation possible by the application of discrete choice. The utility of any activity is obtained by a formula, that can be also taken as the probability.[42] An agent chooses that activity, that has the highest utility and equally that will be realised at the shortest time. First come first served principle will be fulfilled.

---

[39] Kirman (2010).

[40] Kirman (2016) Reviewing Colander and Kuper (2014).

[41] Weaver(1948, p. 70).

[42] Suppes (1961, p. 201) derives that formula too and discusses the term "entropy".

Any action of a trader is changing any state of any trading venue. If a trader places an order, the amount of orders of that share will change. If a buy and a sell order match, generating a price, the actual price quotation has to be adjusted, the number of buyers' share increases and the number of sellers' share decreases. As we use an open order book, all traders are informed of changes to orders and the updated price quotation.

We are convinced that the complete time stamped data set for two weeks provides much more insight how a trading venue works at the microlevel than a time series of not stamped price data for a time span of, let's say, 10 years. Looking 10 years back, we have to accept that the trading landscape has changed. It is up to every researcher to decide if the ten-year-data set fulfils the requirement of belonging to the same population. That is certainly a very interesting and important question, how to handle the issue of emergence and organised complexity in the long run. Every action changes the population under consideration. But in this book we concentrate on reliable modelling of the behaviour of individual agents.

Our approach is realistic because, firstly, it is based on the fact that appropriate data processing capabilities are now available and, secondly, the combination of advanced prospecting studies with the comprehensive mathematical description of human behaviour enables reliable quantitative modelling of the real performance of traders in selecting and placing orders and, moreover, in matching these orders in accordance with the rules and regulations of the trading venue.

The necessary switch from "disorganised complexity to 'organised' complexity" may cause the crises that Kirman and others recognise. David Pines (2014) proposed "*Emergence: A unifying theme for the twenty-first century science*". Robert B, Laughlin and David Pines (2000) obviously address the same issue that might be formulated as: Science has to regard the actions and interactions of individual agents explicitly. The big challenge of "organised complexity" is that the investigation of single activities may not be handled by the hitherto applicable statistical methods. Waren Weaver recognised that difficulty already, and Hayek reaffirmed it later. This challenge -switch from disorganised to organised complexity- touches both natural and social sciences. Robert B. Laughlin (2006, p. 209) recognises the importance of Emergence in physics and states "*the transition to the Age of Emergence brings to an End the myth of the absolute power of mathematics*". Accepting this statement requires "econophysicists" to rethink their program. We keep in mind that organised complexity and emergence address the same issue. Robert B. Laughlin and David Pines think that traditional research orientation should be replaced by a focus on emergent behaviour. We believe that such emergent behaviour in social sciences is modelled by human interacting agents. We have to refer to a reliable description of human behaviour according to the reliable description of activities at the level of atomic structure in physics. For a long time, physicists have assumed that atoms and molecules alike "do not think" (Mann-MacMurray, quoted by Gallegati (2018, p. 32). This behavioural attitude has been assumed in economics for a long time accordingly. That's probably one aspect of Kirman's crises.

4.5 Market Transforms Subjective Values into Objective Prices

Now, after explaining the switch from disorganised to organised complexity, we have to explain the tools we apply in greater detail. Firstly, we have to explain, why we prefer discrete choice compared to expected utility for making decisions under uncertainty. Expected utility is suitable for decisions under risk, but we believe, it does not fit for decisions under uncertainty. It is no doubt that economic and finance decisions are in most of the cases decision under uncertainty. See McFadden's (1999) comprehensive review. He summarises the economists' problem by adapting Oscar Wise's saying: "*Economists know the price of everything and the value of nothing*". According to McFadden (1999), this aphorism characterises the priorities of the disciplines. This aphorism will be quoted completely in chapter 8.2.

In the following, we describe shortly two approaches of human behaviour's quantitative modelling. In this introduction we firstly describe the "expected utility mean–variance" model prevailing until now in finance, and we compare expected utility and then behaviour modelling by their specifics.

An expected utility precursor is Daniel Bernoulli's proposal to evaluate the value of a game by substituting the expected money value by applying a—later so-called—utility function. Daniel Bernoulli used the term "moral expectation". He applied the logarithmic function to evaluate the utilities of the possible payments. The expected utility's value of the possible payments equalised nearly the common figure of money that players were ready to invest in the game. Von Neumann and Morgenstern (1944) took a major step forward in quantifying human behaviour during participating in games. As the title of their book already proclaims, the authors investigate quantification of human behaviour when playing a game. Such a scenario is characterised by complete information about the probabilities of the outcomes and about the possible outcomes itself. It is therefore the scenario of a decision under risk.

Such a scenario is quite different from the human behaviour of acting agents in a common economic situation. "*Choice behaviour can be characterised by a decision process, which is informed by perceptions and beliefs based on available information, and influenced by affect, attitudes, motives, and preferences*" McFadden (1999, p. 74). Neither the outcomes are known nor their probabilities. We come back to this situation later.

Von Neumann and Morgenstern's (1944) publication gave the discussion about human behaviour modelling a big push, even if they added a disclaimer: "*We repeat most emphatically that our theory is thoroughly static. A dynamic theory would unquestionably more complete and therefore preferable. But there is ample evidence from other branches of science that it is futile to try to build one as long as the static side is not thoroughly understood... A static theory deals with equilibria. The essential characteristic of an equilibrium is that it has no tendency to change i.e. that it is not conducive to dynamic developments... Finally let us note a point at which the theory of social phenomena will presumably take a very definite turn away from the existing patterns of mathematical physics*" (p. 44). They did obviously not believe in econophysics. We believe that it is time to break out of the "equilibrium straitjacket" Gallegati (2018). That liberation helps to overcome the crises of economic theory.

Freed from the straitjacket of equilibrium we have to fill out the free space of modelling human behaviour. We suggest that the reliable results of prospect theory help to fill this broad space. We do not rely on ad hoc assumptions of human behaviour. But for the moment, we proceed in comparing the well-established mean variance principle with the—at least in finance and economics—ignored prospect theory and discrete choice.

On the one side, the discussion about the form and type of the utility function was intensified. after Von Neuman and Morgenstern's publication. A big point was further the question, which combinations of probability distribution and utility function resulted at an expected utility expressed by mean and variance of the probability function. Prominent participants were, among others, Friedman, Savage and Marschak. Professor Jacob Marschak tutored Harry Markowitz dissertation.[43]

By a stroke of genius, Harry Markowitz (1952) proposed "portfolio theory" by applying expected utility approach. He proposed that "*investors apply or at least should apply mean variance of the portfolios return*". He proposed further that "*investors like portfolio's return and dislike portfolio's variance*". Investing in a portfolio shall reduce risk by diversification. We stop by this short description, as this is all familiar textbook material.

This risk reduction by diversification may have been important at the time Markowitz was published, but it probably does not reflect the situation today. At that time, the investment industry was essentially a "buy and hold" industry, at least compared by the situation today.

Currently, portfolio revision is as important as portfolio selection. Investors can choose among many trading facilities and trading fees are low. At Markowitz' time, risk management by diversification prevailed and efficient portfolio selection determined minimal variance for a given return or vice versa. This "management by diversification" also became popular in the manufacturing industry under the term "conglomerates" but disappeared again sometime later. The industry realised that management by diversification is not competitive compared to other management styles and recent mathematical results enable to go beyond mean and variance.[44]

The next issue is quantitative modelling of human behaviour when going beyond game scenarios. That is of course relevant for investment decision-making. It is above all relevant in quantitative modelling of economic behaviour. The history of quantitative modelling of human behaviour traces back to Louis Leon Thurston nearly 100 years ago. He proposes to model human decision-making

[43] See Read (2012, p. 177).

[44] See Adcock (2014) and Meckes (2009).

not by evaluating the value of discrete alternatives alone, but by comparison of alternatives.

Research about human behaviour intensified after WWII. One of the first publications was the already mentioned John von Neuman and Oscar Morgenstern. The following research split into two directions. One investigated the real behaviour in specified test situations and was termed "prospect theory". Among the leading experts in prospect theory are Danny Kahnemann, Amos Tversky, Moshe Ben-Akiva and Richard Thaler, to name but a few. With regard to the other direction, which is referred to as "behavioural theoretical research", we would like to mention, beside the precursor Louis Leon Thurstone, Jacob Marschak, R. Duncan Luce, and Kenneth E. Train. Daniel McFadden might deserve a special position because he conducted advanced mathematical research especially about the issue, on how to derive a general utility function from explicit actions. This research has a long history under the heading of "revealed preference". He did research and after a while decided to apply a formula R. Duncan Luce had proposed. Luce himself got inspired by both Thustone's publications and by the army's research on radar detection. It was advantageous to compare simultaneously two alternatives when he had to decide, if a pattern was good or dangerous. Luce (1994, p. 273). Thurstone had proposed already a "*method of paired comparison for social values*" (1927c) and developed a "*Law of Comparative Judgement*" (1927a). Luce combined both research branches successfully and developed a formula how an agent should evaluate alternative actions See Luce (2005, p. 23). The formula was based on theoretical derivations and its practical importance becomes obvious when Daniel McFadden applied the formula to solve the problem of a doctoral student. When implementing a new transportation facility, how will passengers vote? McFadden's successful forecasts, assisted by Luce's principle of Independence from Irrelevant Alternatives, was a convincing success. Under the heading "discrete choice" the technique experienced a successful application in many disciplines when human behaviour should be forecasted.[45]

4.6 Big Data and Big Computer Enhance Order Investigation

Securities trading is a new topic both for practitioners and academics alike. Many textbooks do not cover this topic. Treynor and Wagner (1990) described the investment process as a three-legged stool supported equally by securities research, portfolio management, and securities trading. Of the three "legs", trading is the least understood, least appreciated, and the only leg not considered to be a formal profession. Treynor and Wagner note "*Trading is a learn-by- doing occupation. No*

[45] Thurstone (1927a) and (1927c), see also Luce (2005) and Thurstone (1927b). The widespread application is documented by Haghani et al. (2021).

one studies trading at Harvard Business School. Universities did not offer majors in securities trading." Traders learn on the job.

The situation begins to change. Firstly, there are several venues to carry out a trade. Secondly, there are several ways to sell or acquire securities. Thirdly, trading fees have been reduced. Implicit trading costs have gained importance.

There are several books out describing the performance of exchanges. However, no explicit analytical modelling of performance on the trading venue has yet been published. To avoid any misunderstanding, this is not an omission from the large group of publications that analyse the microstructure of a markets. They do not analyse the actual process of price generation through the matching of orders but are mainly concerned with price time series.

Quite recently Alvin E. Roth's analytical study of matching in two-sided markets has recently honoured with the Nobel Prize. His book contains only cursory remarks on the securities markets. His second book on "two-sided matching", which he published together with Marilda A. Oliveira Sotomayor (1992), also deals with the negotiation of securities, but does not refer to the explicit rules and regulations of a stock exchange or an electronic trading venue. They believe this market is not two-sided in the sense they will speak of, because a broker/trader can change the sides and act in one moment as buyer and in the other moment as seller. This may be true if brokers are involved as intermediaries. On an exchange without brokers, as is the case with electronic exchanges, the trader must submit an offer and is obliged to fulfil this offer until he withdraws it and submits another offer with different conditions. In our scenario—and we believe it is the typical scenario of a current trading venue—the trader submits an offer, and he is tied to this offer until he withdraws and resubmits. Matching takes place between orders clearly labelled as buy or sell. The matching discussion does not cover the decision, if a trader is both, buying and selling. Including intermediaries is indeed a different story. We will discuss a similar problem later, after we have introduced the clear distinction between buyer and seller. Bargaining occurs by withdrawing an order and resubmitting it with other conditions that are more to the liking of the other side.

A main problem of our approach are the circumstances and motives, why a buyer is a buyer and why a seller is a seller. If the trader knows in advance that a buy or sell order will be submitted, he has a competitive advantage.

We investigate firstly the different approaches of decision-making under risk or uncertainty. Then we propose discrete choice to determine how an order will be determined, or to be more precise, which order will be selected according to the technique of discrete choice.

For modelling financial decision-making under uncertainty, we selected the technique of discrete choice. Daniel McFadden—among others—developed discrete choice with reference to prospect theory. We should therefore explain at the beginning, why the application of prospect theory respective discrete choice might be successfully applied in finance.

Decision-making under risk-uncertainty has to be discussed in detail later—applies mainly the principle of expected utility, developed initially by Daniel

Bernoulli. The Royal Swedish Academy of Sciences (2002), pp16 explained the differences among both concepts: "*While expected-utility theory is axiomatic, their (Kahnemann and Tversky,OL) prospect theory is descriptive. It was thus developed in an inductive way from empirical observations, rather than deductively from a set of logically appealing axioms.... Although expected utility theory provides an accurate representation of actual choices in some transparent and simple decision problems, most real-life decision problems are complex and call for behaviourally richer models.... In case of monetary gains and losses, the decision criterion in expected utility... presumes the existence of real valued function u of wealth w, for the decision-maker in the current situation...*".

The most appropriate case for applying expected utility as a decision criterium is buying a lottery ticket. Is the price of the ticket worth the expected lottery gain? The probability of a draw and its result in case are known in advance, disclosed in the conditions of participation. In some games, the expected value of the draws differs significantly from the amount of money players are willing to invest in a ticket, which is particularly evident in the St. Petersburg game. Daniel Bernoulli therefore suggested applying a so-called "moral value" to money. He proposed the logarithmic function of money; and indeed, the expected value of the "moral value lottery" was near the amount, players had been ready to invest in the participation of the St. Petersburg game. A great debate about the appropriate type of utility function is still alive today, at least in the academic world. Professional investors may rely on the so-called "performance presentation standards" applying the time weighted rate of return calculated just on the portfolio's money value at the beginning of the evaluation period, the cash inflows and cash outflow within the evaluation period and the portfolio's final money value. These calculation does not rely on any utility function. Another measure frequently applied is "beta". It relies on mean–variance of the entire portfolio, referring to a so-called market rate of return. We will explain it later in detail. We can assume for our model, that traders do not rely on the expected value of a portfolio's utility. US-performance presentation standards rely in "time weighted rate of return" and do not even discuss the idea of expected utility. In case of expected utility application, the industry may not achieve a unanimous vote about the type of the function and certainly not about the function's parameter values.

Professional traders rely on the current flow of orders. Looking at orders—and above all—at the trades motives and circumstance to place an order, gives a competitive advantage against those who are restricted on the observation of already made prices. Prices are generated by matching orders, according to the trading places rules and regulations. These rules and regulations are quite different for different trading venues. The matching rules are quite transparent at an electronic trading system.

We start with modelling situations where the decision to buy or sell a security is already made and the research department of a bank gives an order to buy or to sell at the trading department. We will investigate the decision of the trader to optimise the order specification. Among the possible order specifications, he must select the one with the highest probability of realisation. This probability is equal to the highest utility.

For some combinations of utility function and probability function, the expected utility resulted from a combination of the mean and variance of the probability function of the outcomes. The discussion about the issue was induced by John von Neumann and Oskar Morgenstern's "Theory of Games and Economic Behaviour". It made formal, axiomatic analysis socially acceptable in economics and psychology and invited laboratory experimentation to test the descriptive validity of axioms. Most of this work concentrated on choice among lotteries, but the ideas spread to other decision-making situations. McFadden (1999, p. 73). Among other locations, Chicago has been a hot spot of the discussion, fired by Milton Friedman, Leonhard Savag and Jacob Marschak. Marschak had earlier recognised that, in considering risk and return, one could realistically confine their descriptions to first moments, known as mean, and second moments, known as variances and covariances. A young doctoral student—Harry Markowitz—benefitted from the discussion among experts. Jacob Marschak's young doctoral student took the chance and developed in a strike of a genius "portfolio theory", first published by Markowitz (1952). Markowitz passed the doctoral exam "after discussion" in 1954.

4.7 Investor Decision-Making Today: Mean Variance vs Prospect Theory

Markowitz proposed at the entrance of his 1952 article that "*the investor does (or should) consider expected return a desirable thing and variance of return an undesirable thing*" (p. 77). This principle remains an undisputed dogma in financial theory to this day. That dogma is reaffirmed by Bernoulli's certainty equivalent—in case of an exponential utility function and a normal probability distribution. In case of other combinations, we get another picture, see chapter 3.4.4. Taking certainty equivalent of lognormal distribution combined with potential utility function, one gets $CE = exp(\mu + \sigma^2/2)$. In case of that combination, variance contributes positively to the certainty equivalent. In case of a lognormal distribution and logarithmic utility function, variance has no impact on the certainty equivalent. This result puts mean variance rule into perspectives. Fluctuations itself are not bad, but their misestimation is risky. Indeed, a share's increasing volatility increases the price of the option, the "Vega" of the option is positive. That result corresponds to the Risk Averse figures.

In case of an exponential utility function, ARA remains constant, RRA increases in case of increasing wealth (see chapter 3.4.2). In case of a potential utility function ARA decreases, RRA remains constant in case of increasing wealth.

These aspects make obvious that efficient risk management requires watching the market situation. One of the riskiest assumptions in financial theory is therefore that markets are efficient and that they clarify risky situations always in favour of the model, as its builders assume.

A detailed observation of the market's performance is therefore necessary. The times that the "efficient market" assumption was enough to sell theoretical financial models disregarding the real performance of markets have gone. Alvin E. Roth proclaims that "*markets are everywhere*". We can add prices made by matching orders, not by throwing a dice or by extrapolating time series of prices.

Dealing with this argument, we must refer to prospect theory, or more general, to ask how human beings really behave. We have progressed from the homo economicus to the homo sapiens, to quote Thaler's headline. That extension is possible, as the mathematical theory of human behaviour has made comparable progress in the last thirty years, even if the discussion lasts nearly 100 years.[46]

The concept of Thurstone's pairwise comparison, extended by Luce and Kahnemann into prospect theory. Then applied by McFadden to solve "Phoebes Problem", an identification of transportation choice quite successfully.

There are certain differences between the two models that make prospect theory consistent with the experimental evidence mentioned earlier in this chapter. Since people evaluate risky prospects based on changes in wealth relative to some reference level, appropriate assumptions about the editing stage would make the model consistent with the common observation that people choose differently depending on how a problem is framed.

The Swedish Academy summarises: Prospect theory and its extensions have taken important steps towards a more accurate description of individual behaviour under risk than expected utility. It now forms the basis for much of the applied empirical work in this field. Kahnemann has been a major source of inspiration behind the recent boom of research in behavioural economics and finance. His research also had a substantial impact on other fields.

4.8 Is There a Change of Paradigm: From Equilibrium to Emergence?

Daniel McFadden's work has been acknowledged by the Nobel Committee in 2000. The observations to be explained are discrete (or qualitative) and cannot be represented by continuous variables. Standard demand theory as well as traditional econometric methods, aimed at explaining variations in continuous variables are generally inappropriate to analyse discrete choice behaviour.

Problems of qualitative choice were initially dealt with work in psychometrics, biometrics and to some extent also econometrics. Early contributions of particular importance are Thurstone (1927a-c), Luce (2005), and Laughlin (2006), who formulated models of discrete probabilistic choice.

[46] See Thurstone (1927a) and (1927c), see also Luce (1994) and Thurstone (1927b).

Prominent scholars both from natural and social science recognise a change of paradigms. Robert B. Laughlin (2006) believes "*science has now moved from the Age of Reductionism to an Ageof emergence, a time when the search for ultimate causes of things shifts from the behaviour of parts to the behaviour of the collective.*" (p. 208). He explains further: "*The Transition to the Age of emergence brings to an end the myth of the absolute power of mathematics*" (p. 209).

Mauro Gallegati "*For a new paradigm, in which quantitative tests are fundamental, and analytical coherence does not derive from axiomatic models, the ABM approach is very promising...even if still immature*"[47] with reference to Farmer and Foley (2009), Stiglitz and Gallegati (2011). Di Guilmi et al. (2020) propose to achieve Markov transition probabilities by solving master equations. We propose to take the transition probabilities from the discrete choice probabilities. This procedure is probably innovative, but simpler.

"*Science develops funeral by funeral*" bluntly stated once Samuelson. Max Planck explained this development: "*A new scientific truth does not triumph by convincing its opponents and making them see the light, but rather because its opponents eventually die, and a new generation grows up with it.*" Alan Kirman (2010), p. 529.

Planck refers to his own experiences: "*It was not without disappointment that I realised that the impression of my dissertation and my habilitation thesis in the physics public of the time was zero. None of his university teachers... had any understanding for the content of his dissertation...Other experts reacted similarly. Helmholtz probably didn't read the paper at all and Kirhhoff explicitly rejected its content.*"[48] Once he participated a competition of the Göttingen University concerning the preservation of energy. He received the award "second to none", not the first award. The prize collegium justified the second place because he did not acknowledge Prof Wilhelm Weber's theory. We have to know that this Professor Weber was the son in law of C.F. Gauss, the big shot in Göttingen.[49] Max Planck himself was ready to acknowledge innovative ideas. He accepted Einstein's famous 1905 paper, and he performed a fair discussion with Boltzmann regarding entropy. "*Among all the physicists of this time Ludwig Boltzmann best comprehended the true importanceof entropy*".[50] In this context he made that remark quoted by Alan Kirman.[51] We will come back to entropy in economics later.

We add here and explain it later in detail: The "meso" layer to connect "micro" and "macro" is a partly complicated mixture of organisational unities; like companies, political parties, families. There may be several layers of activities that

---

[47] Gallegati (2018, p. VIII).

[48] Planck (undated, p. 13).

[49] Planck (1946, p. 45).

[50] Planck (undated, p. 20).

[51] Solow (2005) addresses the same issue, but from a different point of view: "It can become very difficult ever to displace an entrenched model by a better one. Clever and motivated—including ideologically motivated- people can fight a rearguard battle that would make Robert E. Lee like an amateur.", p. 94.

connect micro with macro and that form macro variables out of micro activities. At capital markets, the following activities constitute micro activities. Traders select orders out of the possible set of orders allowed at the trading venue under consideration and submit orders. These orders are matched according to the matching rules prevailing at the trading venue under consideration. The matching enables transactions and generates prices. The share price index may constitute a meso level, maybe XTF-trading constitutes another meso level. The Macro level might be companies' listed stocks, the whole economy, the civic and criminal laws and the government respectively the national and multinational political decision units. For the moment being, it is an open question, how the actions and interactions between these units are modelled and if there are already such models, how reliable such models might be.

That is a huge task and Gallegati has prepared the ground quite thoroughly. We completely agree with Gallegati when he points out the shortcomings of the traditional mainstream. We further completely agree with his assertion that the entire theory must be built on modelling of human activities. He employs the abbreviation ABM.

We reaffirm the assertion that "*the methodology arises from the bottom-up; individual parameters and their distribution are estimated and then evaluated to verify if aggregate regularities emerge when taken together*" Gallegati (2018, p. IX). Procedures, how to summarise the individual activities to a meaningful whole are currently the issue of intensive discussions. Modelling of human behaviour, including psychological aspects of human behaviour, can now be added to traditional economic methods. Such an ABM might fortify the whole theory. It contributes to a solid foundation that is strengthened by contributing behavioural knowledge. That is tested since nearly 100 years, and it is now successfully applied in many disciplines.

This tool exploits the fact that the reliability of evaluating an activity is comparably improved, when a person must evaluate an alternative by comparison among two activities.

Discrete Choice Capabilities to Select Orders

5

Abstract

Chapter 5 describes a market's frame by a Markov process with a discrete state space and a continuous time space: Every individual agent, his/her endowment with shares and money, his/her individual preferences and last but not least, the set of actions feasible to any agent or trader has to be modeled explicitly. These are basic prerequisites to model interactions precisely. This innovative approach exploits the ample data volumes equally available today to the same extent as the computing power. The efficient management of the abundance of data requires methods that go beyond mean and variance of price's time series. Orders are a trader's vital acting tools at markets. The modelling of the trader's decision process applies discrete choice: The utility of placing an order can be transformed in the probability of taking that order: the order under consideration changes the appropriate element in the Markov state of nature. It provides the Markov transition probability of that state under consideration. The connection of an action's probability and a state's transition probability may be termed "Doubly Stochastic Markov Process", (DSMP for short) A. Roth has propagated for some time, that at markets, transactions are generated by matching appropriate opposite incentives. He was awarded the Nobel prize. The time has come to investigate the last mile of trading in finance too, i.e. to investigate order placing and matching. Trading has become a very important risk management tool. It is vital, that the trading facilities do not only exist on paper, but also in reality.

Keywords

Modeling of agents' decision making • Deriving an action's utility • Transforming utility into probability • Explaining open order book • Identification of order types

O. Loistl et al., *Screen Based Trading and Open Order Book*, New Economic Windows,
https://doi.org/10.1007/978-3-031-99052-6_5

5.1 Contractarian Approach to Model Individual Actions

5.1.1 Markets' Vital Function: The Matching of Opposite Orders

Recent discussions postulate that economic modelling rests on individual actions such as a "*culture-dish approach to the study of economic world*" (Tesfatsion 2008). Buchanan (1988) describes analogously market economies as "contractarian system" of actions and interactions. On closer inspection, it becomes clear that orders and the acceptance of such orders are the fundamental activities in a market economy. Investigating the entire order situation, prices are generated by matching orders according to the rules and regulations prevailing at the market segment under consideration, e.g. the famous price time priority. At least in market economies, prices are not dictated by one party alone. We therefore propose to investigate the determinants of order submissions and present statistics showing that the variables determining different order types can be successfully identified, thus proving that the contractarian approach is manageable, at least for market economies. We rely on the complete tick-by-tick order and price data of the Frankfurt Stock Exchanges Xetra for six trading days. But the approach is applicable to any exchange that has the complete tick-by-tick order data available. Furthermore, this approach provides an efficient tool for reliably assessing the issue of best execution.

The postulate that "*any meaningful model of the macro economy must analyse not only the characteristics of the individuals but also the structure of their interactions.*"[1] is well known and nowadays widely accepted: "*All economic reasoning should be based on the actions of individuals*".[2]

The interactions among individual agents shape the behaviour of the whole and have to be regarded. "*There is a large and growing literature on the ideaof emergencein physical, biological, and social systems…In systems that display emergence, the interaction ofautonomous or quasi- autonomous components of the system leads to a higher-level functionality that is not present in any of the individual components*".[3]

However, the concrete modelling of these actions is not yet settled. Two issues may be discussed: Firstly, the question of how actions and interactions can be modelled. That is the issue this book will be dealing with. Secondly, the question of how to model the consistent combination of micro-activities into macro-variables. As the latest discussion convincingly documents, the emerging issue of self-organisation is very promising (See Chapter 8).

Regarding the first question, we propose to follow Buchanan's contractarian view to achieve a realistic modelling of actions and interactions of individual

[1] Colander et al. (2008, p 237, italics in source).

[2] Arrow (1994, p. 4).

[3] Axtell (2007, p. 111). Laughlin (2006) discusses the transition to the Age of Emergence in physics.

agents. Contractarian implies exchange of offers between two parties to buy or sell, e.g. prices do not pertain to actions of individual human beings, at least not in market economies.[4] Prices are not generated by actions of any individual agent alone. Buchanan postulates a "*contractarian paradigm*"... that seeks "*to explain and to understand the behaviour of persons who interact, one with another.*"[5]

5.1.2 Matching of Orders Generates Transaction Prices

Human actions imply choices between feasible alternatives on markets. They are given by the submission of orders or the acceptance of orders already placed at the marketplace.

Transactions generate prices whenever two parties agree to exchange a given quantity of a specified good for a specified amount of money or for the specified amount of another good. The relevant human actions are offers to trade or acceptances of such offers. Modelling prices instead of price generating orders is a shorty, sometimes a very unreliable proxy of the real situation. The history of efficient markets shows that omitting the real trading possibilities is in many situations very risky.

Until recently, the direct empiric investigation of offers to buy or to sell, the motivation to present offers, was quite difficult as data were available for prices only. The investigation of price generating actions has been neglected in academic research. But nowadays, the complete set of offers at a stock exchange is available for academic investigations too. The matching of orders according to the known pricing procedures, e.g. price time priority has to be investigated. Furthermore, offers contain far more reliable signals of agents' reactions to new events than prices as recent investigations document.[6] The results for identifying different orders are a promising first step towards forecasting orders. The results are obtained by discrete choice methods.[7] Three different order forms have been compared: Limit orders (L), Market orders (M) and the special form of Limit Orders "Immediate or Cancel" (LI). It is no surprise that the method's capabilities to identify Limit orders against Limit orders "immediate or cancel" is slightly less than the identification power of other orders.

We investigate Frankfurt Stock Exchanges Xetra System. We rely on time stamped tick-by-tick order data, simulate the emergence of orders and identify by means of discrete choice the determinants of order placing activities. The recently available data files enable to implement this realistic and reliable research design.

---

[4] Arrow (2004, p. 295): Brownian motion [to model prices OL] has no economic significance whatsoever ... So in financial economics you have an analysis based on pattern recognition."

[5] Buchanan (2001, p. 23: defines as "*science of exchanges*").

[6] See Chapter 4.2.

[7] Details see Loistl (2008).

Other recent research results show convincingly that the market participants' reactions to new information are significantly visible in order book adjustment, even if prices do not exhibit such a reaction.

McFadden has investigated the individualistic point of view very successfully.[8] He pursued this research program during the last 25 years.[9] He considered "*in generality the problem of econometric inference on individual behaviour.*"[10] Consequently, he focused on explicit analytical modelling of individuals' decisions, i.e. the choice of a specific activity among several activities, every activity's consequence modelled explicitly.[11] McFadden's Discrete Choice approach has received very affirmative reactions.[12]

We build on a strong basis when applying McFadden's approach of modelling individual decision-making. Regarding modelling interactions, we assume that these interactions of individuals will be mediated by markets.

5.2 Frame of Microstructure Performance

5.2.1 Frame's Discrete Items Express Individual Traders' Endowments and Actions Explicitly

This approach describes the stock (or capital) market by a high dimensional state space: The endowment of each agent with securities is modelled by specific individual data.[13] Furthermore, the individual orders valid on the stock exchange are modelled by an individual dimension. See the detailed description given in Landes and Loistl (1992). Each individual activity of any trader is evaluated by means of discrete choice. We apply the logit approach and derive probabilities for taking individual actions. Any action changes a specific dimension of the state space as defined. The Markov transition probability is controlled by the logit probabilities to take that action.

This concept enables to fulfil Axtell's postulate that the agents' interactions occur within a network. The Markov process and the transition probabilities provide an explicit network structure. The states' transitions are generated by specific actions. Each transition of an individual state is generated by a specific discrete activity. The innovative construction of a doubly stochastic Markov process

---

[8] McFadden (1974, p. 195), "A fundamental concern of economics is the understanding human choice behavior", McFadden (2001).

[9] Manski (2001, p. 17): "McFadden's contemporaneous empirical analyses ... fundamentally changed the way econometricians and empirical researchers thought about the econometric analysis of individual behavior".

[10] Manski (2001, p. 220).

[11] Manski (2001, p. 220): "Applying basic utility theory to the problem of discrete choice, McFadden supposed that each member of a population of interest faces a finite choice set and selects an alternative that maximizes utility."

[12] See the review provided by Manski (2001).

[13] See Kopp Loistl et al. (2008 and Chapter 6).

enables to explicitly determine the state's transition probability by the choice probability to take that specific action generating the state's transition.

Axtell (2007) confirms the view of Kohn (2004) that the hitherto prevailing value paradigm has to be abandoned in favour of the exchange paradigm. "*I have agreed with Kohn that the economics profession is either on the cusp or in the midst of significant methodological innovation. I further agree with him that an empirically accurate depiction of human behaviour is a critical piece of economics, a research stream naturally pursued by economic psychologists and cognitive scientists, while the ability to ramify such specifications to the social level is a core job for the remainder of the economics profession.*"[14]

5.2.2 Integrating the Interaction Part into the Individual Decision Model

Brock and Durlauf concentrate in investigating social interactions, referring "*to the idea that the utility or payoff an individual receives from a given action depends directly on the choices of others in that individual reference group*"[15] Manski (2000) believes that the distinction between these two groups of interactions is not so important nowadays, as "*game theoryrevolution... broke down the sharp distinction that economists had maintained between markets and other social interactions. Game theory encouraged economists to see all interactions as games, with markets as special cases.*"[16] However, even Manski acknowledges a specialisation of modelling interactions in economics. These interactions happen mostly through changes of the market frame, for short MF. The following figure sketches the basic interactions. Trader one, T_1 for short, makes his decision based on the market frame, MF_0. His decision T_1D_1 changes the market frame in MF_1. In this scenario, T_1 receives the information changing the market alone.

Trader T_2 processes this updated information and makes his decision, T_2D_2 and this decision changes the Market Frame, now MF_2. This new data frame is processed by trader T_1, that makes up his mind and chooses T_1D_3. This decision D_3 changes the market frame again, now MF_3. We have to stop now and explain the capital market rule of fair information distribution. The following procedure refers to dissemination of price sensitive information. Price sensitive is defined as a share price that will be affected by the public disclosure of that information.

As we assume an open order book, this new market frame can be and will be processed by other traders too. This information stream is indicated by the arrows from MF_3 to other traders, named T_4, T_3, and T_2. We assume further that traders T_2-T_4 receive the price sensitive information at the same time. However, the processing of that information takes different lengths of time and leads to different

[14] Axtell (2007, p. 119).

[15] Brock and Durlauf (2001, p. 235).

[16] Manski (2000, p. 116).

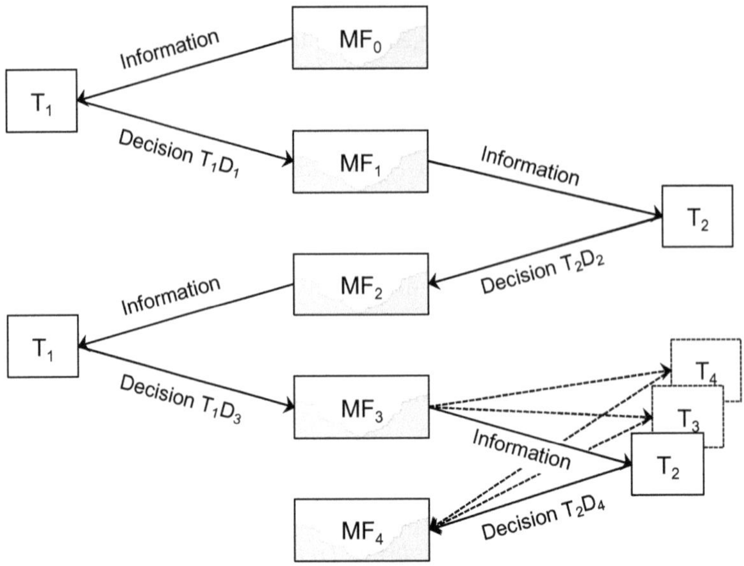

T_i Trader i

T_iD_j Trader i's decision D_j

MF_k Market frame after Decision D_j

The prioritisation of traders I = 2..n is not part of this schedule and will be discussed later.

Fig. 5.1 Market frame and traders' decisions

attractive results. We assume that the trader, who achieved the most attractive result reacts fastest. His decision reaches the market frame. The basic principle of decision and data frame is given in Fig. 5.1.

The big question is the decision D_j of which Trader j will be selected to proceed his order and thus generating a new market frame T_iD_j. Which traders' order will be selected to generate the change of the market frame. The basic rule is "price time priority", a variant of the "first come first serve" principle. The innovative idea is the connection of an actions' utility with the probability to take that action. With regard to Figure 5.1, traders T_2, T_3, T_4 process the information provided by the adjusted market frame MF_3. The selection of the decision to be realised is taken by the following steps:

1. Each trader selects among his feasible actions the one that promises the highest utility for him.
2. The trader whose action promises the highest utility exhibits the highest incentive to react.

Therefore, this trader is the first to place his order at the screen or at the bar. The price time priority rule is connected to the decision rule of selecting the action promising the highest utility. The explicit formal derivation is given in Chapter 6.

We want to fulfil a major critical aspect pointed out by Manski: "***Much recent empirical research conceptualizes interaction processes only in broad terms that lack the clarity of markets and games.***" (Bold letters not in source) We intend to model the details of market interactions. We start with a bottom-up approach, i.e. with modelling the interactions at the microlevel of a stock exchange and implementing the rules and regulations of the stock exchanges under consideration. We will work out how our approach fulfils the basic requirements or dimensions, articulated by Manski[17]:

Stripped to its basics, empirical research has sought to distinguish among three hypotheses:

1. Endogenous interactions wherein the propensity of an agent to behave in some way varies with the behaviour with the group.
2. Contextual interactions wherein the propensity of an agent to behave varies with exogenous characteristics of the group members.
3. Correlated effects wherein agents in the same group tend to behave similarly because they have similar individual characteristics or face similar institutional environments.

5.2.3 Social Interactions Deserve Mediation Features

Brock and Durlauf refer to social interactions: "*By social interactions, we refer to the idea that the utility or payoff an individual receives from a given action depends directly on the choices of others in that individual's reference group, as opposed to the sort of dependence which occurs through the dependence of markets.*"[18]

They apply McFadden's discrete choice approach too, but they restrict their "*analysis to parametric representation of both the social utility term and the probability density of the random utility term. These assumptions will render our model both theoretically and economically tractable.*"

Brock and Durlauf (2001) investigate "*equilibriumproperties under noncooperative decision-making*", so the title of Chapter 3 (p. 239). As we think that Brock and Durlauf provide a very interesting approach dealing with aspects possible under the assumption of an equilibrium, we will propose an alternative that is capable of dealing with individual actions in detail and follows the exchange paradigm to investigating the emergence of market's behaviour on the macrolevel based on the behaviour of individuals at the microlevel without the equilibrium assumption.

[17] Manski (2000, p. 127).

[18] Brock and Durlauf (2001, p. 235).

And last but not least, we try to bring the "*view of economic interactions mediated by networks*" (Axtell 2007) at an operational level with the help of DSMP.

We propose such a network approach, which is both based on the discrete choice approach and consistently integrated into a network. The network is provided by the perhaps high-dimensional state space that describes the market or the social interactions under consideration. The interactions are provided by the state space transitions. The approach enables to model the three hypotheses postulated by Manski[19]: endogenous interactions, contextual interactions and correlated effects in a consistent manner.

We start with the modelling of the possible actions that decision makers can take and proceed with explaining the possible interactions by means of a doubly stochastic process.

5.2.4 Summarising the Proposed Solutions

We summarise the solutions we offer for the problems raised by Axtell[20] as follows:

Requirements	**Proposed Solutions**
Human rational behaviour	Discrete Choice Logit Approach
Interactions in Networks	Doubly Stochastic Markov Process with a High Dimensional State Space (fulfilling IIA proposition)
Individual Human Actions	Placing new or accepting already placed orders
Price Generation	Matching orders according to the exchange rules e.g. price time priority
Intrinsically dynamic	Agents process each change in the market's state of nature and adjust to take appropriate actions
Handling the data issue	Identification of the information relevant for making the individual decisions under consideration.

5.3 Modelling Actions Any Agent Can Take

5.3.1 The Logit Formula

Orders are placed at the market by individual agents, indicating their willingness to buy or to sell a certain quantity for an amount of money chosen. We assume that the limit orders submitted to the exchange express the willingness to pay for the quantity ordered. It is now well-accepted, at least in marketing, that the willingness to pay can be appropriately estimated by the discrete choice approach.

[19] Manski (2000, p. 127).

[20] Axtell (2007, p. 105).

Discrete choice theory developed by McFadden assumes that "a decision maker n faces a choice among j alternatives. [...] The utility that decision maker n obtains from alternative j is U_{nj}. [...] The decision maker chooses the alternative that provides the greatest utility. The behavioural model is therefore: choose alternative i if and only if $U_{ni} > U_{nj}$ for all $j \neq i$. "[21] Further, "*since there are aspects of utility that [may not be] observe[d],* $V_{nj} \neq U_{nj}$,*[the entire] utility is decomposed as* $U_{nj} = V_{nj} + \varepsilon_{nj}$,*where* ε_{nj} *captures the factors that affect utility but are not included in* V_{nj}.*This decomposition is fully general, since* ε_{nj} *is defined as simply the difference between true utility* U_{nj} *and the part of utility that the [observer] captures in* V_{nj}".[22]

In the catallactic capital market model, the stochastic utility $U(a_{ijk}, z)$ of action a_{ijk} of trader i on security j conditional on the actual state z is given by[23]

$$U(a_{ijk}, z) = \Phi(a_{ijk}, z) + \varepsilon_{ijk} \tag{5.1}$$

The representative (deterministic), part $\Phi(a_{ijk}, z)$ of the random utility function U_{ijk} is proposed to take a multifactor functional form, i.e.

$$\Phi(a_{ijk}, z) = \sum_{l} \beta_{il}\phi_{il} \tag{5.2}$$

where β_{il} are termed coupling parameters of the utility potentials ϕ_{il}.[24]

As shown by McFadden (1974) (see also Train [2003]) the probability that agent i chooses to take action $a_{ijk} \in A_i$ (where A_i denotes the set of all actions feasible to agent i) is the probability that the utility of action a_{ijk} is higher than the utilities of all other action alternatives available to the agent i. If the stochastic components ε_{ijk} are assumed to be i.i.d. and to follow an extreme value distribution then following McFadden (1974) and Train (2003), the equation for probability $P(a_{ijk})$ that trader i will choose security j in situation k is given by

$$P(a_{ijk}) = \frac{exp(\Phi(a_{ijk}, z))}{\sum a_{imn} exp(\Phi(a_{imn}, z))} \tag{5.3}$$

This formula is known as Logit model. Marschak (1960) showed that the property of Independence from Irrelevant Alternatives (IIA) of the Logit model implies consistency with utility maximisation. In this regard, Marschak (1960) coined the term stochastic utility maximisation which refers to the utility maximising behaviour in a probabilistic framework when agents choose their next activity.

---

[21] Train (2003, p. 18).

[22] See Train (2003, p. 19).

[23] See Landes and Loistl (1992).

[24] See Loistl et al. (2001, 2002, 2004) for specification of the representative utility function for capital market modelling.

In our research, we determine the waiting time by an approach that might be named doubly stochastic Markov process, analogously to doubly stochastic Poisson process. The assumption of a time-homogeneous conservative Markov process leads to waiting times following an exponential distribution. Its parameter depends on the actual state and is governed by the Markov transition rates. The transition rate, therefore, **is controlled by the probability to take the interacting agent's action that generates the transition**.

5.3.2 Coordination of Information Processing and Action Taking

A further problem has to be discussed: How to handle the huge data volume generated by the individual activities on the market to realise the coordination issue, i.e. how will the market participants process the data available on the market to extract the information to make appropriate decisions.

Human actions imply choices between feasible alternatives on markets. They are given by the feasible submission of orders or the acceptance of orders already placed at the marketplace.

Prices are generated whenever an order to sell matches an order to buy regarding the price limit and the quantity to transact. Once the orders are submitted to the market, the generation of prices is a mere or simple calculation according to the matching rules. Price time priority seems to be the most popular rule.

The major difficulty therefore lies in modelling the forces that govern/control/ generate orders and motivated their revision due to changes in the market's state of nature.

5.3.3 The Milestones

1. Calendar time is not a reliable exogenous yardstick to measure economic activities on markets. They exhibit **asynchronous features** and will be described as **cadlag process**. An equidistant time series feature is not appropriate for describing market activities: **Five minutes in a crash scenario are quite different from five minutes in a calm stock market situation**.
2. **Prices fluctuate around intrinsic values**. That fact is the basic rule at stock market since the centennial publication of Graham and Dodd (1934). It is reaffirmed by their pupil Warren Buffett (see e.g. Warren E. Buffett [2009]), one of the most successful investors of all times. In formal terms this fact may be stated as mean-reverting feature like Ornstein-Uhlenbeck processes. Other tools, however, may incorporate mean reverting as well. This leads again to the nearly forgotten or at least neglected **differentiation between prices and intrinsic values**.

3. Furthermore, at capital markets the **differentiation between prices and orders** prevails. **Orders** are placed at the market by individual agents, indicating their **willingness to buy or to sell** a certain quantity for an amount of money chosen. **Prices are generated** whenever (two) **market participants agreeto exchange the quantity of goods for the amount of money indicated**. Until recently, the theoretical models concentrated on prices were not to blame because there were available price time series only. But the now available ample data bases entailing the entire set of order data require an extended theory comprising the order data too. The intensive discussion about the organisation of the order book, "open or closed" underlines the importance of order information further.
4. Further, actions at capital markets are performed by **interacting human beings governed by their wishes, needs, and fears**. The assumption of the already attained capital market equilibrium has neglected these basic facts for many years. However, the influence and importance of these facts have been reaffirmed by the recent discussion about behavioural finance. It is time to integrating behavioural and quantitative finance into a unique approach. The Catallactics approach is capable of providing such an integrating model. Therefore, I name the approach I am working since many years now **quantitative-behavioural finance**.
5. The **human interactions** are modelled by a **doublystochastic Markov process**: The transition probabilities are determined by the discrete choice logit approach probabilities: The higher the utility of an activity, the higher the probability of taking this activity, and the shorter the corresponding waiting time.

5.4 Model's Capabilities to Explain Real Market Performance

5.4.1 Regulators' View on Best Execution Refers to Orders

Major Regulators are increasingly interested in orders when they have to check if a price is really fair with regard to the specific market situation under consideration. This point of view has been expressed since the National Market System (NMS) has been established: "*Investors must be assured that they are participants in a system which maximizes the opportunities for the most willing seller to meet the most willing buyer.*"[25] Best execution requires "*that investment firms take all sufficient steps to obtain, when executing client orders, the best possible result for their clients*".[26]

The guidelines document that both regulators recognised the availability of big data and that they use it for ample documentation showing that "investment firms

[25] SEC.gov/34-51808, p 13
[26] Esma (2024, p. 6).

Table 5.1 Individual time stamped orders

	ASK	Transaction	BID
Time	# Action Limit (Size)	#Action Limit (Size)	Size (Limit) Action #
10:30:08.35			(36) 97.53 Insertion 7
10:30:09.87	8 Insertion 97.56 (600)		
10:30:11.89	9 Insertion 97.55 (250)		
10:30:11.96			(400) 97.53 Insertion10
10:30:12.56			(300) 97.52 Insertion 21
10:30:12.56	11Accept 97.53(436)	11 97.53 (36) 7	
10:30:12.56		11 97.53 (400) 10	

Note data presented are from Deutsche Börse; Source Loistl et al (2008).

achieve the best possible results for their clients." That obligation to data collections must be translated into precise implementing provisions, to be effective. To ensure the welfare of the general public, it is essential that market participants have a thorough knowledge of both, the market's rules and their interpretation, their practical handling. Analytical knowledge is also useful for such a task. Behavioural expertise is helpful, but especially capital markets do not use the expertise of behavioural economics. Behavioural finance is needed to handle the issue of market regulation.

One major deficit can be addressed already: Both regulators on both sides of the ocean regularly talk about best "execution". This formulation gives the impression that transactions on markets are a one-sided task. But in reality, the event is two sided, a buyer must be joined by a seller. To hit the spot, a trader's order is not executed on one side but is matched on both sides with an opposite order. If an order's execution is the best possible result, it depends on both, the trader's skillfulness as well as on the market situation. The obligations of the trader to bring about a favourable market situation must be regulated. The step from "order execution" to "order matching is—as Alvin E. Roth has shown—possible, but it requires a mental change from a one-sided to a two-sided task.

5.4.2 Dynamic Cumulated Orders Book

The orders for Allianz during the time span between 10:30:08.35 and 10:30:12.56 are given. All the events are time stamped to one hundredth of a second (Table 5.1).

Comprehensive information is provided when we proceed from the individual orders to the cumulated order situation. It is similar to the situation between the frequency distribution and the cumulated probability distribution. The following figures indicate the relations.

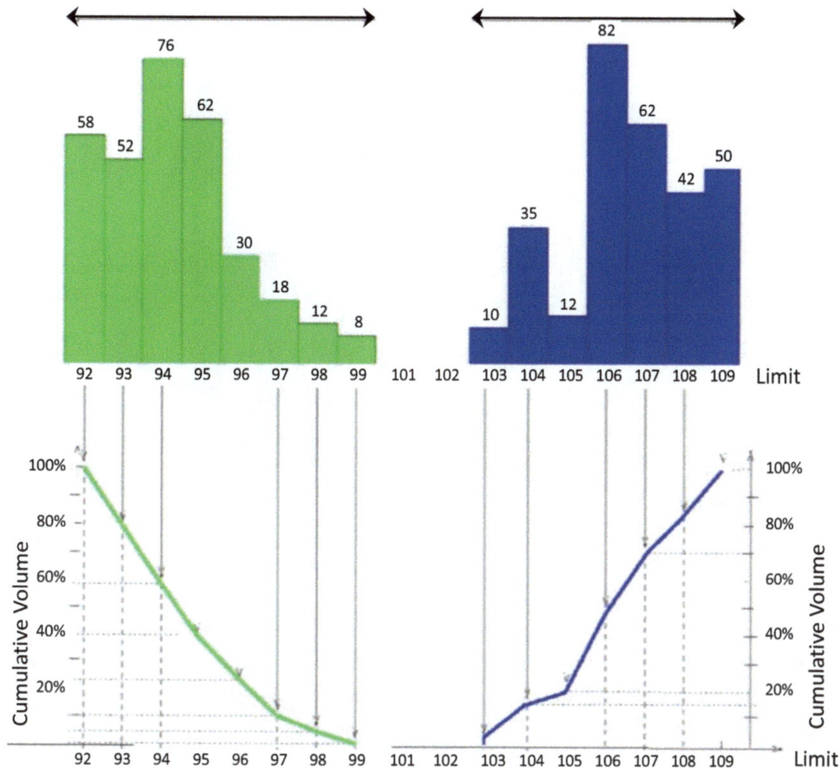

Fig. 5.2 Static cumulated buy and sell orders[27]

5.4.3 Emergence of Cumulated Orders During Trading Time

The upper graphs in Figure 5.2 refer to the individual orders, the graphs below refer to the cumulated order volume, in per cent of the entire order volume, separated for bid and ask volume. Like a cumulated probability distribution, the maximum of both graphs is at 100 per cent. Even more interesting is the figure that emerges when the shapes of both cumulated orders are drafted during the time of order activities in Figure 5.3. We use the picture of two sides of a book. It is indeed the open order book: the one side or page contains the bids, the orders to buy, the other side the asks, the orders to sell. The gap between the orders is the spread, the difference between the cheapest buy limit order and the dearest sell limit order. The gap becomes zero, when a transaction occurs. The buy and sell limit matches. Prices are generated by matching a bid with an ask. Prices are marked by a crossed circle. When a trade happens, the spread becomes zero, either

[27] See Paarsch and Hong (2006) for dealing with cumulative probabilities from discrete distributions. Charts taken from Loistl and Konstantinov (2020)

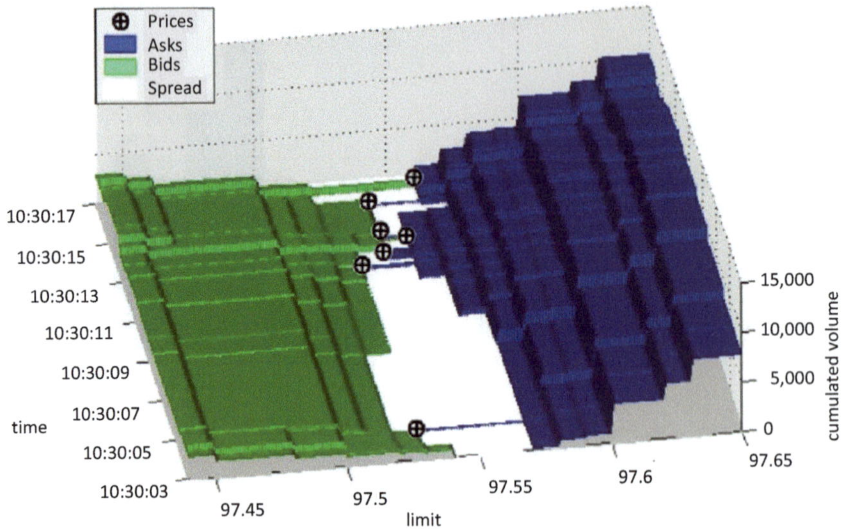

Fig. 5.3 Dynamic cumulated open order book[28]

an ask is reaching to the bid slope or a bid is reaching to the ask slope, thus indicating if the trade is buyer initiated, or seller initiated. Maybe, the initiative is due to the offer's time priority.

5.4.4 Simulated Emergence of Dynamic Order Cumulation

5.4.4.1 Orders Determined According to Random Utility Procedure

Behavioural Finance assumes that psychology is an inherent part of economics. The quantification of such factors traces back at least to Thurstone's (1927a–c), who formulated the law of comparative judgement in an attempt to formalise psychological aspects of decision-making.

Agents' decision-making is controlled by Random utility function U_{ik} for the i-th agent's action a_{ik}—see Equation (5.1):

$$U_{ik} = \Phi_{ik} + \varepsilon_{ik} \tag{5.4}$$

Many years later, McFadden developed Discrete Choice theory (see e.g. McFadden [1974], Train [2003]). It provides a reliable probabilistic framework for modelling individual decision-making behaviour. It has been applied very successfully in different fields of economics. Loistl and Landes (1989), Landes and Loistl (1992)

[28] Chart is taken from Huetl et al. (2006). See also Konstantinov (2020, p. 7).

integrated this approach into Markov Processes thus generating Doubly Stochastic Markov Processes to achieve an isomorphic modelling of capital markets' performance at the order level.

5.4.4.2 The Procedure

Firstly, the change of bid and offer sets during the course of a trading session is investigated. We intend to develop a measure for these sets of orders' dynamic changes. A first choice is the entropy figure. The entropy's history in physics and statistics is discussed in Chapter 7. In economic behavioural choice, this figure is discussed in detail by Luce (2005, p. 11). Its usefulness for selecting the most probable und useful activity has been shown by McFadden (2001). We show that this notion of taking an order is a measure of a state's transformation probability alike.

A question should be answered again: Why should we also look at the orders instead of just analysing the prices? The answer is: Orders determine prices. Not every change in orders is reflected in prices, but this change reflects a change in the market's performance. Orders are therefore a more meaningful measure of market performance than prices. Furthermore, currently valid orders reflect the real trade possibilities, not the past prices.

The simulation is based on the implementation of the isomorphic Xetra trading structure according to the catallactic model presented by Landes and Loistl (1992). The explicit model calibration is given in Huetl et al. (2006).

5.5 Identification of Order Types

5.5.1 Descriptive Statistics of Orders

In this chapter the determinants of the traders' choice for submitting different types of marketable orders are investigated. The research question under consideration is: What are the determinants of the choice of marketable orders?

For the empirical investigation we rely on the data of Frankfurt stock exchange's automated trading system Xetra. Firstly, we present general statistics about the magnitude of different order types. The following table provides descriptive statistics for four different samples, each covering six trading days, from Wednesday to Wednesday each. Insofar, description "week" in the first column is not exact, but serves as proxy description. The sample period covers the entire weekend. The data is thus designed to investigate the real "weekend effect". The headline in the table differentiates the following types of orders. Limit orders, Market orders, Iceberg orders, and Immediate or Cancel orders, described by the abbreviation MTL (Market or limit orders)[29] (Table 5.2).

[29] A comprehensive descriptive statistic of the order situation and the orders' description is provided by Prix et al. (2007, p. 721). The limit order figures in Prix et al. (2007) on p 723 for year 2005 do not match with the figures in Table 3, because it is explicitly referring to "marketable"

Table 5.2 Order types and their magnitude

Type	Limit (%)	Market (%)	Iceberg (%)	MTL (%)	Total (in 1000)	Limit (%)	Market (%)	Iceberg (%)	MTL (%)	Total (in 1000)
Dec. week 2004										
Buy	89.36	5.05	5.57	0.02	229,180.5	89.59	8.68	1.68	0.04	152.2
Sell	88.02	6.02	5.92	0.04	232,637.3	85.16	13.18	1.52	0.14	157.8
Total	88.68	5.54	5.75	0.03	461,817.8	87.33	10.98	1.60	0.09	309.9
Jan. week 2005										
Buy	88.21	5.54	6.24	0.02	299,333.6	86.36	11.72	1.86	0.06	181.3
Sell	88.54	6.16	5.27	0.03	305,900.2	84.17	14.20	1.54	0.09	191.4
Total	88.38	5.85	5.75	0.02	605,233.8	85.24	12.99	1.70	0.07	372.7
Dec. week 2006										
Buy	92.33	3.22	4.42	0.03	294,037.7	92.08	6.72	1.16	0.05	226.6
Sell	90.86	4.55	4.56	0.03	283,239.9	85.94	12.74	1.20	0.12	229.3
Total	91.61	3.87	4.49	0.03	577,277.6	88.99	9.75	1.18	0.09	456.0
Jan. week 2007										
Buy	89.62	4.48	5.84	0.06	350,916.4	88.01	10.39	1.51	0.10	263.1
Sell	89.88	5.13	4.88	0.10	363,768.0	85.20	13.52	1.15	0.13	286.6
Total	89.75	4.81	5.35	0.08	714,684.4	86.54	12.02	1.32	0.12	549.7

Limit orders represent the lion's share, both with regard to volume and number of orders. The iceberg orders differ with regard to the orders' number percentage and with regard to the volume's percentage. The higher volume's percentage figure indicates that the iceberg orders carry an above average volume. The figures are quite similar for the three different time spans. We will therefore concentrate our analysis on the period "Dec. week 2006". The results seem relevant for the other three-time samples too. We will concentrate on the investigation of market orders and limit orders. Limit orders should be differentiated with regard to the time until the order is executed. Marketable limit orders are executed at the market price, non-marketable limit orders are not. The major percentage, some 2/3 of limit orders is cancelled. A limit change is performed by order's cancellation and

orders, as indicated above. Marketable orders are those limit orders that are executed at the required limit exactly.

resubmission. Table 5.3 gives the order situation for every DAX 30 company. The reasons for the differences will be investigated in this chapter.

5.5.2 Order Types to be Investigated

In the following we will investigate the determinants of three order types: Plain Limit Orders ("L/-"), Market Orders ("M/-") and Limit Orders Immediate or Cancel ("L/I")

Table 5.3 gives the magnitude of the three different orders volumes. The lion's share is given by plain limit orders. The order type taking the second largest percentage is limit orders with the specification "immediate or cancelled". Plain market orders are of least magnitude. We will investigate the determinants of these three order types. As can be seen that for both order categories (bids and asks), the volume of the remaining orders is for most DAX companies less than one per cent.

5.5.3 The Statistical Formulas

Limit Order "L/-" versus Market Order "M/-" (L vs M):

$$\text{Market order probability } P(M/-) = \frac{exp(\Phi_i)}{1 + exp(\Phi_i)} \tag{5.5}$$

$$\text{Limit order probability } P(L/-) = 1 - P(M/-) \tag{5.6}$$

Limit Order Immediate or Cancel 'L/I' versus Market Order 'M/-' (LI vs M):

$$\text{Market order probability } P(M/-) = \frac{exp(\Phi_i)}{1 + exp(\Phi_i)} \tag{5.7}$$

$$\text{Limit order IC probability } P(L/I) = 1 - P(M/-) \tag{5.8}$$

Limit order "L/-" versus Limit order Immediate or Cancel "L/I" (L vs LI):

$$\text{Limit order IC probability } P(L/I) = \frac{exp(\Phi_i)}{1 + exp(\Phi_i)} \tag{5.9}$$

$$\text{Limit order probability } P(L/-) = 1 - P(L/I) \tag{5.10}$$

with regression part

$$\begin{aligned}\Phi_i = {} & \beta_{size} size + \beta_{relsize} relsize + \beta_{buysell} buysell + \ldots \\ & + \beta_{dbalance1min} dbalance1min\end{aligned} \tag{5.11}$$

Table 5.3 Percentage of volume executed by different order types

	Marketable Bids (%)				Marketable Asks (%)			
	L/- (%)	L/I (%)	M/- (%)	others (%)	L/- (%)	L/I (%)	M/- (%)	others (%)
Adidas	77.11	18.57	4.09	0.24	80.03	12.05	7.67	0.25
Allianz	77.03	19.59	3.18	0.20	77.32	18.17	4.19	0.32
Altana	79.22	17.70	2.89	0.19	79.80	15.81	4.35	0.04
BASF	77.76	19.18	3.00	0.06	79.34	17.13	3.47	0.06
Hypo Real Estate	73.82	21.22	4.81	0.15	83.51	10.82	5.47	0.21
Bay. Motoren Werke	81.51	15.53	2.91	0.05	84.91	11.90	3.04	0.14
Bayer	74.68	21.72	3.45	0.15	78.62	17.64	3.69	0.06
Commerzbank	79.24	15.00	5.56	0.19	82.28	12.58	4.62	0.51
Continental	75.51	20.22	4.21	0.06	74.59	21.71	3.39	0.32
DaimlerChrysler	77.00	20.51	2.39	0.10	77.95	17.73	3.99	0.33
Deutsche Bank	76.16	21.03	2.67	0.14	74.97	20.84	4.07	0.12
Deutsche Börse	83.06	14.31	2.38	0.26	79.01	15.30	4.91	0.79
Deutsche Post	81.70	13.96	3.81	0.53	79.05	16.42	3.98	0.56
Dt. Telekom	80.85	15.94	3.00	0.21	83.41	12.10	4.36	0.13
E.ON	73.27	23.30	2.64	0.79	79.95	13.28	6.44	0.33
Fresenius Med.	82.70	13.81	3.40	0.09	84.48	12.07	2.87	0.59
Henkel	84.46	13.68	1.86	0.01	81.81	14.29	3.89	0.01
Infineon Tech.	82.85	14.45	1.43	1.27	84.98	9.56	5.19	0.27
Linde	69.98	25.24	4.75	0.03	84.53	12.16	3.13	0.17
Lufthansa	81.52	14.50	3.90	0.08	81.97	11.56	5.98	0.48
MAN	75.04	21.11	3.79	0.06	78.52	17.35	3.78	0.36
Metro	84.60	11.79	3.53	0.08	77.72	17.32	4.75	0.21
Münch. Rückvers.	76.45	18.94	4.57	0.05	75.34	21.25	3.16	0.25
RWE	67.74	29.44	2.62	0.20	80.08	16.35	3.51	0.06
SAP	72.65	22.09	5.17	0.08	80.59	15.62	3.70	0.09
Deutsche Postbank	75.53	18.49	5.75	0.24	81.46	13.04	5.12	0.39
Siemens	76.03	20.53	3.36	0.08	79.06	15.71	4.95	0.28
Thyssenkrupp	81.34	13.38	4.63	0.66	84.08	8.72	6.39	0.81
TUI	80.84	13.90	4.83	0.43	81.50	12.82	5.18	0.51
Volkswagen	87.70	9.65	2.43	0.21	86.69	8.30	4.63	0.38
Min.	67.74	9.65	1.43	0.01	74.59	8.30	2.87	0.01

(continued)

Table 5.3 (continued)

	Marketable Bids (%)				Marketable Asks (%)			
	L/- (%)	L/I (%)	M/- (%)	others (%)	L/- (%)	L/I (%)	M/- (%)	others (%)
1st Qu.	75.52	14.34	2.73	0.08	78.72	12.08	3.70	0.13
Median	77.44	18.53	3.43	0.15	80.06	14.79	4.27	0.28
Mean	78.25	17.96	3.57	0.23	80.58	14.65	4.46	0.30
3rd Qu.	81.52	20.91	4.48	0.23	83.12	17.27	5.08	0.39
Max.	87.70	29.44	5.75	1.27	86.69	21.71	7.67	0.81

Period: December week 2006, January week 007
Order types: (L)imit and (M)arket Order, Order restriction (I)mmediate or cancel
Others: all other Limit and Market Orders

Given order data (e.g. "L/-" with size 17,234) and orderdata2 (e.g. "M/-" with size 2255).

Sampling such that both groups have same size = (0.9∗min(size(orderdata1) size(orderdata2)) (e.g. 2255*0.9).

Combine sampled data into one data set

10-fold cross validation

Divide data set into 10 equal sized parts: 10 data set pairs each with sizes 9/10 and 1/10. For each pair:

Estimate coefficients of binary choice model based on 9/10 of the data by maximum likelihood.

Predict the order type ("L/-" or "M/-") on the remaining 1/10 of the data set. Prediction:

$$\begin{aligned} P(''M/-'') &> 0.5 \rightarrow ''M/-'' \\ P(''M/-'') &\leq 0.5 \rightarrow ''L/-'' \end{aligned} \tag{5.12}$$

5.5.4 The Set of Explanatory Variables

See Table 5.4.

5.5.5 Descriptive Statistics: Outlier Check 0.001

See Table 5.5.

Table 5.4 Variables

Size	order size = number of stocks ordered by order
Relsize	order size divided by volume available at best offer:
buysell	Buy/Sell Flag (1 = Buy order, 0 = Sell Order)
slippage	Max. transaction price – Min. transaction price triggered by order (in Cent)
spread	best ask – best bid (in Cent)
totalspread	vwal ask – vwal bid. vwal = volume weighted limit (in Cent)
bestofferbal	volume at best ask – volume at best bid
totalbal	(total ask volume – total bid volume)/(total ask volume + total bid volume)
entropy	total entropy over the entire orderbook probabilities: bid and ask volumes divided by total (=ask + bid) volume
entropybid	entropy over the bid side of the orderbook probabilities: bid volumes divided by total bid volume
entropyask	entropy over the ask side of the orderbook probabilities: ask volumes divided by total ask volume
daytime	time of the day since 9:00 (in hours) as a fraction of 8.5 (=17:30 – 9:00) hours
ntrades1min	number of observed trades within the last minute
vola1min	price volatility for the last minute (×100)
ncancels1min	number of cancels observed within the last minute
preturn1min	(price at time s – price at time s−1) / (price at time s−1) multiplied by 10,000
dspread1min	(spread at time s – spread at time s−1) / (spread at time s−1) multiplied by 100
dentropy1min	(entropy at time s – entropy at time s−1) / (entropy at time s−1) multiplied by 100
dentropybid1min	(entropybid at time s – entropybid at time s−1) / (entropybid at time s−1) multiplied by 100
dentropyask*1*min	(entropyask at time s – entropyask at time s−1) / (entropyask at time s−1) multiplied by 100
dbalance1min	(balance at time s – balance at time s−1) / (balance at time s−1) multiplied by 100
ntrades5min	number of observed trades within the last 5 minutes
vola5min	price volatility for the last 5 minutes
ncancels5min	number of cancels observed within the last 5 minutes
preturn5min	(price at time s – price at time s−5 min) /(price at time s−5)multiplied by 10 000
dspread5min	(spread at time s – spread at time s−5) / (spread at time s−5) multiplied by 100

(continued)

Table 5.4 (continued)

dentropy5min	(entropy at time s – entropy at time s−5) / (entropy at time s−5) multiplied by 100
dentropybid5min	(entropybid at time s – entropybid at time s−5) / (entropybid at time s−5) multiplied by 100
dentrobpyask5min	(entropyask at time s – entropyask at time s−5) / (entropyask at time s−5) multiplied by 100
balance5min	(balance at time s – balance at time s−5) / (balance at time s−5) multiplied by 100

5.6 The Model's Power to Separating Orders

5.6.1 Significance of Variables' Coefficients: L/- vs L/I vs M/-

See Table 5.6.

As usual, stars indicate the coefficient's significance. The equation's overall significance has not been calculated yet.

5.6.2 The Model's Separating Power

5.6.2.1 Order Determination—Empirical Results: Outlier 0.001

See Table 5.7.

5.6.2.2 Order Determination—Empirical Results: Outlier 0.01

See Table 5.8.

5.7 Summary

5.7.1 The Model's Explanatory Capabilities

The statistics in chapter 5.6.2 reaffirm the validity of the model's analytical description. All three reported empirical results prove that the model can identify order types. The statistics have been performed by adjusting the data set differently to the magnitude of outliers. The first variant skips outliers less than 0.001 and the second variant skips outliers less than 0.01.

In both variants the capabilities to separate different order types according to the procedure described in chapter 5.5.3 are given. Three separation tasks are given:

1. Limit orders against market orders. The results are given in lines 1 and 2.
2. Limit orders "immediate or cancel" against Market orders. The results are reported in lines 3 and 4.

Table 5.5 Outliers statistics

	L/-					L/I					M/-				
	Outls	Min	Med	Mean	Max	Outls	Min	Med	Mean	Max	Outls	Min	Med	Mean	Max
size	19	0	33	54	600	7	0	38	68	507	2	0	6	19	50
relSize	38	0	7	14	1093	8	0	8	33	3490	6	0	0.1	7	625
buySell	0	0	10	5	1.0	0	0	10	6	10	0	0	10	5	1
slippage	17	0	0	2	90	3	0	0	6	100	3	0	0	3	13
nrSlippage	19	0	0	33	595	4	0	0	30	73	–	–	–	–	–
spread	19	10	30	35	160	1	10	30	39	280	3	1	4	49	18
totalSpread	38	83	129	202	687	8	83	131	206	688	6	84	135	222	676
bestOfferBalThisSide	38	−199.5	−16.1	−85	199.4	8	−199.5	−13.1	−7.5	199.3	6	−199.3	−0.4	0	199.7
balanceThisSide	38	−72.0	−0.2	−0.4	713	8	−75.9	−3.9	−38	58.2	6	69.4	25	41	693
entropyThisSide	36	20	30	29	39	8	20	30	30	39	5	2	3	29	38
entropyOtherSide	38	20	30	29	39	8	20	30	29	35	6	2	3	3	39
nTrades5Min	36	9.0	70	81.2	350	7	80	68	77	324	6	8	55	63.5	312
vola5Min	38	7	49	63	331	8	7	49	61.4	330	6	6	4.3	5.2	325
nCancels5Min	34	18	167	198.2	845	7	15	161	184.9	719	5	14	137	160.9	666
preturn5Min	38	−48.2	0	14	783	8	−46.8	0	10	742	5	−49	0	3	58
dspread5Min	36	−120	20	18	520	5	−23	1	11	360	6	−15	0	3	45
dbalance6Min	38	−393	4	5	387	8	−388	14	19	367	6	−356	0.1	0.2	37.8

Table 5.6 Significance of independent variables

	All Orders		Buy Orders		Sell Orders	
	P(L/I)	P(M/-)	P(L/I)	P(M/-)	P(L/I)	P(M/-)
(Intercept)	1.7834***	−2.4349***	0.5053	−1.8606**	5.3081***	−1.8104*
Size	0.0143**	−0.2706***	0.0159	−0.2301***	0.0121***	−0.3463***
relSize	0.0170***	−0.0071*	0.0099	−0.0064	0.0219	−0.0243***
buySell	0.0567	−0.6700***	–	–	–	–
slippage	.2699***	0.5115***	0.4139***	0.6636***	0.3292***	0.5601***
Spread	0.0449**	0.1791***	0.0498	0.1945***	0.0060	0.1472***
totalSpread	0.0038	0.0073	0.0026	−0.0158*	0,0123	0.0149*
bestOfferBalThisSide	0.0006*	0.0028***	1e-04	0.0033***	0.0010**	0.0030***
balanceThisSide	0.0063*	−0.0037	0.0104*	0.0173***	0.0161***	−0.0061
dayTime	0.3017***	−0.3050***	0.3375**	−0.2329	0.2823**	−0.0516
entropyThisSide	0.2660	0.4694**	0.9330**	0.9741**	0.2035	0.2548
entropyOtherSide	−0.9801***	0.7431***	−1.1848***	0.0197	−2.1977***	0.7045*
nTrades5Min	0.0000	−0.0054**	8e-04	−0.0070*	0.0017	−0.0055*
vola5Min	0.0022	−0.0596***	−0.0251	−0.0908***	0.0375*	−0.0099
nCancels5Min	−0.0017*	−0.0001	−0.0020	7e-04	−0.0016	−0.0017
preturn5Min	−0.0033	0.0041	0.0108*	0.0102	−0.0148***	0.0029
dspread5Min	−0.0192*	−0.0178	−0.0213	−0.0013	−0.0053	−0.0209
dbalance5Min	0.0159***	−0.0035	0.0097	0.0028	0.0078	−0.0103

Period: December week 2006

Table 5.7 Discriminating power skipping outliers 0.001

	Outliers 0.001			NumberLeft			All		Bid		Ask	
	All	Bid	Ask	All	Bid	Ask	Mean	Sd	Mean	Sd	Mean	Sd
L vs M												
1	575	277	298	18,134	9,206	8,928	71.5	3.3	70.1	5.4	71.2	3.9
2	84	39	45	2,388	946	1,442	77.7	2.8	73.0	5.0	79.3	3.1
LI vs M												
3	116	61	55	3,559	1,991	1,568	72.3	3.1	65.5	5.4	77.4	3.7
4	84	39	45	2,388	946	1,442	80.1	2.8	76.6	4.2	84.8	3.2
L vs LI												
5	575	277	298	18,134	9,206	8,928	66.8	2.6	62.4	3.8	63.8	4.5
6	116	61	55	3,559	1,991	1,568	54.1	3.1	56.0	3.6	60.5	4.6

Table 5.8 Discriminating power skipping outliers 0.01

	Outliers 0.01			NumberLeft			All		Bid		Ask	
	All	Bid	Ask	All	Bid	Ask	Mean	Sd	Mean	Sd	Mean	Sd
L vs M												
1	2,448	1,233	1,215	1,7110	8,654	8,456	71.2	3.6	70.2	5.1	73.4	4.3
2	299	128	171	2,243	893	1,350	79.7	2.9	75.6	4.3	81.4	3.3
LI vs M												
3	496	296	200	3,356	1,843	1,513	72.8	3.8	68.6	4.7	78.7	3.9
4	299	128	171	2,243	893	1,350	81.5	2.5	76.7	5.7	84.9	3.1
L vs LI												
5	2,448	1,233	1,215	17,110	8,654	8,456	65.9	2.7	63.8	3.8	64.0	4.4
6	496	296	200	3,356	1,843	1,513	51.5	2.9	56.0	3.7	61.6	4.2

3. Plain limit orders vs limit orders "immediate or cancel". The results are reported in lines 5 and 6.

The data adjustments are given in the first rows under the heading "outliers 0.001" and "numbers left", separating the data skipped for "bid" and "ask", resp. "outliers 0.01".

Let's start with the results when outliers less than 0.001 are skipped.

The first row in Table 5.7 refers to the limit orders, 575 orders are skipped, leaving 18,134 limit orders, nearly even for bids (9206) and asks (8928). The second row refers to the market order figures. In total 84 market orders are skipped due to the outlier limitation, leaving 2388 market orders, not really equally split between bids (946) and asks (1442). The figures in the next columns characterised by "mean" give the percentage figures of correctly identified order types. In total 71.5% of all limit orders are correctly classified against market orders. The figures differ slightly when separated according to bids (70.1%) and asks (71.2%).

The second row separates market orders from limit orders according to the probability procedure described in chapter 5.5.3. The separation figures are higher compared to the separation figures given in row 1. The differences are probably caused by the quite lower numbers. A further aspect may be the less varying market orders.

Rows 3 and 4 give the results when separating market orders against Limit orders "immediate or cancel". In total 116 "immediate or cancel" limit orders are skipped due to the outlier limit, leaving in total 3559 (1991 bids and 1568 asks) LI orders. The figures for market orders are the same as in row 2. The identification power is like the identification ratio of L vs M. In total, 72.3% of all LI orders are correctly classified against market orders. The hit rate varies more between bids (65.5%) and asks (77.4%) compared to the "L" results in row 1. The identification capability of M is even stronger compared to the L vs M results: 80.1% for both order categories and for the individual categories. (76.6% for bids and 84.8% for asks). The explanations for the differing identification power must be left to further investigations.

The identification capabilities of L vs LI are lower. Obviously, it is more difficult to separate plain limit orders form LI orders. But even in this case, the model's capabilities, measured by its identification power are convincing.

The results of the investigation given in Table 5.8 when outliers are skipped less than 0.01 are like the outlier 0.001 results. As the figures in rows under heading outliers 0.01 show, more data is skipped. But this adjustment of data did not have a major impact on the results.

5.7.2 Order Identification Capabilities

See Table 5.9.

Table 5.9 Discriminating power based on stratified 10-fold cross validation

	Outliers 0.001			Cases Left			All		Bid		Ask	
	All	Bid	Ask	All	Bid	Ask	Mean	Sd	Mean	Sd	Mean	Sd
L vs M												
1	575	277	298	18,134	9,206	8,928	**71.5**	3.3	**70.1**	5.4	**71.2**	3.9
2	84	39	45	2,388	946	1,442	**77.7**	2.8	**73.0**	5.0	**79.3**	3.1
LI vs M												
3	116	61	55	3,559	1,991	1,568	**72.3**	3.1	**65.5**	5.4	**77.4**	3.7
4	84	39	45	2,388	946	1,442	**80.1**	2.8	**76.6**	4.2	**84.8**	3.2
L vs LI												
5	575	277	298	18,134	9,206	8,928	**66.8**	2.6	**62.4**	3.8	**63.8**	4.5
6	116	61	55	3,559	1,991	1,568	**54.1**	3.1	**56.0**	3.6	**60.5**	4.6

Decision Frame Modelling

6

Abstract

This chapter shows, how DSMP can be applied in interactive decision-making models. The probability to take an action is derived from discrete choice and derives Markov state transition probabilities. At an open order book traders observe and process each change of the decision frame and adjust their decision accordingly. Thus the true interaction process can be pictured step by step. The model' s realistic character will be shown by a comparison of Xetra's rules and regs with DSMP' rules and regs, and comparing NASDAQ and its DSMP version alike.

Keywords

Frame of microstructure to reflect interactions • Formal connection of action's probability with stat's transition probability • Comparison if true rules and regs with model's rules and regs • Both for Frankfurt und Nasdaq trading venue

This chapter presents a comprehensive framework for modelling agent-based interactions on financial markets, integrating micro-level decision-making processes with market-level dynamics. The market's microstructure is modelled as a high-dimensional Markov process with discrete state space and continuous time space. The model's innovation has to be mentioned here. The Markov transition probabilities are available by integrating McFadden's discrete choice concept into the Markov process. The probability of taking an action according discrete choice changes the relevant state space accordingly, thus providing a frames' transition probability. We implement a "Doubly Stochastic Markov Process" (DSMP) to capture endogenous, contextual, and correlated effects in agents' behaviours. The model addresses how decisions emerge from individual utility evaluations, how these decisions affect and are affected by market states, and how price formation results from the interaction of buy and sell orders under stock exchange rules such as price-time priority. Central

O. Loistl et al., *Screen Based Trading and Open Order Book*, New Economic Windows,
https://doi.org/10.1007/978-3-031-99052-6_6

to the approach is the translation of discrete choice probabilities into stochastic state transitions, allowing the timing and coordination of actions to be endogenously modelled. The DSMP circumvents the traditional Markov assumption of fixed transition probabilities by dynamically linking action utilities to reaction rates. By embedding market regulations into the transition structure, we achieve an isomorphic mapping between real-world trading systems—such as Xetra or Nasdaq—and the model. This enables not only realistic simulations of market behaviour but also a solid foundation for deriving robust policy insights. The approach highlights the importance of structured information processing, asynchronous timing, and adaptive behaviour in economic decision-making.

6.1 Interactions of Agents on Markets

6.1.1 Integrating the Interaction Component into the Individual Decision Model

Brock and Durlauf investigate social interactions modelling without mediation by markets.[1] As agents interact by their chosen actions,[2] such interactions can be observed on markets. We therefore intend to model the details of market interactions. We start with a bottom-up approach, i.e. by modelling the interactions at the microlevel of a stock exchange and implementing the rules and regulations of the stock exchanges under consideration.

Brock and Durlauf address interactions. They also apply McFadden's (1974) discrete choice approach.[3] We try to implement the "*view of economic interactions mediated by networks*"[4] at an operational level with the help of DSMP. The network is provided by the Markov Processes' high dimensional state space representing entire set of possible actions and interactions. They are described by the individual states' transitions. The approach enables to model the three hypotheses postulated by Manski[5]: endogenous interactions, contextual interactions and correlated effects in a consistent manner. We start with the modelling of the possible actions that decision makers can take and proceed with modelling interactions by means of a doubly stochastic process.

[1] Brock and Durlauf (2001, p. 235).
[2] Manski (2000, p. 125).
[3] Brock and Durlauf (2001, p. 237).
[4] Axtell (2007, p. 110).
[5] Manski (2000, p. 127).

6.1.2 The Issue of Coordinating Actions and Processing Information

The issue is to settle the question who needs which data set for what sort of decision to make. Complex event stream processing provides the basic concept to handle the data processing issue to coordinate activities. The first step is to realise that not all the data is needed for making any decision. It is important to extract the relevant data. The aggregation embodies not a pure summation of all the data. It is important to have a hierarchical structure of the data. Processing the data to coordinating the agents' activities does not necessarily lead to a complete atomised structure of the economy. Structuring the data adequately is certainly a huge challenge to modelling economic decision processes and to develop adequate, i.e. reliable economic policy instruments based on the real and therefore reliable behaviour of individuals. See the Discussion of IIA in chapter 4.3.

Human actions imply choices between feasible alternatives on markets. They are given by the submission of orders or the acceptance of orders already placed at the marketplace.

Prices are generated whenever an order to sell matches an order to buy regarding the price limit and the quantity to transact. Once the orders are submitted to the market, the generation of prices is a mere or simple calculation according to the matching rules. Price time priority seems to be the most popular rule. The major difficulty therefore lies in modelling the forces that govern/control/generate orders and motivated their revision due to changes in the market's state of nature.

6.2 Explicit Decision Frame[6]

Formally, we assume the stock market to be a time homogenous conservative Markov process $(Z_t)_{t \geq 0}$ in continuous time with values in the discrete countable set Z, the state space. The state vector $z \in Z$, called the market state, is a high-dimensional vector of variables capturing the information attached to the current market status including also variables bearing relevant information of the past[7]: The explicit set of variables might be adjusted to the specific market constellation and to the specific issue to be investigated.

The state vector z is defined as:

$$z = \left(p, p^{of} q^{of}, m, p^{tr}, d^{tr}, x, y, \hat{p}, \hat{p}^{ext}, f_{Synax}\right) \in Z \tag{6.1}$$

$$Z = R_+^J \times R_+^{I \times J} \times Z_+^{I \times J} \times Z^J \times Z^J \times Z^J \times Z_+^{I \times J} R_+^I \times R_+^{I \times J} \times R_+^{I \times J} \times R_+ \tag{6.2}$$

[6] The explicit modelling of the decision scenario is given in chapter 5.3.

[7] A description of the variables is given in Landes and Loistl (1992, p. 212) and Loistl et al. (2004, p. 331).

$\boldsymbol{Z}$ denotes the set of integers, $\boldsymbol{N}$ the set of positive integers, $\boldsymbol{Z}_+$ the set of non-negative integers, $\boldsymbol{R}$ the set of real numbers and $\boldsymbol{R}_+$ the set of non-negative real numbers.

z, which comprises the multi-stock-multi-trader scenario described in this document, entails the following set of vectors, respectively matrices of market data:

$p = (p_j)_{j \in J} \in R_+^J$	p_j = current price of share j
$p^{of} = \left(p_{ij}^{of}\right)_{i \in I, j \in J} \in R_+^{I \times J}$	p_{ij}^{of} = limit of a valid share j offer of trader i
$q^{of} = \left(q_{ij}^{of}\right)_{i \in I, j \in J} \in Z^{I \times J}$	q_{ij}^{of} = quantity of a valid share j offer of trader i
$m = (m_j)_{j \in J} \in Z^J$	m_j = market power of share j
$P^T = \left(P_j^T\right)_{j \in J} \in Z^J$	P_j^T = price trend of share j
$\Delta^T = \left(\Delta_j^T\right)_{j \in J} \in Z^J$	Δ_j^T = counter—trend of share j
$x = (x_{ij})_{i \in I, j \in J} \in Z_+^{I \times J}$	x_{ij} = number of share j held by trader i
$y = (y_i)_{i \in I} \in R_+^I$	y_i = amount of cash (invested in bonds) held by trader i
$\hat{p} = (\hat{p}_{ij})_{i \in I, j \in J} \in R_+^{I \times J}$	$\hat{p}_{ij}$ = intrinsic value estimate of trader i for share j after adjustments during the trading session
$\hat{p}^{ext} = \left(\hat{p}_{ij}^{ext}\right)_{i \in I, j \in J} \in R_+^{I \times J}$	$\hat{p}_{ij}^{ext}$ = intrinsic value estimate of trader i for share j at the start of the trading session
$f_{synax} = (f_{synax}) \in R_+$	f_{synax} = futures quotation; future based on given stock index The "SYNAX" futures quotation is calculated as: $P_{synax} = \sum_j \frac{1}{numberofstocks} p_j$

All variables are described in detail in Loistl et al. (2004).[8] This basic structure refers to the philosophy of fundamental value traders. The empirical investigation reported in chapter 4 has been adjusted to implement the now available tick by tick data. But the description of the core DSMP feature in this chapter is valid for all specifications of the utility function given in (6.3). The basic DSMP relation is given in (6.7) and valid for any specification of $\phi(a_{ijk})$.

[8] Loistl et al. (2004, p. 331).

6.3 Markov State Transition Probabilities Derived From an Action's Discrete Choice Utility: The DSMP Feature

Since the transition probabilities determine the realisation of activities, we can identify the acting agent as the cause of the change in the respective capital market state. Moreover, it can be shown that the waiting time $T(z)$ in a certain state z is exponentially distributed.[9]

Given the market's state of nature z and assuming the logit approach,[10] the probability for selecting an action $a_{ijk'}$ is given by:

$$P(a_{ijk'}|A_{ijk}) = \frac{e^{\Phi(a_{ijk',z})}}{\sum_{a_{ijk}\in A_{ijk}} e^{\Phi(a_{ijk,z})}} \tag{6.3}$$

The probability of selecting action $a_{ijk'}$ is proportional to the deterministic part $\Phi(a_{ijk',z})$ of the action's utility.[11] Starting from the state z, the probability $P(z, z')$ that the next state will be z' is proportional to the transition probability:

$$P(z, z') = \frac{\lambda(z, z')}{\sum_{z^*} \lambda(z, z^*)} \tag{6.4}$$

The Markov process transition probability $\lambda(z, z')$ therefore is controlled by the probability of executing action $a_{ijk'}$, that generates the factual transition from state z to state z'. This connection justifies the term "**Doubly Stochastic Markov Process**", **DSMP** for short.[12] The probability of executing action $a_{ijk'}$ can be formulated as follows:

$$P(a_{ijk'}\text{is the next action to be executed}) = \frac{\lambda_{a_{ijk'}}}{\sum_{a_{ijk}\in A_{ijk}} \lambda_{a_{ijj}}} \tag{6.5}$$

The probability, that the next action to be carried out is $a_{ijk'}$ is given by the ratio between the action's probability of $a_{ijk'}$ to the sum of all the actions' probabilities of all activities $_{ijk}$ defined in the current market state. The expected transition time of an action will be:

$$\frac{1}{\lambda(z, z'(a_{ijk'}))} \tag{6.6}$$

---

[9] See Feller (1968, p. 326) and also Breiman (1969, p. 211).

[10] Train (2003, p. 38) gives a comprehensive description of the logit model.

[11] See Landes and Loistl (1992, p. 214).

[12] We follow the analogy to creating doubly stochastic Poisson processes. See FN 32 in chapter 2

The basic principle of our model can be specified more generally. The greater the utility, the shorter the reaction time and the higher the probability that this action will be realised. The stochastic selection behaviour regarding the set of alternatives is discussed below. Table 6.1 helps illustrate the choice principle, captures the relationship between action's utility, transition probability and reaction time.

To describe the various relationships, a given point in time, t, will again be assumed. The following decision situations are of particular interest[13]:

- Decision behaviour of an agent i regarding a single activity a_{ijk}
- Decision behaviour of an agent i regarding the set of alternatives A_{ij}
- Decision behaviour of an agent i regarding the set of alternatives A_i
- Decision behaviour of the market regarding the set A

In the first row of Table 6.1, the columns are numbered from left to right. Columns 4 to 7 deal with the agents' individual activities: to every agent i a specific set of action alternatives is feasible for a specific share j. These alternatives are buy or sell actions. The specific set of feasible actions depends on the market under consideration and the specific question investigated. When investigating the probabilities to submit specified orders, the set of alternative actions will be different. In the table given above, the individual actions are entered in column 4 with the notation a_{ijk}. Column 5 gives the preference values $\phi(a_{ijk})$ of the action a_{ijk}, while column 6 gives the relevant transition rates $\lambda_{a_{ijk}} = We^{\phi(a_{ijk})}$. The appropriate reaction time $t_{a_{ijk}}$ is obtained based on the transition rate (reaction rate). These times are listed in column 7. The reaction time $t_{a_{ijk}}$ is the realisation of an exponentially distributed random variable with the parameter $\lambda_{a_{ijk}}$.

Columns 8, 9 and 10 describe the selection problem regarding the set of actions in columns 1, 2 and 3: The sets of actions A_{ij}, $i = 1 \ldots N, j = 1 \ldots M$. are given in column 3. The set of actions A_{ij} comprises the individual actions of an agent for a share j. The selection of an action from A_{ij} is subject to the shortest reaction time of all actions from A_{ij}. The minimum reaction times $t_{A_{ij}}^{min}$, $i = 1 \ldots N, j = 1 \ldots M$ are determined in column 8.

The sets of actions A_i, $i = 1 \ldots N$ are given in column 2. The set of actions A_i comprises all actions of an agent i for all shares j, $j = 1 \ldots M$. This is given by the union $A_i = A_{i1} \cup A_{i2} \ldots \cup A_{iN}$. The choice of an action from A_i is again subject to the shortest reaction time of all actions from A_i. The relevant minimum reaction times $t_{A_i}^{min}$, $i = 1 \ldots N$ are given in column 9.

The sets of actions A_i of all agents i, $i = 1 \ldots N$ are summarised in column 1 by uniting them to form a total alternative amount $A = A_1 \cup A_2 \ldots \cup A_N$. Column 10 gives the minimum reaction time t_A^{min} for all actions from A. The action with which the minimum is reached will be performed next. In this way, only one action can take place at a time. For details see Landes and Loistl (1992).

[13] The following description is adapted from Loistl et al. (2001, p. 275).

Table 6.1 Reaction rates and reaction times

1	2	3	4	5	6	7	8	9	10
A	A_i	A_{ij}	a_{ijk}	$\Phi_i(a_{ijk})$	$\lambda_{a_{ijk}} = We^{\Phi_i(a_{ijk})}$	$t_{a_{ijk}}$	$t^{min}_{A_{ij}}$	$t^{min}_{A_i}$	t^{min}_A
			a_{111}	$\Phi_i(a_{111})$	$\lambda_{a_{111}}$	$t_{a_{111}}$			
		A_{11}	a_{112}	$\Phi_i(a_{112})$	$\lambda_{a_{112}}$	$t_{a_{112}}$			
			$\vdots$	$\vdots$	$\vdots$		$t^{min}_{A_{11}}$		
			a_{121}	$\Phi_i(a_{121})$	$\lambda_{a_{121}}$	$t_{a_{121}}$			
	A_1	A_{12}	a_{122}	$\Phi_i(a_{122})$	$\lambda_{a_{122}}$	$t_{a_{122}}$			
			$\vdots$	$\vdots$	$\vdots$	$\vdots$	$t^{min}_{A_{12}}$		
		$\vdots$	$\vdots$	$\vdots$	$\vdots$	$\vdots$	$\vdots$		
		$\vdots$	$\vdots$	$\vdots$	$\vdots$	$\vdots$	$\vdots$		
			a_{1M1}	$\Phi_i(a_{1M1})$	$\lambda_{a_{1M1}}$	$t_{a_{1M1}}$			
		A_{1M}	a_{1M2}	$\Phi_i(a_{1M2})$	$\lambda_{a_{1M2}}$	$t_{a_{1M2}}$			
			$\vdots$	$\vdots$	$\vdots$	$\vdots$	$t^{min}_{A_{1M}}$	$t^{min}_{A_1}$	
	$\vdots$	$\vdots$	$\vdots$	$\vdots$	$\vdots$		$\vdots$	$\vdots$	
A	$\vdots$	$\vdots$	$\vdots$	$\vdots$	$\vdots$		$\vdots$	$\vdots$	
			a_{N11}	$\Phi_i(a_{N11})$	$\lambda_{a_{N11}}$	$t_{a_{N11}}$			
		A_{N1}	a_{N12}	$\Phi_i(a_{N12})$	$\lambda_{a_{N12}}$	$t_{a_{N12}}$			
			$\vdots$	$\vdots$	$\vdots$		$t^{min}_{A_{N1}}$		
			a_{N21}	$\Phi_i(a_{N21})$	$\lambda_{a_{N21}}$	$t_{a_{N21}}$			
	A_N	A_{N2}	a_{N22}	$\Phi_i(a_{N22})$	$\lambda_{a_{N22}}$	$t_{a_{N22}}$			
			$\vdots$	$\vdots$	$\vdots$		$t^{min}_{A_{N2}}$		
		$\vdots$	$\vdots$	$\vdots$	$\vdots$		$\vdots$		
		$\vdots$	$\vdots$	$\vdots$	$\vdots$		$\vdots$		
			a_{NM1}	$\Phi_i(a_{NM1})$	$\lambda_{a_{NM1}}$	$t_{a_{NM1}}$			
		A_{NM}	a_{NM2}	$\Phi_i(a_{NM2})$	$\lambda_{a_{NM2}}$	$t_{a_{NM2}}$			
			$\vdots$	$\vdots$	$\vdots$	$\vdots$	$t^{min}_{A_{NM}}$	$t^{min}_{A_N}$	t^{min}_A

The following relation links the logit approach and the stochastic process:

$$\lambda\left(z, z'\left(a_{ijk'}\right)\right) = W \cdot e^{\Phi\left(a_{ijk',z}\right)} \tag{6.7}$$

This fundamental connection is possible since both approaches have the same structure. The probability of selecting action a_{ijk} is (assuming the logit model), proportional to $e^{\phi\left(a_{ijk',z}\right)}$. Landes and Loistl (1992)[14] break down the whole transition probabilities into single components determined by behavioural attitudes. Since the transition probabilities control the realisation of activities, we can thus integrate the acting agents into the factors that cause a change in the natural states of the capital markets. Furthermore, it can be shown that the waiting time $T(z)$ for which the continuous-time and time-homogeneous Markov process remains in state z, is exponentially distributed with the state-dependent parameter.[15] Table 6.1 shows the transition probabilities in row 6, which are determined by the actions' utilities. Row 7 shows the waiting time of the Markov process that remains in the considered state, calculated by the parameter of the exponential distribution for each feasible action. In rows 8–10 the actions characterised by the minimal waiting times are computed: In row 8 the minimal waiting time among the actions feasible for an agent and a stock, in row 9 an agent's overall minimal waiting time and in row 10, the overall minimal waiting time action is determined. This action is realised and the market's state of nature changed accordingly. This procedure enables the time spans' endogenous and asynchronous modelling between two events, e.g. the submission of an order. The importance of timing specification has recently been affirmed.[16] Furthermore, under the assumption that the transition probability for the transition from state z to state y at any time exists, it can be shown that the transition probabilities can be decomposed component by component. Consequently, the process has instantaneously independent transition components.[17] The DSMP's IIA property follows from this decomposition principle:

The action's probability $P(z, z')$ is proportional to the state's transition probability $\lambda\left(z, z'\left(a_{ijk'}\right)\right)$.

The following basic relationship between the utility of an action and the waiting time until the action is carried out can be proved. The greater the utility of an action, the faster the reaction of the trader and the shorter the expected reaction time of the trader to carry out this action.[18]

The specification of the transition probabilities of a Markov process with continuous time and discrete state space is generally achieved by a system of differential

[14] Landes and Loistl (1992, p. 227).
[15] Feller I (1968, p. 326), Breiman (1969, p. 211), and Landes et al. (1989, p. 71).
[16] ESMA (2024, p. 222).
[17] Landes et al. (1989, p. 106).
[18] Loistl et al. (2001, p. 279) and Landes and Loistl (1992, p. 223).

equations. The evolution of the market state z is represented by the time evolution of the probability function of z, $P_t(z)$, which obeys the so-called master equation[19]:

$$\frac{dP_t(z)}{dt} = \sum_{z' \neq z} \lambda(z, z') \cdot P_t(z') - \sum_{z' \neq z} \lambda(z', z) \cdot P_t(z) \tag{6.8}$$

The master equation is one of the displacement equations that are usually used to describe dynamic systems.[20] To draw up the master equation, all transition rates in the process must be given. The approach can take the specific rules and regulations of the stock market under consideration into account. For example, an isomorphic modelling of the stock markets' microstructure is explained in chapter 6.5.

We do not intend to solve the master equation analytically (see the next chapter 6.4). The relation between the master equation, Itô and Stratonovich integration conditions is discussed in detail in van Kampen (2007).[21]

6.4 DSMP Circumvents Markov's Principle of Constant Transition Probabilities

In principle, Markov processes have constant transition probabilities. Our model circumvents this condition by the integration of discrete choice into the Markov process constructing DSMP. For the first moment, it is an incompatible combination of conflicting attributes. But the combination works: Firstly, calculate the logit probability of an action that generates the change of a specific state of nature. Secondly, borrow the probability of that action—that changes the state of nature under consideration—for the Markov probability of that state's change.

[19] Landes and Loistl (1992, p. 215).

[20] Haken (1983a, p. 80) and Van Kampen (2007, p. 96).

[21] Van Kampen (2007, p. 232), see also Haken (1983b, p. 143). The positioning of the weighting points makes the difference: Ito proposes weighting the argument at the beginning of the interval, Stratonowitch proposes weighting by averaging the arguments at the beginning and the end of the interval. Ito's "feature is very useful when making mathematical transformations. On the other hand, it has turned out that in many applications this choice (i.e. Itô's formula) does not represent the actual process well." Haken (1983b, p. 145).

As Table 6.1 specifies, this change of the state of nature requires an update of any trader's evaluation of his own activities. This assumption is in accordance with the real behaviour of traders. Whenever a trader observes a change in an order on the market, this new information is used to check whether the traders' own order backlog needs to be adjusted. Traders do not wait until the prices change. They adjust their orders as soon as information about an event, including the modification of an order, is disclosed on the exchange.[22] Modelling this adaptive behaviour makes it possible to model the emergence of markets. The adaptation of prices is an ambiguous event. Watching prices mixes the behaviour of buyers and sellers. And above all: it is a waste of time to wait until prices adjust to the new information. Time is very costly at exchanges.

6.5 Isomorphic Modelling of Real Trading Venues

In the following Tables 6.2 and 6.3, the modelled feature is compared with the real situation on the stock exchange under consideration. The comparison refers to the situation in the 1990s. When analysing the current situation, the structures of the models may need to be adapted to reflect developments in the meantime.[23] The main purpose of this comparison is to illustrate the capabilities of the approach and to confirm the isomorphic modelling of the stock exchange under consideration. Of course, the modelling of each market may require adjustments in detail, but certainly without a revision of the basic structure of DSMP.

[22] See Kopp, Loistl et al. (2008).

[23] Loistl et al. (2002, p. 205). The results' details will not be reported. The simulation affirmed the relevance for real situations: Nasdaq's operating efficiency of SOES has been confirmed by the simulation results and Xetra's advantage regarding medium and block size orders. The simulation results confirmed problems for other trading sections. These results explain Nasdaq's efforts to implement Super Montage and Deutsche Börse's efforts to improve trading conditions for retail investors. See Loistl et al. (2002, p. 215).

Table 6.2 DSMP Xetra Modelling

Xetra Rules & Regulations	DSMP Xetra Modelling
Type of Market Maker	
One type of market maker, a so-called designated sponsor. The designated sponsor's performance is assessed by the stock exchange. The performance rating code created is published quarterly and is part of a remuneration scheme	One type of market maker, a designated sponsor. The designated sponsor statistics are used to create a rating code
Alternative Trading Systems (ATS)	
No ATS are connected into the trading platform	No ATS
Market Access	
All market participants have equal non-discriminatory access	One access level for all traders
Tick Size	
Tick size for all stocks is one cent	Tick size for all stocks is one cent
Market Participants and Stocks Tradable	
Over 70 designated sponsor and more than 5,500 different stocks, potentially millions of investors	Both the number of designated sponsors and the number of stocks and investors is limited. These limits are imposed by the capacity of the computers the simulation will run on, and reasonably short simulation run times. The key aspect is that KapSyn investors may have different behavioural attitudes, the number of investors within a group with the same attitudes is not subject to any reasonable limitation
Trading System Characteristics	
Continuous trading in connection with an opening auction, none, one, or several intraday auctions, and a closing auction. For each trading segment the trading phase is defined, market participants are informed in an auction plan	Trading starts with an opening auction, followed by continuous trading. Continuous trading might be interrupted by intraday auctions. At the end of continuous trading, a closing auction is initiated. The number of auctions is a parameter which can be set prior to starting the simulation
Market Transparency	
During continuous trading the order book is open, i.e. all price limits and order volumes are displayed. In auctions, by contrast, the order book remains partially closed. Market participants obtain only the best bid and ask quotes	For continuous trading either an open or a closed order book can be chosen by setting a corresponding parameter prior to starting the simulation. In auctions only the best bid and ask limits are visible

Table 6.3 Nasdaq Modelling

Nasdaq Rules & Regulations	DSMP Nasdaq Modelling
Type of Market Maker	
Numerous different investment firms with different types of market makers (Retail, Wholesale, …)	One type of market maker for regular market making and one market maker representing the ATS, no difference between wholesale and retail
Alternative Trading Systems (ATS)	
More than ten different ATS	One ATS
Market Access	
Three different access levels (Level 1: trading and all quotes, Level 2: all quotes, Level 3: only the best quotes)	Only two levels (Level 1: trading and all quotes, Level 2: all quotes).
Tick Size	
On April 9, 2001, the Nasdaq stock market switched to a decimal increment, i.e. reduced tick size to one cent.	Tick size for all stocks can be fixed at the range between \$1 and \$0.001, this is a parameter which can be changed prior to starting the simulation.
Market Participants and Stocks Tradable	
Over 6,000 market maker and more than 6,000 different stocks, potentially millions of investors	Both the number of market makers and the number of stocks and investors is limited. These limits are imposed by the capacity of the computers the simulation will run on, and reasonably short simulation run times. The key aspect is that KapSyn investors may have different behavioural attitudes, the number of investors within a group with the same attitudes is not subject to any reasonable limitation
Trading System Characteristics	
Different trading systems such as SOES, ACES and SelectNet, negotiations between investors and market makers over the phone	The information exchange resembles SelectNet, orders below 1,000 shares are immediately executed (emulating SOES), no SOES or time lag resulting from phone negotiations

Entropy and Economic Efficiency 7

Abstract

A big role becomes entropy in decision-making according Suppes' and Luce' approach. In analogy the Bose Einstein hypothesis we derive an operational definition of an efficient market by means of entropy: Nobody has an incentive for acting to improve his/her position. The market shows the highest entropy figure.

Keyword

Short explanation of entropy's different meaning • Entropy and market's operational definition of efficiency

This chapter explores the concept of entropy as a unifying measure of uncertainty, with applications spanning thermodynamics, information theory, and economics. Building on the work of Shannon and Jaynes, it introduces entropy as a tool for modelling decision-making and market behaviour under limited information. By defining new metrics—Activity Efficiency (AEI) and Information Efficiency of Markets (IEM)—the chapter offers a novel way to understand how information shapes economic actions and market equilibrium. The term entropy underwent a further change in meaning with the issue of "high dimensional probability", hdp for short. For the innovative use of the term "entropy" in connection with this topic see chapters 7.6 and 8.2. In chapter 7.1, we discuss entropy's development from physics till information theory and its innovative application to handle well known economic issues. In the next chapter, we will sketch the application of the recently developed tools of high dimensional probability to tackle open economic problems. Furthermore, we discuss hdp's capabilties to analyse economic issues that have

It is partly an updated and extended version of Loistl and Veverka (2005).

O. Loistl et al., *Screen Based Trading and Open Order Book*, New Economic Windows,
https://doi.org/10.1007/978-3-031-99052-6_7

to be tackled when giving up the equilibrium paradigm, like self organisation, resilience and learning.

7.1 Meanings of Entropy

7.1.1 Entropy in Physics

The term entropy is used in several disciplines and seems to have quite different meanings at the first glance. However, the use of the same term in different disciplines is based on analogies. Just to drop the milestones: Historically, the term entropy was introduced in physics by Clausius to have a measure of mechanical thermodynamics (see Petz 2001, p. 83). Boltzmann developed the famous formula. Shannon found the formula's analogy with information entailed in an event. Jaynes reversed the question and asked which probability distribution fits the information entailed in the data under consideration. He brought forward the issue of maximal entropy. The distribution that is related to the data under consideration and provides the maximum entropy that best fits the data must be selected. Luce provides a switch to the probabilistic basis.

Maxwell and Tait[1] favoured a probabilistic interpretation of thermodynamic order. This idea was brought forward by Poincaré—after Tait's monitoring[2]—and Boltzmann. Poincaré approached the problem by first reflecting on the concept of probability: as early as 1896 he gave a lecture on the "nature of probability", a second edition was published in 1912. His doubts about probability are still relevant today: "*How shall we know that two possible cases are equally probable?*".[3] Thurstone (1927) proposed the idea of using a comparison of two events to estimate probability. R. Duncan Luce[4] took up this idea and proposed "independence from irrelevant alternatives". Daniel McFadden (2000) built on this idea and developed the efficiently applicable "random utility" concept. See Chapter 5 and 6. Poincaré, the "impatient genius",[5] thought about "probability" all the time.[6] Boltzmann, without further questioning the meaning of "probability" made use of the frequentist concept.[7] He derived a formula for entropy by investigating the "permutabilities of all possible state distributions"[8] of molecules. We refer to the

[1] See Gray (2013, p. 514).
[2] Mazliak (2013) report in more details that exchange of arguments, p. 34.
[3] Poincaré (1899), reported and translated by Mazliak, p. 37.
[4] Luce (2005, p. 27).
[5] Verhulst (2012). Biography's title.
[6] See Del Vecchio (2016).
[7] Boltzmann (1877), throughout the entire paper and explicit p. 149. Klir (2006, p. 91) reports several entropy formulas and discusses their interpretations.
[8] Boltzmann (1877, p. 148).

derivation provided by Sommerfeld.[9] Using Sterling's formula to convert permutations in logarithms and substitute $n_i! \sim \log n_i! = n_i \bullet (\log n_{i-1})$, then get the basic, well known, formula for entropy.

$$\log w = const - \sum n_i \log n_i \tag{7.1}$$

This is not exactly the formula that Boltzmann achieved, but this common notation is explained by Sommerfeld,[10] for example. Petz (2001, p. 2), gives a short but consistent derivation of entropy formulas used in different disciplines. It is a scientific coincidence that both Boltzmann and Poincaré each taught a student who were both pioneers in the evaluation of mathematical option pricing methods: Vinzenz Bronzin and Louis Bachelier. Bronzin visited Boltzmann's lectures in Vienna, then lived in Trieste. His "Theorie der Prämiengeschäfte" (1908) applied a frequentist probability concept like that Boltzmann applied to derive the entropy formula. Louis Bachelier was Poincaré's doctoral student. He had after some other positions finally a chair at the university of Besancon. But as far as we know, neither Bachelier nor Bronzin was active in financial business. Both published books on mathematics and economics that also touched on issues related to the application of probability, but neither of them referred to the techniques of stochastic processes.

The consequences of maximum entropy in nuclear physics, which is attained at 0° Kelvin, were derived by Bose and Einstein as early as 1925 through theoretical considerations (see Anglin and Ketterle (2002, p. 211). Ketterle (2002) and others were awarded the Nobel Prize in Physics in 2001 for the empirical proof of this theoretically derived situation, known as Bose–Einstein condensation.

7.1.2 Entropy in Information Theory

Von Neumann (1932/1968, p. 191) also did a lot of mathematical work in the field of quantum physics and entropy. This experience gave rise to the second important meaning of entropy: Shannon was looking for a suitable term when he was concerned with calculating the information capacity of a coding system. Von Neumann suggested the term entropy because, firstly, it is the same formula and, secondly, nobody knows exactly what entropy means in physics, as Shannon describes von Neumann's reasoning (see Tribus and McIrvine [1971], cited in Petz [2001, p. 90]). Shannon (1948) had many degrees of freedom in the interpretation of his formula by choosing the term entropy.

---

[9] Sommerfeld (1952, p. 206).

[10] Sommerfeld (1952, p. 206).

Shannon (1948) defined the entropy of a discrete probability distribution with probabilities $p_1, \ldots, p_k$ attached to the discrete events as

$$H(p_1, p_2, \ldots, p_k) = -\sum_{i=1}^{k} p_i \log p_i \tag{7.2}$$

A special case of interest is the uniform distribution where $p_i = \frac{1}{k} \forall i$; in this case, through a classical theorem of Shannon, we know that $H(p_1, p_2, \ldots, p_k)$ attains its maximum value $\log k$ (see Shastri and Govil 2001, p. 73).

7.1.3 Entropy and Statistics

The next big step was taken by Jaynes (1957). He connected entropy to statistics and introduced the concept of (constrained) maximum entropy. Conrad (2004) points out that "*[t]he principle of maximum entropy leads to the selection of a probability distribution which is consistent with our knowledge […]*" (p. 2). The higher the entropy of a probability distribution, the higher the risk associated with this distribution with regard to a possible surprise compared to the beliefs. We illustrate this relation by means of the uniform distribution and discrete events. The implications of Jaynes' (1957) maximum entropy with restrictions (see also Conrad 2004) for modelling the microstructure of capital markets deserve further investigation (see Chapter 8).

7.1.4 Entropy of Selected Probability Distributions

The uniform distribution was proposed by Laplace in case of complete ignorance, i.e. if there is no reason to do otherwise. As Conrad (2004) states: "*If we apply Laplace's principle and find through experiment that the outcomes do not fall out uniformly, then there is information about the situation which we did not consider. Usually, this new information can be described as some type of constraint. How do we select a suitable probability distribution considering our new knowledge, which is no longer a state of complete ignorance? There is an extension of the principle of insufficient reason which tells us what to do. It is the principle of maximum entropy*" (p. 1).

Even when we work with discrete probabilities for discrete choices, we provide results that relate to continuous probability distributions, which points to the usefulness of entropy as a measure of risk[11]:

1. The unique probability distribution maximising entropy (in Shannon's sense) is the uniform distribution. In the case of discrete probabilities, the unique

[11] See also Conrad (2004, p. 3).

maximum-entropy distribution is the uniform distribution, whose entropy is $\log n$, where n is a counting measure. As mentioned before, in physics the state of nature exhibiting highest entropy is given by the Bose–Einstein condensation. In chapter 7.4 we show that our model provides a consistent interpretation to both, physics and information theory, by referring to efficient capital markets.

2. If the probability distribution is Gaussian with variance σ^2, the entropy is
   $H(p) = \frac{1}{2}\left(1 + \log\left(2\pi\sigma^2\right)\right)$
   The entropy of a normal distribution is independent of its mean.
3. For an exponential distribution with mean λ the entropy is $H(p) = 1 + \log(\lambda)$.
   "[F]or an experiment with positive outcomes whose mean value is known, the most conservative probabilistic model consistent with that mean value is an exponential distribution" (Conrad 2004, p. 3).

The entropy measure, as Soofi (1994) states, "*[...] summarises the uncertainty associated with a distribution [...] in terms of concentration of probabilities*".[12]

7.2 Entropy and Random Utility

7.2.1 Maximum Entropy and Actions Probability Formula

"The [maximum entropy] procedure extends Laplace's principle of insufficient reason for assigning probabilities. For example, if information is given that the die is loaded such that the average outcome is [given], then the [maximum entropy] method [...] gives the [maximum entropy] probabilities by"

$$\pi \bullet \left(x_j\right) = \frac{e^{(\beta x_j)}}{\sum_{h=1}^{6} e^{(\beta x_h)}} \tag{7.3}$$

Soofi (1994, p. 1247). This formula is well known in discrete choice modelling. It provides the probabilities of individual activities in case a logit model is valid.

Our approach can integrate entropy concepts into financial issues. We can measure the efficiency of a capital market state based on the entropy of the Markov probabilities associated with that state.

7.2.2 Entropy and Market Efficiency

The application of the entropy concept to capital market issues has been discussed for quite a while.[13] Foley (1994) has already stated that "*the maximum entropy*

[12] Ehsan S. Soofi (1994, p. 1245).

[13] One of the first applications to markets has been, up to our knowledge, Foley (1994) and Soofi (1994). Nijkamp and Reggiani (1988) relate the entropy concept explicitly to discrete choice.

market transaction distribution can be viewed as the statistical equilibrium for the market" (p. 322). We extend the application of maximum entropy to deriving a "no activity conclusion" at an operational level.

Shannon's (1948) concept of unconstrained entropy is sufficient to determine operationally two extreme market situations: pure insider knowledge and pure ignorance. In the first case, entropy is zero and the agent with insider knowledge is (almost) certain to carry out the activity in question; in the second case, entropy reaches a maximum and the agents have no incentive to do anything.

A simple but obvious analogy between the entropy in physics and in economy refers to trades: The vigour of trades—how easily money flows between people is analogous to the temperature: If entropy is high, things go slow, if entropy is low, trades get hectical.

7.2.3 Entropy Equals the Actions' Probability

We consider the decision situation of an individual agent i^*, given his/her feasible actions $k \in K = \{1, \ldots, L\}$ on the shares $j \in J = \{1, \ldots, M\}$. How great is her/his incentive to execute a feasible activity a_{i^*jk} out of the set of all activities A_{i^*jk} feasible to him/her?

The application of the concept of Shannon's (1948) entropy definition in Eq. (7.2) to the distribution of his/her actions' execution probability given in chapter 6.3, Eq. 6.3) provides an appropriate measure:

$$AEI\left(A_{i^*jk}, z\right) = -\frac{1}{\log(M \bullet L)} \sum_{a_{i^*jk'} \in A_{i^*jk}} \left(\frac{\lambda_{a_{i^*jk'}}}{\sum_{a_{i^*jk'} \in A_{i^*jk}} \lambda_{a_{i^*jk}}} \bullet \log \frac{\lambda_{a_{i^*jk'}}}{\sum_{a_{i^*jk'} \in A_{i^*jk}} \lambda_{a_{i^*jk}}} \right) \quad \forall j \in J, k \in K \tag{7.4}$$

for a given i^*. The sum of the term in parentheses corresponds to the entropy definition in Eq. (7.2) using the actions' execution probability in Eqs. 6.3 and 6. 4). Dividing by the entropy's maximum value (see chapter 7.2.1, Eq. 7.3) scales AEI to the unit interval [0; 1].

If an agent i^* attaches to any activity $k \in K$ on any share $j \in J$ equal utility, there is no incentive for him/her to execute any action; he/she is indifferent to all feasible actions. Activity efficiency of (this) individual reaches its maximum $AEI = 1$. If, in contrast, an actions' a_{i^*jk} utility motivates agent i^* to disregard all his/her other feasible actions, activity efficiency of (this) individual reaches its minimum $AEI = 0$. There is no incentive for him/her to do anything else than a_{i^*jk}.

7.3 Definition of Information Efficiency of Markets and Examples

7.3.1 Definition

Consider now the decision situation of all agents $i \in I = \{1, \ldots, N\}$ in the current market state, given their respective feasible actions $k \in K = \{1, \ldots, L\}$ on the shares $j \in J = \{1, \ldots, M\}$. Analogous to the construction of AEI, we define an activity efficiency measure over the entire set of activities A_{ijk} feasible to the agents in the market as

$$IEM(A_{ijk}, z) = -\frac{1}{\log(N \bullet M \bullet L)} \sum_{a_{ijk'} \in A_{ijk}} \left(\frac{\lambda_{a_{ijk'}}}{\sum_{a_{ijk} \in A_{ijk}} \lambda_{a_{ijk}}} \bullet \log \frac{\lambda_{a_{ijk'}}}{\sum_{a_{ijk} \in A_{ijk}} \lambda_{a_{ijk}}} \right)$$
$$\forall i \in I, j \in J, k \in K \tag{7.5}$$

and refer to it as the information efficiency of markets (IEM). Also, IEM is scaled to the unit interval [0; 1].

In the sense of catallactics, IEM incorporates the information flow between the agents through their acting and interacting in the market and covers the intensity of the competition for information among the market participants. While AEI might be interpreted as intra-agent activity efficiency, IEM might be understood as inter-agent activity efficiency.[14]

The two extreme market situations of pure insider knowledge and pure ignorance are characterised, respectively, discussed below.

7.3.2 Pure Insider Knowledge, Minimum Entropy and Minimum Information Efficiency of Markets

The situation of an insider can be formulated by means of DSMP and entropy as follows. If one single agent i' knows that an event happened with price impact on share j in case of public knowledge and an activity k to exploit the price impact

[14] In the general case, for any subset of activities the activity efficiency given the current capital market status is then defined as:

$AE(A, z) = -\frac{1}{\log(\#A)} \sum_{a_{ijk'} \in A} \left(\frac{\lambda_{a_{ijk'}}}{\sum_{a_{ijk} \in A} \lambda_{a_{ijk}}} \bullet \log \frac{\lambda_{a_{ijk'}}}{\sum_{a_{ijk} \in A} \lambda_{a_{ijk}}} \right)$ where $\#A$ denotes the number of elements in the set A. The economic foundation of the selection of the activity subset A is decisive for the economic relevance of the efficiency measure derived.

in advance, with all other agents $i\forall i \neq i\prime$ having no knowledge and therefore no motivation to trade (given the information available to them), then

$$P\left(a_{ijk\prime}|A_{ijk}\right) = 1$$

and $P\left(a_{ijk}|A_{ijk}\right) = 0 \forall a_{ijk} \neq a_{ijk\prime}$

which leads to $IEM\left(A_{ijk}, z\right) min\left(p_{a_{111}}, \ldots, p_{a_{ijk\prime}}, \ldots, p_{a_{NML}}\right) = 0$

There is no doubt that agent $i\prime$ realises activity $a_{ijk\prime}$, exploiting the insider information; information efficiency of the markets reaches a minimum. The concept of IEM therefore provides the possibility to implement regulations on such insider-driven activities at an operational level.

7.3.3 Pure Ignorance, Maximum Entropy and Maximum Information Efficiency of Markets

In the situation of pure ignorance all agents $i \in I = \{1, \ldots, N\}$ have equal motivation to execute any of the actions $k \in K = \{1, \ldots, L\}$ with respect to any of the shares $j \in J = \{1, \ldots, M\}$, that is,

$$P\left(a_{ijk}|A_{ijk}\right) = \frac{1}{N \bullet M \bullet L} \forall a_{ijk} \in A_{ijk}$$

and $IEM\left(A_{ijk}, z\right) max\left(p_{a_{111}}, \ldots, p_{a_{ijk\prime}}, \ldots, p_{a_{NML}}\right) = 1$

Any action $a_{ijk} \in A_{ijk}$ provides the same utility. None of the actions is superior or inferior to another. The agents remain undecided and are unable to take any action. Information efficiency of markets reaches a maximum.

In order to clarify our concepts of AEI in Eq. (7.4) and IEM in Eq. (7.5), Table 7.1 assigns the activity efficiency states of capital markets into the dynamic market process.

In the first row, the columns are numbered from left to right. Columns 1 to 4 break down the set of all feasible activities in the current market state for each agent $i \in I = \{1, \ldots, N\}$ with respect to the available shares $j \in J = \{1, \ldots, M\}$ considering the feasible actions $k \in K = \{1, \ldots, L\}$. The preference value $\Phi\left(a_{ijk}\right)$, which is the deterministic part of the utility (see chapter 5.3), attached to each feasible activity a_{ijk} is given in column 5. The corresponding transition rate $\lambda_{a_{ijk}}$ of the Markov process for the transition from state z to state $z\prime$ generated by the action a_{ijk} (see chapter 6.3) is determined in column 6.

In column 7 the activity efficiency of individuals $\mathrm{AEI}\left(A_{i^*jk}, z\right)$ is classified as an application of the concept of Shannon's (1948) entropy to the distribution of execution probabilities defined over the set of an individual agent's i^* feasible actions; the actions' execution probabilities are determined by the transition rates as given in Eqs. 6.3 and 6.4.

Table 7.1 Assignment of activity efficiency states into the dynamic market process

1	2	3	4	5	6	7	8
A	A_i	A_{ij}	a_{ijk}	$\Phi(a_{ijk})$	$\lambda_{a_{ijk}} = We^{\Phi(a_{ijk})}$	$AEI(A_{i^*jk}, z)$	$IEM(A_{ijk}, z)$
			a_{111}	$\Phi(a_{111})$	$\lambda_{a_{111}}$		
		A_{11}	a_{112}	$\Phi(a_{112})$	$\lambda_{a_{112}}$		
			:	:	:		
			a_{121}	$\Phi(a_{121})$	$\lambda_{a_{121}}$		
	$\boldsymbol{A_1}$	A_{12}	a_{122}	$\Phi(a_{122})$	$\lambda_{a_{122}}$	$\boldsymbol{AEI(A_{1jk}, z)}$	
			:	:	:		
		:	:	:	:		
		:	:	:	:		
			a_{1M1}	$\Phi(a_{1M1})$	$\lambda_{a_{1M1}}$		
		A_{1M}	a_{1M2}	$\Phi(a_{1M2})$	$\lambda_{a_{1M2}}$		
			:	:	:		
	:	:	:	:	:	:	
$\boldsymbol{A}$	:	:	:	:	:	:	$\boldsymbol{IEM(A_{ijk}, z)}$
			a_{N11}	$\Phi(a_{N11})$	$\lambda_{a_{N11}}$		
		A_{N1}	a_{N12}	$\Phi(a_{N12})$	$\lambda_{a_{N12}}$		
			:	:	:		
			a_{N21}	$\Phi(a_{N21})$	$\lambda_{a_{N21}}$		
	$\boldsymbol{A_N}$	A_{N2}	a_{N22}	$\Phi(a_{N22})$	$\lambda_{a_{N22}}$	$\boldsymbol{AEI(A_{Njk}, z)}$	
			:	:	:		
		:	:	:	:		
		:	:	:	:		
			a_{NM1}	$\Phi(a_{NM1})$	$\lambda_{a_{NM1}}$		
		A_{NM}	a_{NM2}	$\Phi(a_{NM2})$	$\lambda_{a_{NM2}}$		
			:	:	:		

Finally, column 8 gives the information efficiency of markets IEM(A_{ijk}, z) as application of the entropy concept to the distribution of execution probabilities defined over the set of all activities feasible to the agents in the market; the actions' execution probabilities are again determined by the transition rates as given in Eq. 6.8.

7.4 Market Equilibrium as Bose–Einstein Condensation

The analogy between entropy in physics and entropy on the capital markets can be taken one step further: When entropy in physics is as its highest, Bose–Einstein condensation occurs and the atoms collapse. This situation occurs at (almost) 0° Kelvin.

If entropy attains maximum at capital markets, market equilibrium occurs and the market participants' individuality collapses. That is, buyers and sellers on markets lose their identity, their individual preference structures vanish, and they become faceless, will-less entities; there is a phase transition from unique to uniform personalities. In the sense of catallactics, no interaction among individuals is possible. The differentiation between intrinsic values and observable prices collapses; no trades occur. The individuals' activities are irrelevant, because the individuals became will-less.

The DSMP model therefore disentangles the so-called Grossmann and Stiglitz (1980) paradox of (informationally) efficient markets at an operational market microstructure level.[15] If all agents share the same information, i.e. all states of nature have the same transition probabilities, then the agents are indifferent to the possible actions, and in fact, to put it in other words, nobody takes any action.

We are convinced that the concept of entropy in physics gives an analogue result in economics, maximum entropy of the Markov process determines perfectly efficient markets. Furthermore, the entropy concept can also provide a concept for measuring the risk of a prospect whose outcome is described by a probability distribution, since the entropy of the normal distribution depends, for example, on the variance of the distribution, but not on the mean of the distribution. This issue deserves further investigation in future research.

7.5 Entropy and Economic Efficiency—Two Suggestions

7.5.1 Entropy and Logit Model's Probability

Finally, we want to point out an identity of the formulas used in both discrete choice and maximum entropy calculations.

Uniform distributed utility. Informationally efficient capital markets ($IEM_{max} = 1$) are determined if no agent is motivated to take any action, that is, the agents are indifferent to all feasible actions; so, all the feasible actions have the same execution probability

$$\mathrm{P}\left(a_{ijk}|A_{ijk}\right) = \frac{1}{N \bullet M \bullet L} \forall a_{ijk} \in A_{ijk} \tag{7.6}$$

[15] See Grossman and Stiglitz (1980, p. 403), and for an updated view Stiglitz (2002, p. 466).

where the number of agents N multiplied by the number of available shares M multiplied by the number of actions L feasible to each agent on the available shares is the number of feasible actions in the market.

As the actions' execution probability can also be formulated as in Eq. 6.6, Eq. (7.6) implies that the same utility is attached to all feasible activities $a_{ijk} \in A_{ijk}$:

$$\Phi_{111}(a_{111}, z) = \cdots = \Phi_{ijk'}(a_{ijk'}, z) = \cdots = \Phi_{NML}(a_{NML}, z) \quad (7.7)$$

Any agent attaches the same utility to any action on any share. None of the actions is superior or inferior to another. The agents remain undecided and are unable to take any action.

Non-uniform distributed utility. For a prospect exhibiting at least two different utility values for the activities $a_{ijk} \in A_{ijk}$ another interesting similarity in the entropy and discrete choice formulas may be noticed.

For each probability distribution P on $\Phi_{ijk}(a_{ijk}, z)\forall a_{ijk} \in A_{ijk}$ the corresponding expected value of this function is[16]

$$E[\Phi] = \sum_{ijk} p(\Phi_{ijk}) \bullet \Phi_{ijk} \quad (7.8)$$

which is between $\min_{ijk}\lfloor\Phi_{ijk}\rfloor$ and $\max_{ijk}\lfloor\Phi_{ijk}\rfloor$. Choose any Φ^* such that $\min_{ijk}\lfloor\Phi_{ijk}\rfloor \le \Phi^* \le \max_{ijk}\lfloor\Phi_{ijk}\rfloor$. What probability distribution P on $\Phi_{ijk}(a_{ijk}, z)\forall a_{ijk} \in A_{ijk}$ satisfies $\Phi^* = \sum_{ijk} p(\Phi_{ijk}) \bullet \Phi_{ijk}$ and maximises entropy?

When $\Phi_{111}(a_{111}, z) = \cdots = \Phi_{ijk'}(a_{ijk'}, z) = \cdots = \Phi_{NML}(a_{NML}, z)$, the expected value condition is void; maximising entropy without restrictions leads to uniform distribution.

What if there are at least two different utility values? Conrad's (2004) Theorem 10 provides the answer: "*If the Φ_{ijk} are not all equal, then for each Φ^* between $\min_{ijk}\lfloor\Phi_{ijk}\rfloor$ and $\max_{ijk}\lfloor\Phi_{ijk}\rfloor$, there is a unique distribution Q on $\Phi_{ijk}(a_{ijk}, z)\forall a_{ijk} \in A_{ijk}$ which satisfies the condition $\Phi^* = \sum_{ijk} p(\Phi_{ijk}) \bullet \Phi_{ijk}$ and has maximum entropy. It is given by the equation*

$$Q(\Phi_{ijk}) = \frac{e^{-\beta\Phi_{ijk'}}}{\sum_{ijk} e^{-\beta\Phi_{ijk}}} \quad (7.9)$$

for a unique extended real number $\beta \in [-\infty, \infty]$ which depends on Φ^*" (p. 8, notation of variables from authors).

[16] The following considerations are adapted from Conrad (2004, p. 8).

Interestingly, the same formula describes the probability of selecting action $a_{ijk'}$ according to the logit model of discrete choice

$$\mathrm{P}\left(a_{ijk'}|\mathrm{A}_{ijk}\right) = \frac{e^{\Phi\left(\mathrm{a}_{ijk'},z\right)}}{\sum_{a_{ijk}\in \mathrm{A}_{ijk}} e^{\Phi\left(\mathrm{a}_{ijk},z\right)}} \tag{7.10}$$

where $\Phi\left(\mathrm{a}_{ijk'}, z\right)$ is the deterministic part of utility (see Train 2003, p. 39).

7.5.2 Entropy and Aggregation of Individual Decisions to Collective Decisions

Let us conclude with indicating an application of entropy to (capital) markets capable of handling an issue unresolved in economics until now: the question of how to proceed from individual decisions to collective decisions. Or in a more technical sense, how to explore the relationship between (micro) discrete choice theory and macro theory based on global figures. In environmental economics such a relationship has been investigated by Nijkamp and Reggiani (1988).

It is left for future investigations if entropy provides the means to properly shift from the individual to the collective (see Buchanan 2001, p. 30). Maybe Buchanan's (2001) postulate will be adequately managed by the combined application of discrete choice and entropy and as stated above, its integration into rational belief equilibria. Buchanan's (2001) remark underlines that the consistent interrelation of individual decisions and aggregated global data is an essential issue in economics. That has probably been the core issue in the Hayek-Keynes clash.[17] The debate focused on different issues and the opponents were at different stages of finding the appropriate instruments. Keynes and his followers applied the recently developed calculus of variation methods to model macroeconomic problems. The connections to micro-economic reality were explained verbally. A consistent logical foundation was missing. Hayek, on the contrary, tried to develop a model with quantitative consistent connection of real micro behaviour with macro-economic functions. He failed. He was too far ahead of his time. Keynes and his followers were successful and did not care about the issue Hayek was searching for but could not find. He could not even address the issue by quantitative terms properly. He acknowledged that impossibility and wrote a book without maths: The "road to serfdom" was a great success.

[17] See Wapshott (2011).

7.6 High-Dimensional Probability to Model Stochastic Processes

With the advent of big data and big computers, probability theory also experienced a new upswing, frequently under the heading "high-dimensional probability", hdp for short. EEorts to grasp the phenomenon of stochastic processes have taken a great leap forward. A comprehensive understanding requires expertise in set and measure theory. That knowledge is beyond our scope. We will confine to verbal explanations and sketch the capabilities of this approach to tackle economic problems, mostly by quotes from experts, and hope that this description provides a reasonable information to the reader.

The discussion itself has a long history of development: Chaining, originated from Kolmogorov (1958), (1959), developed by Dudley, Fernique, others and made operational by Talagrand (2010), (2021), is a powerful technique in high dimensional probability for bounding the expected suprema of random processes while taking into account the dependencies between their random variables in a multiscale manner using maximal inequality. (Asadi and Abbe (2020, p5).

8 Outlook

Abstract

The outlook sketches the future development. We review the current discussion to modify the equilibrium assumption. Recent results (Talagrand 2021; Vershynin 2025) of identifying peaks and troughs of stochastic processes will enable to implement the interaction of agents and thus to model the self-organisation of markets. Adam Smith experiences justice with this approach. He did neither in "Moral Sentiments"(1759) nor in "Wealth of Nations"(1776) refer to any "equilibrium" when he used the term "invisible hands."

Keywords

Emancipation from overriding equilibrium • New concept "entropy numbers" to evaluate interactions • Possibilities to model markets' self-organisation

The Outlook wraps up the continued reliance on equilibrium models in economics, emphasising the shift towards agent-based approaches that incorporate self-organisation, emergence and resilience. It emphasises that economic outcomes are driven by individual agents pursuing their goals within legal and social frameworks, rather than by overarching equilibria. Drawing on game theory, discrete choice models, and Markov processes, the Outlook advocates for a bottom-up approach to economic modelling. It also explores new mathematical tools, such as entropy numbers and generic chaining, to better understand the resilience of economic systems under stochastic conditions. These innovations offer a promising departure from traditional models, providing more accurate insights into economic dynamics and extreme events.

O. Loistl et al., *Screen Based Trading and Open Order Book*, New Economic Windows,
https://doi.org/10.1007/978-3-031-99052-6_8

8.1 Econophysics II 1: From the Overriding Equilibrium to Agents' Objectives

Emergence, interactions, self-organisation and resilience will dominate the discussion in social sciences. The assumption of achieving a general equilibrium is controversial. The defence of the equilibrium assumption with reference to Adam Smith is treacherous. He does not use the term "equilibrium", at least not anywhere near the famous expression "invisible hands", neither in "Wealth of Nations"[1] nor in "Moral Sentiments".[2] According to von Neumann and Morgenstern, dynamic disequilibrium is "unquestionable more preferable",[3] and Gallegati postulates that economy is "freed from the equilibrium straitjacket".[4]

Recently, authors have interpreted the expression of the invisible hands as metaphor for self-organisation, which was already in use before Adam Smith: "*Without the deeper and wider emergence of notions of self-organisation... it would be hard to explain, why it spread so widely so fast.*"[5] Given these strong statements, we wonder, why the assumption of equilibrium can still maintain such a strong position?

The difficulties of simultaneously striving for individual benefit and a general equilibrium are already evident in Adam Smith, when he admits that "*he intends only his own gain... led by an invisible hand to promote an end which was no part of his intention*". Achieving a result other than the intended one can be caused by interactions with other actors.

In the reality of democratic societies, there is no force that overrides the pursuit of individual benefit. That is different in autocratic societies where the will of the dictator is decisive. In democratic societies, individual agents pursue individual goals, interact with each other in compliance with social rules and legal regulations—and may fail to achieve their own goals in the process. In living societies, social and legal control mechanisms ensure that everyday life runs smoothly.

The tension between individual goals and statutory provisions does indeed exist. In reality, there is no overriding rule that prescribes the achievement of an equilibrium. Statutory provisions must be complied with, but these provisions leave

---

[1] "*By preferring the support of domestick[!] to that of foreign industry he intends only his security; and by directing that industry in such a manner as its produce may be of greatest value, he intends only his own gain, and he is in this, as in many other cases, led by an invisible hand to promote an end which was no part of his intention*", Smith (1776), II, p 35.

[2] "*They consume little more than the poor, and in spite of their natural selfishness and rapacity, tho' the sole end which they propose from labours of all the thousands whom they employ, be the gratification of their own vain and insatiable desires, they divide with the poor the produce of all their improvements. They are led by an invisible hand to make nearly the same distribution of the necessaries of life, which would have been made, had the earth been divided into equal portions among all its inhabitants, and thus without intending it, without knowing it advance the interest of the society, and afford means to the multiplication of the species.*", Smith (1759), p 350.

[3] Von Neuman and Morgenstern(1944), p 44.

[4] Gallegati (2018), p 53.

[5] Shehan and Wahrman (2015), p 230.

enough room to pursue individual goals. This may be different in centrally planned economies. They suppress individual decisions in a similar way to equilibrium economies. Resilience addresses the issue of how long an economy runs smoothly and how strong the extremes are in the event of a disruption and how quickly they are equalised.

According to welfare theory, a society reaches the highest level of prosperity or wealth in a state of equilibrium. Quants like to use the equilibrium assumption because it is much easier to model than dynamic disequilibrium. Equations are easier to handle than inequations,[6] and dealing with an equilibrium does not seem to require comprehensive factual knowledge about the actual performance of a society.

The latest developments emancipate themselves from a global equilibrium and use a bottom-up approach. In the first step, the activities of individual agents are modelled, then the matching rules are designed and finally it is checked how the matching of the opposing wishes works. Alvin E. Roth (2015) and (2018) breaks fresh ground by applying game theoretic tools to investigate this bottom-up issue. The basic scenario is a bipartite matching in orders to achieve mutual equilibrium between the individuals. The overall scenario is determined by these individual actions, not by an overriding equilibrium force. The individual agents pursue their own goals and observe the matching rules. They are not forced to achieve an overall equilibrium, however this may be defined. There is no such operational guidance for an individual market participant anywhere. The guiding principle of achieving a market-clearing situation guides the developers of the trading rules. Scharfenaker and Foley[7] provide an overview of the various regulations that must be observed.

In our opinion, however, the role of institutions does not primarily consist of "negative feedback". We favour "guidance through statutory provisions". The modelling of the agents' activities must reflect these possibilities and limitations. Successful modelling of actions must consider the assumption of "Independence from Irrelevant Alternatives".[8] As Luce explains in detail, alternatives between which the agent can choose must be precisely described in terms of their effects and must be precisely differentiated from one another.[9]

The economic frame that is decisive for the agents' decision-making must be explicitly stated. In our model, this is the state space of the Markov process. According to the precise modelling of Markov state space - continuous time space

[6] The British mathematician Hardy was once asked, if he would sell his soul to the devil for an equation. He answered: "*Not for an equation, but for an inequation*". This statement is ascribed to other scientists too, like P. A. Samuelson. But we think, the ascription to Hardy is plausible. He has published 6 volumes about inequalities. Samuelson has not published any book about this topic.

[7] Scharfenaker and Foley (2017), Abstract, p 1. Landini et al. (2020) provide a comprehensive mathematical analysis of the tension between individual freedom of choice and general equilibrium.

[8] See Luce (2005), chapter 5 and Appendix.

[9] That is not given in the famous case of "another blue bus" example.

and discrete state space – it makes sense to link the Markov state space with the actions of the agents. The model specifies, which action changes which state space (see chapter 5.2) and the utility of an action corresponds to the probability of the action. The probability of a change in a state space can be determined by the probability of this action. The tedious calculation of a master equation to obtain the transition probability is obsolete. For ease of reference, the logit formula is repeated here. For details on derivation, see chapters. 5.2 and 5.3. For a given market state z and assuming the logit approach[10,11] the probability for choosing an action $a_{ijk\prime}$ is given by:

$$P\left(a_{ijk\prime}|A_{ijk}\right) = \frac{e^{\Phi\left(a_{ijk\prime,z}\right)}}{\sum_{a_{ijk} \in A_{ijk}} e^{\Phi\left(a_{ijk,z}\right)}} \tag{8.1}$$

The probability of choosing the action $a_{ijk\prime}$ is proportional to the deterministic part $\Phi\left(a_{ijk\prime,z}\right)$ of the utility of the action.[12] Starting from state z, the probability $P(z, z\prime)$ that the next state will be $z\prime$ is proportional to the transition probability:

$$P(z, z\prime) = \frac{\lambda(z, z\prime)}{\sum_{z^*} \lambda(z, z^*)} \tag{8.2}$$

Kirman[13] applies the structure of the logit formula but with different meanings of the variables. With his formula, he obtains the probabilities that "buyer i will visit seller "j.

The consequences of an agent's action must be modelled as accurately as possible. In portfolio selection, the number of possible investment alternatives is given, for example, by the number of shares within an index, e.g. the DAX. If another share is included in the index, the entire calculation must be carried out again. In the case of electronic trading, the open order book reflects exactly the consequences of an action (See chapter 5.2.2 and especially Fig. 5.1). In another decision scenario, modelling the exact consequences of an agents' actions is of course not so easy.

The extension of the model is primarily a matter of working out the factual details. The extensions to capture the different attitudes of the agents are primarily a question of the parameters of the utility function and, of course, a question of the capacity of data storage and computer performance. First and foremost,

---

[10] This formula is connected to the term "entropy". The different meanings have been discussed by Boltzmann (1877), Shannon (1948), Jaynes (1957), Suppes (1961), Luce (2005) and with a quite different meaning Talagrand (2021) and van Handel (2018). Train (2003), pp 38, gives a comprehensive derivation of the logit model.

[11] See Landes and Loistl (1992), pp 214

[12] See Landes and Loistl (1992), pp 214.

[13] Kirman (2011), p 23.

knowledge of how the market works is required. In addition, the dynamics of market developments go beyond the possibilities of modelling using static framework equations.

Taking advantage of the opportunities offered by innovative investment tools and ignoring the hidden dangers created by these regulatory loopholes leads to speculative bubbles. The bursting of speculative bubbles highlights the risks of the new instruments and makes it possible to manage these risks.

Such questions are at the centre of the resilience discussion. It is a balancing act between too little and too much control; too little regulation leaves room for too much (i.e. too much loss-making) speculation. Too strict regulations prevent the development of (technological) progress that can benefit the general public. Every regulatory authority has to solve this task when an innovative tool is introduced on the capital market. In many cases, the introduction of innovative financial instruments poses a challenge for regulatory authorities such as SEC or FTC. They have to act skilfully to avoid loss-making speculation. In other cases, the authorities are not so successful. So far, it has been difficult to draw up analytical guidelines.

This task requires in-depth factual knowledge of what is really happening. This seems to be a competitive disadvantage for mathematicians. According to the curriculum of their discipline, they are not trained to trade on the stock markets. Mathematical economics does not have much to do with the real economic situation. "*Generally speaking, formalists write for one another*"[14].

To analyse this question, let us start with two famous quotes. Jevons calls for the use of mathematics to model economic problems: "*If economics is a science at all, it must be a mathematical one*"[15]. On the other hand, Alfred Marshall recognises that the recognition of a factual technical problem can be misguided by the inadequate modelling possibilities of the mathematical methods used. He proclaims to "*use mathematics as a shorthand language, rather than an* ***engine*** *of inquiry*"[16]. But in economic research, maths is often used as the engine of investigation. This misleading application was favoured by the fact that opinions on economic phenomena have long been ambiguous. There was no guidance through precise and standardised economic knowledge. The well-known London joke from the 1920s and 1930s illustrates the diversity of opinions: "*When five economists get together, you hear six different opinions, and two of them are from Keynes*"[17]. Schumpeter provides an insightful explanation of this quote: "*The new men came to face our*

[14] Solow (2005), p 90.

[15] Jevons (1981).

[16] An ample quote from the letter to Bowley goes as follows:"*...But I know I had a growing feeling in the later years of my work that a good mathematical theory dealing with economic hypothesis was very unlikely to be good economics and I went more and more on the rules: (1) Use mathematics as a shorthand language, rather than as an engine of inquiry (2) Keep them till you have done (3) Translate into English (4) Then illustrate by examples that are important in real life (5) Burn the mathematics (6) If you can't succeed in (4), burn (3). The last I did often.*".

[17] Caldwell (1995), p 9.

problems from very different angles and with very different acquirements, full of impatience to clear the ground and to build entirely anew.“[18]

The quants utilised this freedom and defined problems to be investigated according to their abilities in mathematical methods. Instead of adapting their methods to the solution of precisely defined economic problems, the quants adapted the problem under consideration so that they could apply the methods with which they had been trained. Thus, providing a competitive advantage over economists who are not trained in these methods. In the discussion at the presentation of these quantitative models, questions about the economic impact or justification of the quantitative models were dismissed as old fashioned and outdated. On the other hand, each quantitative approach was given scientific weight a priori.

As a result, the quantitative models were not compared with reality from the outset by means of an analytical discussion. The main argument was and is that the statistical tests reveal the reliability of a model. This line of retreat must be questioned if the statistical test had to prove statements that do not correspond to the theoretical model. McCloskey and Ziliak (1996) provide a comprehensive synopsis of statistical inefficiencies. In between the statistical software's handling has been improved. However, the central question of whether the statistical model's assumptions are also present in reality is often only answered formally. Max Planck was realistic about the possibilities of statistics. “*It is in the nature of statistics that they often have the first, but never the last word to say.*“[19] A famous example is the “market portfolio” of portfolio theory. Theoretically, it includes all securities on the market, but in empirical tests various indices serve as a substitute for the market. Another famous example is the “successful” test that the value of a company is independent of the capital structure. The derivation of the theoretical model is based on a tautology: the independence of the company is already contained in the initial assumptions; the flow of capitalised earnings is independent of the capital structure. It took a while for the finance community to discover this circular argument. It was not discovered by statistical tests but by analytical considerations. Opler et al. (1997) described capital structure's impact on a company's earnings power - and on company's value. Landes and Loistl (1991) simulated capital structure's impact on earnings power, bankruptcy risks and on company's value as well.

A breakthrough in professional modelling was Daniel McFadden's successful application of Discrete Choice to predict human decisions between given alternatives. He was inspired by a student who asked him a real-life exam question. Which line of transport will a customer choose? He applied a formula developed by R. Duncan Luce[20] and by Patrick Suppes[21]. The groundbreaking success leads to the application of this formula to evaluate the probability of choosing one alternative from several alternatives.

[18] Schumpeter (1933), p 10.

[19] Planck (1914), p 98.

[20] Luce (2005).

[21] Suppes (1961), p 199.

This model of human decision-making has largely prevailed, but not in the world of economics and finance. This is all the more surprising as the term "agent-based modelling" is commonly used but does not refer to "Discrete Choice".

8.2 Econophysics II 2: Entropy Numbers to Evaluate Interactions' Resilience

James Buchanan gave once "*game theory … the top rank*"[22]. His assessment requires a change of game theory's goal: Giving up the equilibrium restriction and applying other mathematical tools.

That undertaking demands other mathematical tools, as von Neumann and Morgenstern already proposed in the 1940s: "*the theory of social phenomena will presumably take a very definite turn away from the existing patterns of mathematical physics… The emphasis on mathematical methods seems to be shifted more towards combinatorics and set theory.*"[23]

We recognise now—some 80 years after von Neumann Morgenstern's far-sighted forecast—that adequate methods are in the making. These methods imply a switch from continuous smooth functions to case-by-case considerations, requiring discrete mathematical and set theoretic tools[24].

It has long been understood that the behaviour of suprema of random processes is intimately connected with the geometry of their sets. Due to M. Talagrand, it "*has culminated in a remarkable general theory that captures the precise connection between the underlying probabilistic and geometric structures. For example, the classic result in this theory...provides a sharp geometric characterisation of the suprema of Gaussian processes.*" (van Handel 2018, p. 1764).

Kolmogorov (1958), (1959) invented the most important idea to bound stochastic processes: chaining. This wonderfully eOicient method answers with little eOort a number of basic questions. (Talagrand 2021, p. VIII).

Kolmogorov also introduced the concept of chaining by applying measure theoretic tools. It was treated as a remote subject till the work of Talagrand. His results were made more accessible by other publications. Just to name three recently published books, all three of them bearing the same title "High-Dimensional Probability" (hdp for short): Van Handel (2016), Tropp (2023) and Vershynin (2025). Even if a comprehensive understanding requires expertise in measure theory, we will refrain from measure theoretic arguments and limit ourselves to verbal description, mainly quoting experts. We hope that these quotes inform about the hdp's core possibilities to analyse central economic problems, like self-organisation and resilience.

A key feature of hdp is the non-asymptotic analysis of large probability models, e.g. the classical limit theorems are not adequate. (Topp 2023, p. 3). It has become

[22] Buchanan (2001), p 27.

[23] Von Neumann and Morgenstern (1944), p 45.

[24] Details see chapter 4.4.

apparent that the quantitative estimates and not the limit behaviour of empirical processes are of central importance in Data Science. (Bartl and Mendelson (2025), p. 1) - and in problems of organised complexity alike. Hdp's capabilities fulfil the requirements already articulated by prominent scholars like Von Neumann/ Morgenstern (1943) who pointed towards the necessity of measure theoretic technics when going beyond equilibrium, and Warren Weaver (1948) and F.A. Hayek (1974) who articulated the necessity to analyse economic problems in a discrete setting. A continuous modelling is not suitable for reliably capturing economic issues like emergence and selforganisation.

Surprisingly, in discrete high-dimensional probability, the most basic phenomenon is that, under fairly weak assumptions, a random variable typically takes values close to its mean. This result is valid whenever the distribution has finite second moments. It uses variance to summarise the fluctuations of the distribution, the smaller the variance, the sharper the concentration. (Topp (2023), p. 4).

Furthermore, Kolmogorov (1958) transplanted Shannon's notion of entropy from the theory of information into the theory of dynamical systems. (Ivanov 2015, p. I).

The concept of entropy numbers is applicable and useful in characterising the behaviour of stochastic processes since it represents the uncertainty, ambiguity, and disorder of the process without being restricted to the forms of the theoretical distributions. (Namdari and Li (2019)).

"Entropy numbers and covering numbers are important standard tools for quantifying the compactness of operators." (Simon Fischer, (2020) p. 1).

"The metric entropy is equivalent to the number of bits to encode points in a set K. (Vershynin (2025),p. 129).

Chaining is called "the workhorse of the modern approach of approximating stochastic processes" (Polllard 2025,p3).

"Majorising measures provide bounds for the supremum of stochastic processes. They represent the most general possible form of chaining argument going back to Kolmogorov" (Talagrand 1996a, p. 1049).

Talagrand "discovered that one could replace majorising measures by a suitable variation on the usual chaining arguments". (Talagrand (2010), p. 2).

The adequate mathematical tools will lead to concentration inequalities for many nonlinear functions. (Joel A. Tropp (2023) p. 2). The basic principle underlying modern concentration theory was enunciated by Michel Talagrand: "A random variable that depends (in a 'smooth' way) on the influence of many independent variables (but not too much on any of them) is essentially constant. This statement will of course be quantified by inequalities." (Talagrand (1996b), p. 2).

When giving up the equilibrium paradigm, the question "what else?" can be directed towards "High Dimensional Probability". The issue is now quite common in advanced probability discussions and used e.g. in machine learning. Again, Talagrand broke fresh ground by "Mean Field Models for Spin Glasses" (2010), (2011), thus providing for Parisi's formula, discussed "In a flight of Starlings. The wonder of complex Systems" (2023) a solid derivation. This scientific achievement was doubly honoured with the award of the Nobel Prize to Parisi on the one hand

and the Abel prize to Talagrand on the other. David Gamarnik commented this fact and quips "The scientific value of one formula is worthy two major prices" (2025). It is definitely designed to investigate issues in self-organisation and resilience.

The perspective is furthermore emphasised by using the possibilities offered by DSMP, the combination of Markov Process and Discrete Choice. It provides utilities as well as the realisation probabilities of individual actions. Thus, exploiting the capabilities of "hdp", high-dimensional probabilities. The entire construct is thus founded on the solid basis of real behaviour.

A further approximation to real human behaviour concerns learning, i.e. the adaptation of behavioural parameters to current events. The human ability to draw consequences for one's own behaviour from experience is the subject of a heated debate[25].

As history teaches us, every generation must make its own experiences. Knowledge is not always passed on to the next generation, as can be clearly observed by economic speculative bubbles.

The modelling of speculative bubbles can either apply deterministic or stochastic tools. Deterministic modelling may have different degrees of abstraction. Some investors will recognise the risks of the newly emerging opportunity and avoid the exposure. They will act accordingly and avoid such investments. Other, unexperienced agents believe they can take a big chance and take the risks. It depends, e.g. on the ratio of experienced to inexperienced investors whether a bubble forms and eventually bursts. The reliable exact modelling of such a behaviour is a big challenge.

Modelling by stochastic tools seems to make promising progress. Until quite recently, the modelling was restricted to figures describing the global stochastic behaviour. Expression of the general stochastic movements relied on mean and variance, of course further developed to e.g. GARCH in different Variants.[26] It was assumed that the agents or elements do not interact, i.e. react to other agents' activities.

Observing the requirements of self-organisation and emergence, the fundamental principle of ergodicity is no longer appropriate. They can fix neither the time points of peaks nor that of troughs, at least not under the basic assumption of traditional probability theory.

Talagrand's[27] research results will change the situation. Recently obtained advanced results can discuss upper and lower bounds of stochastic processes.

He is called the "*mathematician who tamed randomness*"[28]. That might be seen as fulfilment of the big shots' postulate like von Neumann and Morgenstern, Warren Weaver and F.A. Hayek made nearly some 80 years before. Indeed, Talagrand developed methods to forecast the maxima/minima of stochastic processes. He relies on the principle of "chaining", already introduced by Kolmogorov, specified

[25] See e.g. Lopez de Prado (2018).

[26] Lopez de Prado (2018) provides a comprehensive synopsis.

[27] See Talagrand (2021).

[28] Castelvecchi (2024).

by Talagrand to Generic Chaining. Based on these figures, Talagrand sharpens the range within maxima or minima of stochastic processes will occur. The handling of these results requires knowledge of a new field in mathematics that is called entropy numbers. Ramon van Handel shows that classical chaining bounds on the suprema of random processes in terms of entropy numbers can be systematically improved when the underlying set is convex.[29] The term "entropy numbers" is obviously quite common among theoretic experts already.[30] These results break fresh ground. We can only guess, how and when these results will be as operational instruments improve the handling of capital markets performance. But one is for sure, the application will come, the door is open. As Hilbert asserted, where there is a need, there will be a method. It is up to economic and finance experts to articulate these needs.

Talagrand explains: "*The 'classical theory of processes' deals mostly with the case where T is a subset of the real line or of $\mathbb{R}^n$. Our most important index sets are 'high-dimensional'. ...Our specific goal is to demonstrate the impact and the range of modern abstract methods*".[31]

The Finance community is not yet familiar with this concept, but the familiarisation with these long postulated instruments will more than make up the effort. After all, they can be used to deal with economic issues that have long been and increasingly urgently required attention.

[29] Van Handel (2016), Van Handel (2018).

[30] "*Entropy numbers ... of sets and operators are well known geometric notions, which found many applications in various fields of mathematics, statistics, and computer science*" Kossaczka and Vybíral (2020), see also Temlyakov (2020), Prochno et al. (2024).

[31] Talagrand (2021), Preface VII.

References

Adcock, C., Eling, M., Loperfrido. N.: Skewed Distributions in finance and Actuarial ScienceUniversity of St Gallen. Working Papers on Risk management and Insurance No. 122 (2012)

Adcock, C., Shutes, K.: On the multivariate extended skew-normal, normal-exponential and normal-gamma distributions. J. Stat. Theory Pract. **6**, 636–664 (2012)

Adcock, C.J.: Mean-Variance-skewness efficient surfaces, Stein's lemma and the multivariate extended skew-Student distribution. Eur. J. Oper. Res. **234**, 392–401 (2014)

Aitchison, J., Brown, J.A.C.: The Lognormal Distribution. Cambridge (1957)

Allais M.: The foundations of a positive theory of risk involving risk and a criticism of the postulates and Axioms of the American School. In: Allais M., Hagen. O. (eds.) Expected Utility Hypotheses and the Allais Paradox. Contemporary Discussions of Decisions under Uncertainty with Allais' Rejoinder, pp. 27–145. D. Reidel Publishing Dordrecht (1979)

Allais M., Hagen O. (eds.): Expected Utility Hypotheses and the Allais Paradox. Contemporary Discussions of Decisions under Uncertainty with Allais' Rejoinder. D. Reidel Publishing Dordrecht (1979)

Alireza, N., Zhaojun (Steven) Li: A review of entropy measures for uncertainty quantification of stochastic processes, Adv. Mech. Eng. **11**, 1–14 (2019)

Amir R. A., Emmanuel A.: Chaining Meets chain rule: Multilevel Entropic Regularization and Training of Neural Networks, J. Mach. Learn. Res. **21**, 1–32 (2020)

Anglin, J. R., Ketterle, W.: Bose-Einstein condensation of atomic gases. NATURE **416**, 14 March 211–217 (2002)

A.N. Kolmogorov: A new Metric Invariant of Transitive Dynamical Systems and of Automorphisms of Lebesque Spaces, in: A.N. Kolmogorov's and Y.G. Sinai's Papers introducing (1958)

A.N. Kolmogorov: On the entropy per unit of time as a metric invariant of automorphism, in: A.N. Kolmogorov's and Sinai's papers, l.c. 9–13 (1959)

A.N. Kolmogorov: On the entropy per unit of time as a metric invariant of automorphism, in: A.N. Kolmogorov's and Sinai's papers, l.c. 9–13 (1959)

A.N. Kolmogorov: Addendum to the paper about dynamical systems, in: Kolmogorov, A.N. theory of information and theory of algorithms, reprinted in: Kolmogorov's and Sinai's papers, l.c. p.8 (1987)

Arrow, K.J.: Aspects of the Theory of Risk Bearing. Yrjö Jahnsson Lectures, Yrjö Jahnsson Foundation (1965)

Arrow, K.J.: Methodological individualism and social knowledge. Am. Econ. Rev. **84**(2), 11–19 (1994)

O. Loistl et al., *Screen Based Trading and Open Order Book*, New Economic Windows, https://doi.org/10.1007/978-3-031-99052-6

Arrow, K.J.: Interview in: Colander D., Holt, R.P.F., Rosser, Jr, J.B.: The Changing Face of Economics: Conversations with Cutting Edge Economists, pp. 291–307. University of Michigan Press (2004)

Axtell, R.L.: The complexity of exchanges. Econ. J. **115**, F193–F210 (2005)

Axtell, R.L.: What economic agents do: how cognition and interaction lead to emergence and complexity. Rev. Austrian Econ. **20**, 105–122 (2007)

Axtell, R.L., Young, P.H.: Interview in: Colander, D., Holt, R.P.F., Rosser, Jr, J.B.: The Changing Face of Economics: Conversations with Cutting Edge Economists, pp. 251–290. University of Michigan Press (2004)

Bachelier, M.L.: Théorie de La Speculation. Annales scientifiques de É.N.S. 3 e série, tome 17, pp. 21–86. http://www.org/item?id=ASENS_3_17_21_0 (The Theory of speculation, translated by D. May (1900)) (1900)

Beja, A., Hakansson, N.H.: From orders to trades: some alternative market mechanisms. In: Bloch, E., Schwartz, R.A. (eds.) Impending Changes for Securities Markets: What Role for Exchanges, pp. 144–161. JAI Press, Greenwich, CT (1979)

Bierwag, G.O.: The rationale of the mean-standard deviation analysis: Comment. Am. Econ. Rev. **64**, 431–433 (1974)

Black, F.: Business Cycles and Equilibrium, p. 179. John Wiley & Sons (2009)

Black, F.: Living up to the model. Risk **3**(3), 11–13 (1990)

Black, F., Scholes, M.: The pricing and options and corporate liabilities. J. Polit. Econ. **81**, 637–654 (1973)

Bleher, J., Bleher, M., Dimpfl, T.: From orders to prices: a stochastic description of the limit order book to forecast intraday returns, arXiv:2004.11953v2[q-fin.TR] 4 May 2021 (2021)

Boltzmann, L.: Über die Beziehung zwischen dem zweiten Hauptsatze der mechanischen Wärmetheorie und der Wahrscheinlichkeitsrechnung respektive den Sätzen über das Wärmegleichgewicht: In: Boltzmann, L. (1905): Entropie und Wahrscheinlichkeit, pp. 137–196 (1877)

Boltzmann, L.: Entgegnung auf die wärmetheoretischen Betrachtungen des Herrn Zermelo. In: Entropie und Wahrscheinlichkeit, l.c., pp. 231–242 (1896)

Boness, J.A.: Elements of a theory of Stock-Option Value. J. Polit. Econ. **72**, 163–175 (1964)

Börse Frankfurt: Orderzusätze und Ordertypen-der feine Unterschied. Deutsche Börse AG. https://www.boerse-frankfurt.de>ordertypen-und-zusaetze (2019). Accessed 13 October 2024

Bouchaud, J.-P., Potters, M.: Theory of Financial Risks. From Statistical Physics to Risk Management. Cambridge (2000)

Breiman, L.: Probability and Stochastic Processes: With a View Towards Applications. Houghton Mifflin Company, Boston (1969)

Brock, W.A., Durlauf, S.N.: Discrete choice with social interactions. Rev. Econ. Stud. **68**(2), 235–260 (2001)

Bronzin, V.: Theorie der Prämiengeschäfte. Franz Deuticke, Leipzig und Wien (1908)

Buchanan, J.M.: A contractarian paradigm for applying economic theory. Am. Econ. Rev. **65**, 225–230 (1975)

Buchanan, J.M.: The contractarian political economy and constitutional interpretation. Am. Econ. Rev. **78**, 135–139 (1988)

Buchanan, J.M.: Game theory, mathematics, and economics. J. Econ. Methodol. **8**(1), 27–31 (2001)

Buffett, W.: Letter to the Shareholders of Berkshire Hathaway Inc Feb (1988)

Buffett, W.: Letter to the Shareholders of Berkshire Hathaway Inc Feb (2003)

Buffett, W.: Letter to the Shareholders of Berkshire Hathaway Inc Feb (2009)

Buffett, W.: Letter to the Shareholders of Berkshire Hathaway Inc Feb (2010)

Caldwell, B.: The Collected Works of F.A. Hayek, Volume IX: Contra Keynes and Cambridge, Essays, Correspondence. in: B. Caldwell (eds.). The University of Chicago Press, Chicago (2010)

CBOE VIX: CBOE VIX. Volatility Index. Methodology (2024)

CBOE: CBOE Volatility Index, Mathematics Methodology, CBOE (2025)

Castelvecchi, D.: Mathematician who tamed randomness wins Abel prize. Nature **627**, 28 March, 714–715 (2024)
Claude, E. S.: The Mathematical Theory of Communication, reprinted in: Claude E. Shannon and Waren Weaver (1949), l.c. pp31–125, (1949)
Claude, E. S. Warren, W.: The mathematical theory of communication, The University of Illinois Press, Urbana, tenth printing (1964)
Colander, D.: New millenium economics: how dit it get this way, and what way is it? J. Econ. Perspect. **14**, 121–132 (2000)
Colander, D.: Complexity and the History of Economic Thought. Middlebury College Economics Discussion Paper No 08-04. Department of Economics Middlebury College, Middlebury (2008)
Colander, D., Holt, R.P.F. Rosser, Jr., J.B.: The Changing Face of Economics. Conversations with Cutting Edge Economists. University of Michigan Press, Ann Arbor (2004)
Colander, D., Howitt, P., Kirman, A., Leijonhufvud, A., Mehrling, P.: Beyond DSGE models: Toward an empirically based macroeconomics. Am. Econ. Rev. Pap. Proc. **98**, 236–240 (2008)
Colander, D., Kuper, R.: Complexity and the Art of Public Policy: Solving Society's Problems from the Bottom Up. Princeton University Press, Princeton and Oxford (2014)
Conrad, K.: Probability Distributions and Maximum Entropy (2004). http://math.uconn.edu/~kconrad/blurbs/entropy.pdf
Cont, R., Tankov, P.: Financial Modelling with Jump Processes. Chapman & Hall, London (2004)
Cox, D.A.: Some statistical models related with series of events. J. Roy. Stat. Soc. **17**, 129–164 (1955)
Dalko, V., Wang, M.H.: High-Frequency Trading: Order-Based Innovation or Manipulation? (2020). https://link.springer.com/article/10.1057/s41261-019-00115-y
Daniel B., Shahar M.: Uniform Mean Estimation Via Generic Chaining, arXiv:2502.15116v1 [math.PR] 21 Feb 2025
Das, A., Singh, R.: Discrete choice experiments—a unified approach. J. Stat. Plan. Inference **205**, 193–202 (2020)
David, G.: Turing in the Shadows of Nobel and Abel: An Algorithmic Story Behing Two Recent Prices, Notices of the American Mathematical Society, May 2025
David P.: Chaining. Version: 3jul25. printed: 5 July (2025)
de Prado, M.L.: Advances in Financial Machine Learning. John Wiley & Sons, Hoboken, N.J. (2018)
del Vecchio Junior, J.: Chance and probability in Poincaré's epistemology. Philosophia Scientiae **20–2**, 177–196 (2016)
Degiannakis, S., Filis, G., Hassani, H.: Forecasting global stock market implied volatility indices. J. Empir. Financ. **46**, 111–129 (2018)
Demeterfi, K., Derman, E., Kamal, M., Zou, J.: A guide to volatility and variance swaps. J. Deriv., summer 1999, 9–32 (1999)
Derman, E., Taleb, N.N.: The illusions of dynamic replication. Quantitative Finance **5**(4), 323–326 (2005)
Deutsche Börse: Designated Sponsor Guide, Version 13.1, www.xetra.com (2023)
Deutsche Börse: Market Model for Trading Venues Xetra, T7 Release 12.1 Version 1.0 (2024)
Deutsche Bundesbank: Bedeutung und Wirkung des Hochfrequenzhandels am deutschen Kapitalmarkt, Monatsbericht Oktober 2016, pp. 38–61 (2016)
Di Guilmi, C., Gallegati, M., Landini. S., Stiglitz, J.F.: An analytical solution for network models with heterogeneous and interacting agents. J. Econ. Behav. Organ. **171**, 189–220 (2020)
Dunbar, N.: Inventing Money: The Story of Long-Term Capital Management and the Legends Behind It. Wiley, New York (2000)
Eichengreeen, B., Park, D., Shin, K.: Economic Resilience: Why some countries recover more robust than others from shocks. Econ. Model. **136**, 1–16 (2024)
ESMA: European Securities and Market Authority. Consultation Paper. Guidelines on transaction reporting, reference data, order record keeping & clock synchronization, 23 December I ESMA/2015/1909 (2015)

ESMA: European Securities and Market Authority. Consultation Paper. Technical Standards specifying the criteria for establishing and assessing the effectiveness of investment firms' order execution policies, 16 July, www.esma.europa.eu (2024)

Eucken, W.: Grundlagen der Nationalökonomie, 9th edn. Springer, Berlin (1989)

Farmer, J.D., Foley, D.: The economy needs agent-based modelling. Nature **460** 6 August, 685 (2009)

Fassas, A.P., Siriopoulos, C.: Implied volatility indices—a review. Quartely Rev. Econ. Financ. **79**, 303–329 (2021)

Feldstein, M.S.: Mean-variance analysis in the theory of liquidity preference and portfolio selection. Rev. Econ. Stud. **35**, 5–12 (1968)

Feller, W.: An Introduction to Probability Theory and its Application, Vol. I, 3rd edn. Wiley, New York (1968)

Fischer, B., Wermers, R.: Performance Evaluation and Attribution of Security Portfolios. Academic Press, Oxford (2013)

Fisher, I.: Mathematical Investigation in the Theory of Values and Prices. Econ. J., 108–112 (1892)

Fisz, M.: Wahrscheinlichkeitsrechnung und Mathematische Statistik, 2nd edn. VEB Deutscher Verlag der Wissenschaften, Berlin (1962)

Foley, D.K.: A statistical equilibrium theory of markets. J. Econ. Theory **62**(2), 321–345 (1994)

Francioni, R.: Exchange organizations: thoughts and reflections. In: Francioni, R., Schwartz, R.A. (eds.), Equity in Transition. The Value Chain, Price Discovery, Regulation and Beyond, pp. 3–14. Springer (2017)

Francioni, R.: An Exchange and its value chain: In: Francioni, R., Schwartz, R.A. (eds.), Equity in Transition. The Value Chain, Price Discovery, Regulation and Beyond, pp. 15–69, Springer (2017)

Francioni, R., Reck, M., Schwartz, R.A.: Secondary Markets: Trading, Price Discovery, and Order Matching. Springer International Publishing, Cham (2017)

Francioni, R., Schwartz, R.A. (eds.): Equity Markets in Transition. The Value Chain, Price Discovery, Regulation, and Beyond. Springer International Publisher, Cham (2017)

Gallegati, M.: Beyond Econophysics (not to mention mainstream economics). Eur. Phys. J. Spec. Top. **225**, 3179–3185 (2016)

Gallegati, M.: Complex Agent Based Models. Springer Nature Switzerland (2018)

Gallegati, M., Kirman, A.: 20 Years of WEHIA: a journey in search of a safer road. J Econ Behav. Organ. **157**, 5–14 (2019)

George J. K.: Uncertainty and Information. Foundations of a Generalized Information theory, Wiley interscience, Hoboken (2006)

Gradsteyn, I.S., Ryzhik, I.M.: Tables of Integrals, Series, and Products. Academic Press, Boston (2007)

Graham, B., Dodd, D.L.: Security Analysis. McGraw-Hill, New York (1934)

Grasselli, M.R., Kirman, A., Hayes, W.: Editorial: a sytemic recovery. J. Risk Financ. Manag. **15**, 578. https://doi.org/10.3390/jrfm15220578 (2022)

Gray, J.: Henri Poincaré. A Scientific Biography. Princeton University Press, Princeton and Oxford (2013)

Grinold, R.C., Kahn, R.N.: Active Portfolio Management: A Quantitative Approach for Providing Superior Returns and Controlling Risk. MacGraw-Hill, New York (2000)

Grossman, S.J., Stiglitz, J.E.: On the impossibility of informationally efficient markets. Am. Econ. Rev. **70**, 393–408 (1980)

Gunnarsson, E.S., Isern, H.R., Kaloudis, A., Risstad, M.: Prediction of realized volatility and implied volatility indices using AI and machine learning: a review. Int. Rev. Financ. Anal. **93**, 1–20 (2024)

Haghani, M., Bliemer, M.C.J., Hensher, D.A.: The landscape of econometric choice modelling. J. Choice Model. **40**, 1–40 (2021)

Haken, H.: Synergetics. An Introduction, Nonequilibrium Phase Transitions and Self-Organization in Physics. Chemistry and Biology, 3rd edn. Springer, Berlin (1983a)

Haken, H.: Advanced Synergetics. Instability Hierarchies of Self-Organizing Systems and Devices. Springer, Berlin (1983b)
Haug, E.G., Taleb, N.T.: Option traders use (very) sophisticated heuristics, never the Black-Scholes-Merton formula. J. Econ. Behav. Organ. **77**, 97–106 (2011)
Hautsch, N.: Modelling Irregularly Spaced Financial Data. Springer, Berlin (2004)
Hayek, F.A.: The Pretence of Knowledge. Prize Lecture, Lecture in the Memory of Alfred Nobel. https://www.nobelprize.org/prizes/economic-sciences/1974/hayek/lecture/ (1974)
Hayek, F.A.: The Pretense of Knowledge, Nobel Memorial Lecture, held December 11, 1974. Swed. J. Econ., 433–442 (1975)
Hayek, F.A.: The Keynes Centenary: the Austrian Critique. The Economist June 11, 45–48, 1983 reprinted in: Caldwell, B. (ed.) The Collected Works of F.A. Hayek, Volume IX: Contra Keynes and Cambridge, Essays, Correspondence. Chicago University Press, Chicago, 247–255 (1995)
Huetl, M., Loistl, O., Prix, J.: Financial Market Micro Jumps Modeled by Doubly Stochastic Markov Process. Paper Presented at AMAMEF Workshop on Financial Modeling with Jump Processes, Palaiseau France, 6 September–8 September (2006)
Hull, J.C.: Options, Futures, and Other Derivatives, 3rd edn. Upper Saddle River, NJ (1997)
Hull, J.C.: Options, Futures, and Other Derivatives, 4th ed, Upper Saddle River, NJ (2000)
Hwang, J., Lay, S., Lippman, A.: Nonparametric multivariate density estimation: a comparative study. IEEE Trans. Signal Process. **42**(10), 2795–2810 (1994)
Ilinski, K.: Physics of Finance. Gauge Modelling in Non-equilibrium Pricing. New York (2001).
Jarrow, R. (2001): Default Parameter Estimation Using Market Prices. Financial Analysts Journal September/October, 75–92 (2001)
Jaynes, E.T.: Information theory and statistical mechanics II. Phys. Rev. **108**(2), 171–190 (1957)
Jevons. W.S.: The Theory of Political Economy. https://www.econlib.orglibrary/YPDBooks/Jevons/jvnPE.html?chapter_num=5#book-reader (1871)
Jianxi, G., Baruch, B., Albert-Laszlo, B.: Universal resilience pattern in complex networks, Nature, vol 530, February 307–312 (2016)
Joel, A. Tropp Probability in High Dimensions, ACM 217 /Caltech CMS Lecture Notes 2021, Pasadena, March 2021, Corrected March 2023 / Winter 2023, https://doi.org/10.7907/mxr0-c422
Joscha, P., Mathias, S., Jan, V.: Entropy numbers of finitedimensional Lorentz space embeddings, arXiv: 2404.06058v2 [math.FA] 14 ct (2024)
Ketterle, W.: Nobel lecture: When atoms behave as waves: Bose-Einstein condensation and the Atom Laser. Rev. Mod. Phys. **74**, 1131–1151 (2002)
Kingman, J.F.C.: Poisson Processes. Oxford University Press, reprinted (2002)
Kirman, A.: The economic crises is a crises for economic theory. Cesifo Econ. Stud. **56**(4), 498–533 (2010)
Kirman, A.: Learning in agent-based models. East. Econ. J. **37**, 20–27 (2011)
Kirman, A.: Complexity and economic policy: A paradigm shift or a change in perspective? A review essay on David Colander and Roland Kuper's complexity and the art of public policy. J. Econ. Lit. **54**(2), 534–572 (2016)
Kirman, A., Laisney, F., Pezanis-Christou, P.: Relaxing the symmetry assumption in participation games: a specification test for cluster-heterogeneity. Exp. Econ. **26**, 850–878 (2023)
Klir, G.J.: Uncertainty and Information: Foundations of Generalized Information Theory. Wiley Interscience, Hoboken, N.J. (2006)
Kohn, M.: Value and exchange. Cato J. **24**, 303–339 (2004)
Kopp, E., Loistl, O., Huetl, M.: The Influence of Real-Time Stock-Specific Messages on Liquidity, Returns, and Trading Behaviour. Paper Presented at the 4th AFFI International Conference, Yasemine-Hamamet, Tunisia (2008)
Kossacká, M., Vybíral, J.: Entropy numbers of finite-dimensional embeddings. Expo. Math. **38**, 319–336 (2020)
Kreps, D.M.: Multiperiod Securities and the Efficient allocation of Risk: A Comment on the Black-Scholes Option Pricing Model, The Economics of Information and Uncertainty. University of Chicago Press (1982)

Kurz, M., Beltratti, A.: The equity premium is no puzzle. In: Kurz, M. (ed.) Endogenous Economic Fluctuations. Studies in the Theory of Rational Beliefs, pp. 283–315. Springer, Berlin (1997)

Kurz, M., Jin, H., Motolese, M.: Determinants of stock market volatility and risk premia. Ann. Finance **1**, 109–147 (2005)

Landes, T., Loistl, O., Reiss, W.: The market microstructure and the dynamic pricing of financial assets. In: Loistl, O. Landes, T. (eds.) The Dynamic Pricing of Financial Assets, pp. 53–108. McGraw-Hill, Hamburg (1989)

Landes, T., Loistl, O.: Capital structure, principal/agency-relation and the value of the corporation: a simulation study, OMEGA. Int. J. Manag. Sci. **19**, 291–303 (1991)

Landes, T., Loistl, O.: Complexity models in financial markets, applied stochastic models and data analysis. Spec. Issue Financ. **8**, 209–228 (1992)

Landini, S., Gallegati, M., Rosser Jr., J., B.: Consistency and incompleteness in general equilibrium theory. J. Evol. Econ. **30**, 205–230 (2020)

Landsman, Z., Neslehova, J.: Stein's Lemma for elliptical random vectors. J. Multivar. Anal. **99**, 912–927 (2008)

Laughlin, R.B.: A Different Universe. Reinventing Physics from the Bottom Down. Basic Books, New York (2006)

Laughlin, R.B., Pines, D.: The Theory of Everything, https://www.pnas.org/doi/full/10.1073/pnas.97.1.28 (2000)

LeBaron, B., Tesfatsion, L.: Modeling macroeconomics as open-ended dynamic systems of interaction agents. Am. Econ. Rev. Pap. Proc. **98**, 246–250 (2008)

Lee, C., Ready, M.: Inferring trade direction from intraday data. J. Finance **46**(2), 733–746 (1991)

Lo, A.W., MacKinlay, A.C., Zhang, J.: Econometric models of limit-order executions. J. Financ. Econ. **65**, 31–71 (2002)

Loistl, O.: The erroneous approximation of expected utility by means of a Taylor's series expansion: analytic and computational results. Am. Econ. Rev. **66**, 904–910 (1976)

Loistl, O.: Kapitalmarkttheorie. Oldenburg, München (1994)

Loistl, O.: Implementation issues: Transaction costs in German equity markets. In: Squires, J.R (ed.) ACFA continuing Education: Global Portfolio Management, pp. 84–93. Charlottesville (1996)

Loistl, O.: Modeling of Agent Based Financial Markets. Combining the Paradigms of Exchange, Emergence and Organized Complexity. Paper presented at InterSymp 2008, 20th International Conference on Systems Research, Informatics & Cybernetics, July 24th, 2008 (2008)

Loistl, O.: Does mean variance portfolio management deserve expected utility's approximative affirmation? Eur. J. Oper. Res. **247**, 676–681 (2015)

Loistl, O., Konstantinov, G.S.: Interactions and interconnectedness shape financial market research. J. Financ. Data Sci. Spring, 1–13 (2020)

Loistl, O., Landes, T. (eds.): The Dynamic Pricing of Financial Assets. McGraw Hill, Hamburg (1989)

Loistl, O., Schossmann, B., Vetter, O.: Xetra efficiency evaluation and Nasdaq modelling by KapSyn. Eur. J. Oper. Res. **135**, 270–295 (2001)

Loistl, O., Schossmann, B., Vetter, O., Veverka, A.: A comparison of transaction costs on Xetra and on Nasdaq. Quant. Financ. **2**, 199–216 (2002)

Loistl, O., Schossmann, B., Veverka, A.: Tick size and spreads: The case of Nasdaq's decimalization. Eur. J. Oper. Res. **155**, 317–334 (2004)

Loistl, O., Vetter, O.: KapSyn. Computer Program for Evaluating the Operating Efficiency of a Stock Market's Microstructure, Version 3.0 (1999)

Loistl, O., Veverka, A.: Entropy and Capital Market Efficiency, Working Paper Vienna University of Economics and Business, Department Finance and Statistics, Chair Investmentbanking and Catallactics (2005)

Luce, R.D.: Thurstone and sensory scaling: Then and now. Psychol. Rev. **101**(2), 271–277 (1994)

Luce, R.D.: Individual choice behavior. A theoretical analysis. Dover Publication. It is an unabridged replication of the work originally published by John Wiley & Sons, Inc. New York 1959 (2005)

Luckham, D.: The Power of Events. An Introduction to Complex Event Processing in Distributed Enterprise Systems. Addison-Wesley, Boston (2002)
Nikolai, V. I.: Translator's Preface, A.N. Kolmogorov's and Y.G. Sinai's Papers introducing Entropy of Dynamical Systems, http://nikolaivivanov.com 2015
Madan, D.B., Carr, P.C., Chang, E.C.: The Variance Gamma Process and Option Pricing. Eur. Finance Rev. **2**, 79–105 (1998)
Madan, D.B.: Purely Discontinuous Asset Price Processes. University of Maryland, Working Paper (1999)
Madhavan, A.: Market Microstructure: A Practitioner's Guide. Financ. Anal. J. September/October 2002, 28–42 (2002)
Madhavan, A., Panchapagesan, V.: Price discovery in auction markets: A look inside the black box. Rev. Financ. Stud. **13**, 627–658 (2000)
Manahov, V., Hudson, R., Urquhart, A.: High-frequency trading from an evolutionary perspective. Financial markets as adaptive systems. Int. J. Financ. Econ. **24**, 943–962 (2018)
Manski, C.F.: Economic analysis of social interactions. J. Econ. Perspect. Summer 2000, **14**, 3, 115–136 (2000)
Manski, C.F.: Daniel McFadden and the econometric analysis of discrete choice. Scand. J. Econ. **103**(2), 217–229 (2001)
Markowitz, H.: Portfolio selection. J. Financ. **7**(1), 77–91 (1952)
Marschak, J.: Binary choice constraints on random utility indications. In: Arrow, K. (ed.) Stanford Symposium on Mathematical Methods in Social Sciences. Stanford University Press, pp. 207–240, Stanford, C.A. (1960)
Marshall, A.: Letter to Bowley 1906. The letter was copied by Eric Rasmussen from pages 427–428 of Memorials of Alfred Marshall, edited b A.C. Pigou. One edition is: New York, A.M. Kelley, 1966, HB 103 M3 (1966)
Marshall, A.: Principles of economics, 8th edn. Macmillan, London (1920)
Mazliak, L.: Poincaré and probability. Lettera Mathematica, **1**, 33–39 (2013)
McCloskey, D., Ziliak, N.S.: The standard error of regressions. J. Econ. Lit. **34**, 97–114 (1996)
McFadden, D.: Conditional logit analysis of qualitative choice behavior. In: Zarembka, P. (ed.) Frontiers in Econometrics, pp. 105–142. Academic Press (1974)
McFadden, D.: Rationality for economists? J. Risk Uncertain. **19**, 73–105 (1999)
McFadden, D.: Economic choices. Am. Econ. Rev. **91**, 351–378 (2001)
McFadden, D.: Revealed stochastic preference. A synthesis. Econ. Theory **26**, 245–264 (2005)
Meckes, E.: On Stein's method for multivariate normal approximation. IMS Collections, High Dimensional Probability V: The Luminy Volume Vol. 5, pp. 153–178 (2009)
Meent, R., Mandjes, M., Pras, A.: Gaussian traffic everywhere? Working Paper, Centrum voor Wiskunde en Informacia, Amsterdam (NL) (2006)
Michel, T.: Majorizing Measures: The Generic Chaining, The Annals of Probability, **24**, 1049–1103 Special Invited Paper. (1996a)
Michel, T.: A new look at independence, Special Invited Paper, The Annals of Probability, Vol 24, 1, 1–34 (1996b)
Michel, T.: The Geneneric Chaining. Upper and Lower Bounds of Stochastic Processes, Springer Berlin Heidelberg (2010)
Michel, T.: Upper and Lower Bounds for Stochastic Processes. Decomposition Theorems, Springer Nature Switzerland (2021)
Myerson, R.B.: Probability Models for Economic Decisions. home.unichicago.edu/rmyerson/teaching/util 206.pdf. Accessed 30 April 2015 (2015)
Neftci, S.N.: An Introduction to the Mathematics of Financial Derivatives, 2nd edn. Academic Press, San Diego (2000)
Neubeerger, A.: The Log Contract. A New Instrument to Hedge Volatility, 74–80 (1994)
Nijkamp, P., Reggiani, L.: Entropy, spatial interaction models and discrete choice analysis: static and dynamic analogies. Eur. J. Oper. Res. **36**, 186–196 (1988)

Nobel Prize Committee: The scientific contributions of James Heckman and Daniel McFadden, Advanced information on the Bank of Sweden Prize. In: Economic Sciences in Memory of Alfred Nobel 2000 (www.kva.se) (2000)

NYSE, leaflet nyse.com/equities

O'Hara, M.: Presidential address: liquidity and price discovery. J. Financ. **58**, 1335–1354 (2003)

Opler, T.C., Saron, M., Titman, S.: Designing capital structure to create shareholder value. J. Appl. Corp. Financ. **10**, 21–32 (1997)

Paarsch, H.J., Hong, H.: An Introduction to the Structural Econometrics of Auction Data. Cambridge Mass MIT Press (2006)

Petz, D.: Entropy, von Neumann and the von Neumann entropy. arXiv:math-ph/0102013v1 9 Feb 2001 (2001)

Pines, D.: Emergence: A unifying theme for the 21st century science. Santa Fe Institute, Oct 31 (2014)

Planck, M.: Zur Geschichte der Auffindung des physikalischen Wirkungsquantums, in: Roos und Hermann, l.c. pp. 11–24 (undated)

Planck, M.: Dynamische und statistische Gesetzmässigkeiten, speech at anniversary of Berlin University Foundation, in: Roos und Herman, l.c. pp. 87–101 (1914)

Planck, M.: Zur Geschichte der Auffindung des physikalischen Wirkungsquantums. Naturwissenschaften **31**, 153–159 (1943)

Planck, M.: Persönliche Erinnerungen aus alten Zeiten, Die Naturwissenschaften, Hft 8 v.30 Oktober 1946, in: Roos und Herman, l.c. pp. 41–54 (1946)

Platanakis, E., Sakkas, A., Sutcliffe, C.: Harmful Diversification: Evidence from Alternative Investments. ICMA Centre, Henley Business School, University of Reading, Discussion Paper Number: ICM-2017-09 (2017)

Pratt, J.W.: Risk aversion in the small and the large. Econometrica **32**, 122–135 (1964)

Pressacco, F., Serafini, P.: The origins of the mean-variance approach in finance: revisiting de Finetti 65 years later. Decisions Econ. Finan. **30**, 19–49 (2007)

Prix, J., Loistl, O., Hütl, M.: Algorithmic trading patterns in Xetra orders. Eur. J. Financ. **13**, 717–739 (2007)

Prochno, J., Sonnleitner, M., Vybiral, J.: Entropy Numbers of Finite Dimensional Lorentz Space Embeddings (2024)

Raiffa, H.: Decision Analysis, Introductory Lectures on Choices under Uncertainty, 2nd edn. Addison-Wesley, Massachusetts (1970)

Ramon V. H.: Probability in High dimensions. APC 550 Lecture Notes Princeton University (2016)

Read, C.: The Portfolio Theorists. Von Neuman, Savage, Arrow, and Markowitz. Palgrave MacMillan, United Kingdom (2012)

Rinne, H.: Taschenbuch der Statistik, 2nd edn. Harri Deutsch, Thun (1997)

Roman, V.: High Dimensional Probability. An Introduction with Applications in Data Science, second Edition, https://www.math.uci.edu/~rvershyn/ (2025)

Roos, H., Hermann, A. Herausgeber: Max Planck: Vorträge, Reden Erinnerungen, Springer Berlin (2001)

Roth, A.E.: Who Gets What and Why. The New Economics of Matchmaking and Market Design. Houghton Mifflin Harcourt, New York (2015)

Roth, A.E.: Marketplaces, markets, and market design. Am. Econ. Rev. **108**, 1609–1658 (2018)

Roth, A.E., Sotomayor, M.A.O.: Two-sided Matching. A Study In Game-Theoretic Modelling and Analysis. Cambridge University Press (1992)

The Norwegian Academy of Science and Letters, Abelprisen (2025)

The Royal Swedish Academy of Sciences: Bose-Einstein condensation in Alkali Gases. Advanced Information on the Nobel Prize in Physics (2001)

The Royal Swedish Academy of Sciences: Foundations of Behavioral and Experimental Economics: Daniel Kahnemann and Vernon Smith. Advanced information on the Prize in Economic Sciences, 17 December 2002 (2002)

Samuelson, P.A.: The fundamental approximation theorem of portfolio analysis in terms of means, variances and higher moments. Rev. Econ. Stud. **37**, 537–542 (1970)

Scharfenaker, E., Foley, D.K.: Quantal response statistical eqilibrium in economic interactions theory and estimation. Entropy **19**(444), 2–15 (2017)
Schneeweiß, H.: Entscheidungskriterien bei Risiko. Springer, Berlin (1967)
Schumpeter, J.: The common sense of econometrics. Econometrica **1**(1), 5–12 (1933)
Schumpeter, J.: Geschichte der ökonomischen Analyse. Vandenhoeck & Rupprecht, Göttingen (1965)
SEC: SEC.gov/34-51808 Regulation NMS
SEC: Supplemental Information and Reopening of Comment period for Amendments Regarding the Definition of exchange (2023a)
SEC: Regulation Best Execution Proposed Rule Release No. 34-96496; file No. S7-32-22 (2023b)
SEC: Alternative Trading System ("ATS") List June 2024 (2024a)
SEC: Disclosure of Order Execution Information, Final rule (2024b)
Shannon, C.E.: A Mathematical Theory of Communication. Bell System Technical Journal 27, 379–423, https://doi.org/10.1002/j.1538-7305.1948.tb01338.x (1948)
Sheehan, J. Wahrman, D.: Invisible Hands. Self-Organization and the Eighteenth Century. The University of Chicago Press, Chicago (2015)
Simon, F.: Some new bounds on the entropy numbers of diagonal operators, J. Approx. Theory, **252**, 1–14 (2020)
Sinn, H.W.: Entscheidungen bei Ungewissheit. Mohr, Tübingen (1980)
Sirignano, J.A.: Deep learning for limit order books. Quantitative Finance **19**, 549–570 (2019). https://doi.org/10.1080/14697688.2018.1546053
Sjoerd, D.: Tail bounds via generic chaining, Electron. J. Probab. **20**, #53, 1–29 (2015)
Solow, R.M.: How did economics get that way & what way did it get? Daedalus **134**(4), 87–100, http://www.accessmy library.com.coms2/summary0826-12127142 ITM (2005)
Sommerfeld, A.: Vorlesungen über theoretische Physik, Band V Thermodynamik und Statistik. Dietrich'sche Verlagsbuchhandlung, Wiesbaden (1952)
Soofi, E.S.: Capturing the intangible concept of information. J. Am. Stat. Assoc. **89**, 1243–1254 (1994)
Soros, G.: The new Paradigm of Financial markets. The Credit Crisis of 2008 and what it means. Public Affairs, New York (2008)
Stiglitz, J.E.: Information and the change in the paradigm in economics. Am. Econ. Rev. **92**, 460–501 (2002)
Stiglitz, J.E., Gallegati, M.: Heterogeneous interacting agent models for understanding monetary economies. East. Econ. J. **37**, 5–12 (2011)
Suppes, P.: Behavioristic foundations of utility. Econometrica **29**(2), 186–202 (1961)
Talagrand, M.: Mean Field Models for Spin Glasses, Volume I: Basic Examples. Springer, Berlin (2010)
Talagrand, M: Mean Field Models for Spin Glasses, Volume II: Advanced Replica-Symmetry and Low Temperature. Springer, Berlin (2011)
Talagrand, M.: Upper and Lower Bounds for Stochastic Processes. Decomposition theorems. Springer Nature, Switzerland (2021)
Temlyakow, V.: A Remark on Entropy Numbers, arXiv:2008.13030v 1 [math.NA] 29 Aug (2020)
Tesfatsion, L.: Agent-based computational economics: a constructive approach to economic theory. In: Tesfatsion, L., Judd, K.L. (eds.), Handbook of Computational Economics, Volume 2: Agent-Based Computational Economic Series. North-Holland, Amsterdam (2008)
Thaler, R.: The end of behavioral finance. Financ. Anal. J. **55**(6), 12–17 (1999)
Thaler, R.: From Homo Economicus to Homo Sapiens. J. Econ. Perspect. **14**, 133–141 (2000)
Thaler, R.: From Cashews to Nudges: The Evolution of Behavioral Economics. Prize Lecture, The Nobel Prizes, December 8, 488–515 (2017)
Thorp, E.: Optimal gambling systems for favorable games. Rev. Int. Stat. Inst. **37**, 273–293 (1969)
Thorp, E.: Options in Institutional Portfolios: Theory and Practice. Center for Research in Security Prices, Graduate School of Business, Proceedings, Seminar on the Analysis of Security Prices, **20** (1) May 15–16 (1975)
Thurstone, L.L.: The law of comparative judgement. Psychol. Rev. **34**, 273–286 (1927a)

Thurstone, L.L.: Three psychological laws. Psychol. Rev. 424–432 (1927b)
Thurstone, L.L.: The method of paired comparisons for social values. J. Abnorm. Soc. Psychol. **21**, 384–400 (1927c)
Train, K.E.: Discrete Choice Methods with Simulations. Cambridge University Press, Cambridge (2003)
Treynor, J.L., Wagner, W.H.: Implementing of portfolio building: execution. In: Maginn, J.L., Tuttle, D.L. (eds.) Managing Investment Portfolios: A Dynamic Process. Warren, Gorham & Lamont, Boston (1990)
Tsiang, S.-C.: The rational of the mean-standard deviation analysis, skewness preference and the demand for money. Am. Econ. Rev. **62**, 354–371 (1972)
van Handel, R.: Changing, Interpolation, and Convexity, arXiv:1508.05906v2 [math.PR] 26 Feb (2016)
van Handel, R.: Chaining, interpolation and convexity II: the contraction principle. Ann. Probab. **46**, 1764–1805 (2018)
Van Kampen, N.G.: Stochastic Processes in Physics and Chemistry, 3rd edn. Elsevier, Amsterdam (2007)
Verhulst, F.: Henri Poincaré Impatient Genius. Springer, New York (2012)
Vogel, H.L.: Financial Market Bubbles and Crashes. Features, Causes, and Effects, 2nd edn. Palgrave Macmillan, Cham Switzerland (2018)
von Neumann, J.: Mathematische Grundlagen der Quantenmechanik. Springer Verlag, Berlin (unveränderter Nachdruck der ersten Auflage) 1968 (1932)
von Neumann, J., Morgenstern, O.: Theory of Games and Economic Behavior. Princeton University Press, Princeton (1944)
Wapshott, N.: Keynes Hayek. The Clash That Defined Modern Economics. W.W. Norton&Company, New York (2011)
Warren, W.: Recent Contributions to the Mathematical Theory of Communication, reprinted in: Claude E. Shannon and Warren Weaver (1949), The Mathematical Theory of Communication, pp1–28, University of Illinois Press, Urbana 1964 (1949)
Weaver, W.: Science and complexity. Am. Sci. **36**, 536–544 (1948)
Wertenbroch, K., Skiera, B.: Measuring consumers' willingness to pay at the point of purchase. J. Mark. Res. **39**, 228–241 (2002)
Witold, B.: CHAIN—Generic chaining approach to the regularity of stochastic processes: Reg.No: 2019/35/B/ST1/04292; Principal Investigator: Dr hab. Witold Marek Bednorz (2019)
Y.G. Sinai: On the concept of entropy for a dynamic systems, in A.N. Kolmogorov's and Sinai's papers, l.c. p 12–14 (1959)
Ya. G. Sinai: Metric Entry of Dynamical System, Mathematics Department, Princeton University, Princeton, New Jersey, U.S.A. (2007)
Zhang, X., Huang, Y., Xu, K., Xing, L.: Novel Modelling Strategies for High-frequency Stock Trading Data. arXiv:2212.00148v1 [stat.AP] 30 Nov 2022 (2022)
Zhang, Z., Lim, B., Zohren, S.: Deep learning for market by order data. App. Math. Financ. **28**(1), 1–17 (2021)
Zuckerman, G.: The Man Who Solved the Market. How Jim Simons Launched the Quant Revolution. Penguin Random House (2019)

Index

A
Active portfolio management strategy, 12
AI, 60
Algorithmic trading. *See* Algo trading
Algo-Trading, 12
Alternative Trading Systems, 9, 31, 151, 152
Arbitrage, 1, 15, 21, 25, 27
Arrow-Debreu formula, 21

B
Behavioural finance, 2, 31, 125
Bernoulli, D., 30, 32, 34, 37, 38, 106, 110, 111
Bernoulli Principle, 34, 38
Biometrics, 112
Black and Scholes, 19–21, 23–27
Bose-Einstein interpretation, 4
Brokers, 9, 11, 14, 17, 32, 58, 109

C
Cadlag process, 124
Catallactics, 23, 123, 128, 159, 162
Chicago Board Options Exchange, 21
Constant-initial-cushion, 73, 90

D
Decision frame, 2, 14, 15, 20, 30, 97, 98
Designated sponsor, 3, 11, 19, 151
Discrete choice, 4, 5, 15, 59, 96, 99, 101, 104, 106–109, 113, 117, 118, 121, 122, 125, 141, 142, 145, 149, 157, 162–164, 167
Discrete Choice theory, 127
Disorganised complexity, 100, 101, 103–105
Doubly Stochastic Markov Process, 4, 23, 122, 127, 141, 145
Doubly Stochastic Poisson Processes, 23
DSMP. *See* Double Stochastic Markov Process
Dynamic disequilibria, 1

E
Econometrics, 112
Econophysics, 107
Efficient market hypothesis, 5, 31
Electronic trading, 3, 5, 8, 11, 15, 17, 23, 32, 58, 61, 109, 110, 170
Emergence, 2, 9, 16, 30, 103, 105, 113, 116, 117, 121, 150, 167, 168, 175
Entropy, 4, 5, 15, 104, 113, 127, 134, 135, 153–164, 167, 170, 176
Equilibrium, 1, 7, 8, 15, 16, 18, 30, 49, 102, 106, 107, 121, 125, 153, 158, 162, 167–169, 173
Equilibrium condition, 18
Equilibrium straitjacket, 107, 168
ESMA, 65, 91, 148
Exchange, 4, 9–11, 14, 19, 23, 31, 58, 59, 85, 89, 90, 96–99, 109, 116–119, 121, 122, 125, 129, 141, 142, 150–152, 154
Expected utility value, 33, 34, 38, 46, 47, 49, 50

F
Frankfurt Stock Exchange, 3, 4, 32, 58, 61, 116, 117

G
Game theory, 17, 119, 167, 173
GARCH, 175

O. Loistl et al., *Screen Based Trading and Open Order Book*, New Economic Windows,
https://doi.org/10.1007/978-3-031-99052-6

Gaussian kernels, 71
Generalised Information Theory, 100

H
Hedge funds, 12
Hedge portfolio, 24, 25

I
IIA, 30, 32, 98, 99, 102, 122, 123, 148
Integrated Active Asset Management, 12
Intercontinental Exchange, 11
Invariance principles, 105

K
KapSyn model, 162
Kernel density estimates, 71

L
Logit approach, 99, 118, 125, 145, 148, 170
Logit Choice, 30
London Stock Exchange, 11
Long-Term Capital Management, 21

M
Markets microstructure, 4
Markov process, 23, 30, 100, 118, 124, 125, 143, 145, 148, 149, 160, 162, 169
Markov transition rates, 124
Matching, 2, 3, 5, 10, 11, 15, 17, 19, 53, 58–61, 77, 91, 96, 98, 102, 104, 105, 109, 110, 112, 114, 116, 117, 124, 126, 127, 143, 169
Microstructure, 4, 23, 91, 96, 97, 109, 149, 156, 162
MIFID, 91

N
Nasdaq, 3, 9, 59, 142, 150, 152
National Market System, 31, 125
Nobel Prize, 3, 4, 91, 109, 155
NYSE, 9, 11, 19, 32

O
Options, 10, 19, 24, 25, 27, 31
Order types, 19, 61, 63–65, 116, 129, 131, 132, 135, 139
Organised complexity, 2, 59, 100–106
Ornstein-Uhlenbeck processes, 124

P
Poisson process, 96, 124
Portfolio management, 12, 33, 107, 108
Portfolio theory, 33, 39, 43, 107, 111, 172
Price time priority, 3, 10, 14, 54, 61, 68, 104, 116, 117, 122, 124, 143
Price time priority rule, 3, 10, 54, 104
Prospect theory, 30, 104, 107–110, 112
Psychometrics, 112

Q
Quadratic utility functions, 33
Quantitative-behavioural finance, 125

R
Random utility approach, 5
Risk-free portfolio, 20, 21, 23–26

S
Safety equivalent, 34
Security and Exchange Commission, 9
Security Exchange Act, 9
Self Regulating Organisations, 9
Shares, 8–10, 13, 19–21, 24, 39, 58, 65, 75, 79, 97–99, 104, 146, 152, 158–160, 163, 170
Slippage, 13, 82, 83, 90, 134, 136, 137
State space transitions, 122
Stein's lemma, 39
Stochastic process, 20, 21, 25, 122, 142, 148
Stochastic utility maximisation, 123
Synergetics, 23

T
Taylor series, 33, 34, 39, 41, 43, 46
Trading venue, 10, 17, 18, 53, 58, 99, 104, 105, 109, 114

U
Utility formula, 5, 15

X
Xetra, 3, 5, 9–11, 15, 19, 23, 32, 58, 59, 61, 63–65, 82, 90, 97, 116, 117, 128, 129, 142, 150, 151

MIX
Papier aus verantwortungsvollen Quellen
Paper from responsible sources
FSC® C105338

If you have any concerns about our products,
you can contact us on
ProductSafety@springernature.com

In case Publisher is established outside the EU,
the EU authorized representative is:
Springer Nature Customer Service Center GmbH
Europaplatz 3, 69115 Heidelberg, Germany

Printed by Libri Plureos GmbH
in Hamburg, Germany